THE FIRST AND SECOND
BOOK OF THE KINGS

THE IGNATIUS CATHOLIC STUDY BIBLE

REVISED STANDARD VERSION
SECOND CATHOLIC EDITION

THE FIRST AND SECOND
BOOK OF THE KINGS

With Introduction, Commentary, and Notes

by

Scott Hahn and Curtis Mitch

with

Mark Giszczak

and

with Study Questions by

Dennis Walters

IGNATIUS PRESS   SAN FRANCISCO

Original Revised Standard Version, Catholic Edition:
Nihil Obstat: Thomas Hanlon, S.T.L., L.S.S., Ph.L.
Imprimatur: +Peter W. Bartholome, D.D.
Bishop of Saint Cloud, Minnesota
May 11, 1966

Introduction, commentaries, and notes:
Nihil obstat: Ruth Ohm Sutherland, Ph.D., Censor Deputatus
Imprimatur: +The Most Reverend Salvatore Cordileone
Archbishop of San Francisco
March 20, 2017

The *nihil obstat* and *imprimatur* are official declarations that a book or pamphlet
is free of doctrinal or moral error. No implication is contained therein that those
who have granted the *nihil obstat* and *imprimatur* agree with the contents,
opinions, or statements expressed.

Second Catholic Edition approved by the
National Council of the Churches of Christ in the USA

Cover art: The prophet Elijah ascending into heaven on the fiery chariot
16th century, by an unknown Flemish artist
Beaune, Abbey of Carmes.
© DeA Picture Library / Art Resource, NY

Cover design by Riz Boncan Marsella

Published by Ignatius Press in 2017

CONTENTS

INTRODUCTION TO THE IGNATIUS STUDY BIBLE

by Scott Hahn, Ph.D.

You are approaching the "word of God". This is the title Christians most commonly give to the Bible, and the expression is rich in meaning. It is also the title given to the Second Person of the Blessed Trinity, God the Son. For Jesus Christ became flesh for our salvation, and "the name by which he is called is The Word of God" (Rev 19:13; cf. Jn 1:14).

The word of God is Scripture. The Word of God is Jesus. This close association between God's *written* word and his *eternal* Word is intentional and has been the custom of the Church since the first generation. "All Sacred Scripture is but one book, and this one book is Christ, 'because all divine Scripture speaks of Christ, and all divine Scripture is fulfilled in Christ'[1]" (CCC 134). This does not mean that the Scriptures are divine in the same way that Jesus is divine. They are, rather, divinely inspired and, as such, are unique in world literature, just as the Incarnation of the eternal Word is unique in human history.

Yet we can say that the inspired word resembles the incarnate Word in several important ways. Jesus Christ is the Word of God incarnate. In his humanity, he is like us in all things, except for sin. As a work of man, the Bible is like any other book, except without error. Both Christ and Scripture, says the Second Vatican Council, are given "for the sake of our salvation" (*Dei Verbum* 11), and both give us God's definitive revelation of himself. We cannot, therefore, conceive of one without the other: the Bible without Jesus, or Jesus without the Bible. Each is the interpretive key to the other. And because Christ is the subject of all the Scriptures, St. Jerome insists, "Ignorance of the Scriptures is ignorance of Christ"[2] (CCC 133).

When we approach the Bible, then, we approach Jesus, the Word of God; and in order to encounter Jesus, we must approach him in a prayerful study of the inspired word of God, the Sacred Scriptures.

Inspiration and Inerrancy The Catholic Church makes mighty claims for the Bible, and our acceptance of those claims is essential if we are to read the Scriptures and apply them to our lives as the Church intends. So it is not enough merely to nod at words like "inspired", "unique", or "inerrant". We

have to understand what the Church means by these terms, and we have to make that understanding our own. After all, what we believe about the Bible will inevitably influence the way we read the Bible. The way we read the Bible, in turn, will determine what we "get out" of its sacred pages.

These principles hold true no matter what we read: a news report, a search warrant, an advertisement, a paycheck, a doctor's prescription, an eviction notice. How (or whether) we read these things depends largely upon our preconceived notions about the reliability and authority of their sources—and the potential they have for affecting our lives. In some cases, to misunderstand a document's authority can lead to dire consequences. In others, it can keep us from enjoying rewards that are rightfully ours. In the case of the Bible, both the rewards and the consequences involved take on an ultimate value.

What does the Church mean, then, when she affirms the words of St. Paul: "All Scripture is inspired by God" (2 Tim 3:16)? Since the term "inspired" in this passage could be translated "God-breathed", it follows that God breathed forth his word in the Scriptures as you and I breathe forth air when we speak. This means that God is the primary author of the Bible. He certainly employed human authors in this task as well, but he did not merely assist them while they wrote or subsequently approve what they had written. God the Holy Spirit is the *principal* author of Scripture, while the human writers are *instrumental* authors. These human authors freely wrote everything, and only those things, that God wanted: the word of God in the very words of God. This miracle of dual authorship extends to the whole of Scripture, and to every one of its parts, so that whatever the human authors affirm, God likewise affirms through their words.

The principle of biblical inerrancy follows logically from this principle of divine authorship. After all, God cannot lie, and he cannot make mistakes. Since the Bible is divinely inspired, it must be without error in everything that its divine and human authors affirm to be true. This means that biblical inerrancy is a mystery even broader in scope than infallibility, which guarantees for us that the Church will always teach the truth concerning faith and morals. Of course the mantle of inerrancy likewise covers faith and morals, but it extends even farther to ensure that all the facts and events of salvation history are accurately presented for us in the Scriptures. Inerrancy is our guarantee that the

---

[1] Hugh of St. Victor, *De arca Noe* 2, 8: PL 176, 642: cf. ibid. 2, 9: PL 176, 642–43.
[2] *DV* 25; cf. Phil 3:8 and St. Jerome, *Commentariorum Isaiam libri xviii*, prol.: PL 24, 17b.

words and deeds of God found in the Bible are unified and true, declaring with one voice the wonders of his saving love.

The guarantee of inerrancy does not mean, however, that the Bible is an all-purpose encyclopedia of information covering every field of study. The Bible is not, for example, a textbook in the empirical sciences, and it should not be treated as one. When biblical authors relate facts of the natural order, we can be sure they are speaking in a purely descriptive and "phenomenological" way, according to the way things appeared to their senses.

Biblical Authority Implicit in these doctrines is God's desire to make himself known to the world and to enter a loving relationship with every man, woman, and child he has created. God gave us the Scriptures not just to inform or motivate us; more than anything he wants to save us. This higher purpose underlies every page of the Bible, indeed every word of it.

In order to reveal himself, God used what theologians call "accommodation". Sometimes the Lord stoops down to communicate by "condescension"— that is, he speaks as humans speak, as if he had the same passions and weakness that we do (for example, God says he was "sorry" that he made man in Genesis 6:6). Other times he communicates by "elevation"—that is, by endowing human words with divine power (for example, through the Prophets). The numerous examples of divine accommodation in the Bible are an expression of God's wise and fatherly ways. For a sensitive father can speak with his children either by condescension, as in baby talk, or by elevation, by bringing a child's understanding up to a more mature level.

God's word is thus saving, fatherly, and personal. Because it speaks directly to us, we must never be indifferent to its content; after all, the word of God is at once the object, cause, and support of our faith. It is, in fact, a test of our faith, since we see in the Scriptures only what faith disposes us to see. If we believe what the Church believes, we will see in Scripture the saving, inerrant, and divinely authored revelation of the Father. If we believe otherwise, we see another book altogether.

This test applies not only to rank-and-file believers but also to the Church's theologians and hierarchy, and even the Magisterium. Vatican II has stressed in recent times that Scripture must be "the very soul of sacred theology" (*Dei Verbum* 24). As Joseph Cardinal Ratzinger, Pope Benedict XVI echoed this powerful teaching with his own, insisting that "the *normative theologians* are the authors of Holy Scripture" (emphasis added). He reminded us that Scripture and the Church's dogmatic teaching are tied tightly together, to the point of being inseparable: "Dogma is by definition nothing other than an interpretation of Scripture." The defined dogmas of our faith, then, encapsulate the Church's

infallible interpretation of Scripture, and theology is a further reflection upon that work.

The Senses of Scripture Because the Bible has both divine and human authors, we are required to master a different sort of reading than we are used to. First, we must read Scripture according to its *literal* sense, as we read any other human literature. At this initial stage, we strive to discover the meaning of the words and expressions used by the biblical writers as they were understood in their original setting and by their original recipients. This means, among other things, that we do not interpret everything we read "literalistically", as though Scripture never speaks in a figurative or symbolic way (it often does!). Rather, we read it according to the rules that govern its different literary forms of writing, depending on whether we are reading a narrative, a poem, a letter, a parable, or an apocalyptic vision. The Church calls us to read the divine books in this way to ensure that we understand what the human authors were laboring to explain to God's people.

The literal sense, however, is not the only sense of Scripture, since we interpret its sacred pages according to the *spiritual* senses as well. In this way, we search out what the Holy Spirit is trying to tell us, beyond even what the human authors have consciously asserted. Whereas the literal sense of Scripture describes a historical reality—a fact, precept, or event—the spiritual senses disclose deeper mysteries revealed through the historical realities. What the soul is to the body, the spiritual senses are to the literal. You can distinguish them; but if you try to separate them, death immediately follows. St. Paul was the first to insist upon this and warn of its consequences: "God ... has qualified us to be ministers of a new covenant, not in a written code but in the Spirit; for the written code kills, but the Spirit gives life" (2 Cor 3:5–6).

Catholic tradition recognizes three spiritual senses that stand upon the foundation of the literal sense of Scripture (see CCC 115). **(1)** The first is the *allegorical* sense, which unveils the spiritual and prophetic meaning of biblical history. Allegorical interpretations thus reveal how persons, events, and institutions of Scripture can point beyond themselves toward greater mysteries yet to come (OT) or display the fruits of mysteries already revealed (NT). Christians have often read the Old Testament in this way to discover how the mystery of Christ in the New Covenant was once hidden in the Old and how the full significance of the Old Covenant was finally made manifest in the New. Allegorical significance is likewise latent in the New Testament, especially in the life and deeds of Jesus recorded in the Gospels. Because Christ is the Head of the Church and the source of her spiritual life, what was accomplished in Christ the Head during his earthly life prefigures what he continually produces in his members through grace. The allegorical sense builds up the virtue of faith. **(2)** The second is the *tropological* or *moral* sense, which reveals how the actions of God's people in the Old Testament and the life of Jesus in the New Testament prompt us to form virtuous habits in our own lives. It therefore draws from Scripture warnings against sin and vice as well as inspirations to pursue holiness and purity. The moral sense is intended to build up the virtue of charity. **(3)** The third is the *anagogical* sense, which points upward to heavenly glory. It shows us how countless events in the Bible prefigure our final union with God in eternity and how things that are "seen" on earth are figures of things "unseen" in heaven. Because the anagogical sense leads us to contemplate our destiny, it is meant to build up the virtue of hope. Together with the literal sense, then, these spiritual senses draw out the fullness of what God wants to give us through his Word and as such comprise what ancient tradition has called the "full sense" of Sacred Scripture.

All of this means that the deeds and events of the Bible are charged with meaning beyond what is immediately apparent to the reader. In essence, that meaning is Jesus Christ and the salvation he died to give us. This is especially true of the books of the New Testament, which proclaim Jesus explicitly; but it is also true of the Old Testament, which speaks of Jesus in more hidden and symbolic ways. The human authors of the Old Testament told us as much as they were able, but they could not clearly discern the shape of all future events standing at such a distance. It is the Bible's divine Author, the Holy Spirit, who could and did foretell the saving work of Christ, from the first page of the Book of Genesis onward.

The New Testament did not, therefore, abolish the Old. Rather, the New fulfilled the Old, and in doing so, it lifted the veil that kept hidden the face of the Lord's bride. Once the veil is removed, we suddenly see the world of the Old Covenant charged with grandeur. Water, fire, clouds, gardens, trees, hills, doves, lambs—all of these things are memorable details in the history and poetry of Israel. But now, seen in the light of Jesus Christ, they are much more. For the Christian with eyes to see, water symbolizes the saving power of Baptism; fire, the Holy Spirit; the spotless lamb, Christ crucified; Jerusalem, the city of heavenly glory.

The spiritual reading of Scripture is nothing new. Indeed, the very first Christians read the Bible this way. St. Paul describes Adam as a "type" that prefigured Jesus Christ (Rom 5:14). A "type" is a real person, place, thing, or event in the Old Testament that foreshadows something greater in the New. From this term we get the word "typology", referring to the study of how the Old Testament prefigures Christ (CCC 128–30). Elsewhere St. Paul draws deeper meanings out of the story of Abraham's sons, declaring, "This is an allegory" (Gal 4:24). He is not suggesting that these events of the distant past never really happened; he is saying that the events both happened *and* signified something more glorious yet to come.

The New Testament later describes the Tabernacle of ancient Israel as "a copy and shadow of the heavenly sanctuary" (Heb 8:5) and the Mosaic Law as a "shadow of the good things to come" (Heb 10:1). St. Peter, in turn, notes that Noah and his family were "saved through water" in a way that "corresponds" to sacramental Baptism, which "now saves you" (1 Pet 3:20–21). It is interesting to note that the expression translated as "corresponds" in this verse is a Greek term that denotes the fulfillment or counterpart of an ancient "type".

We need not look to the apostles, however, to justify a spiritual reading of the Bible. After all, Jesus himself read the Old Testament this way. He referred to Jonah (Mt 12:39), Solomon (Mt 12:42), the Temple (Jn 2:19), and the brazen serpent (Jn 3:14) as "signs" that pointed forward to him. We see in Luke's Gospel, as Christ comforted the disciples on the road to Emmaus, that "beginning with Moses and all the prophets, he interpreted to them in all the Scriptures the things concerning himself" (Lk 24:27). It was precisely this extensive spiritual interpretation of the Old Testament that made such an impact on these once-discouraged travelers, causing their hearts to "burn" within them (Lk 24:32).

Criteria for Biblical Interpretation We, too, must learn to discern the "full sense" of Scripture as it includes both the literal and spiritual senses together. Still, this does not mean we should "read into" the Bible meanings that are not really there. Spiritual exegesis is not an unrestrained flight of the imagination. Rather, it is a sacred science that proceeds according to certain principles and stands accountable to sacred tradition, the Magisterium, and the wider community of biblical interpreters (both living and deceased).

In searching out the full sense of a text, we should always avoid the extreme tendency to "over-spiritualize" in a way that minimizes or denies the Bible's literal truth. St. Thomas Aquinas was well aware of this danger and asserted that "all other senses of Sacred Scripture are based on the literal" (*STh* I, 1, 10, *ad* 1, quoted in CCC 116). On the other hand, we should never confine the meaning of a text to the literal, intended sense of its human author, as if the divine Author did not intend the passage to be read in the light of Christ's coming.

Fortunately the Church has given us guidelines in our study of Scripture. The unique character and divine authorship of the Bible call us to read it "in the Spirit" (*Dei Verbum* 12). Vatican II outlines this teaching in a practical way by directing us to read the Scriptures according to three specific criteria:

1. We must "[b]e especially attentive 'to the content and unity of the whole Scripture'" (CCC 112).

2. We must "[r]ead the Scripture within 'the living Tradition of the whole Church'" (CCC 113).

3. We must "[b]e attentive to the analogy of faith" (CCC 114; cf. Rom 12:6).

These criteria protect us from many of the dangers that ensnare readers of the Bible, from the newest inquirer to the most prestigious scholar. Reading Scripture out of context is one such pitfall, and probably the one most difficult to avoid. A memorable cartoon from the 1950s shows a young man poring over the pages of the Bible. He says to his sister: "Don't bother me now; I'm trying to find a Scripture verse to back up one of my preconceived notions." No doubt a biblical text pried from its context can be twisted to say something very different from what its author actually intended.

The Church's criteria guide us here by defining what constitutes the authentic "context" of a given biblical passage. The first criterion directs us to the literary context of every verse, including not only the words and paragraphs that surround it, but also the entire corpus of the biblical author's writings and, indeed, the span of the entire Bible. The *complete* literary context of any Scripture verse includes every text from Genesis to Revelation—because the Bible is a unified book, not just a library of different books. When the Church canonized the Book of Revelation, for example, she recognized it to be incomprehensible apart from the wider context of the entire Bible.

The second criterion places the Bible firmly within the context of a community that treasures a "living tradition". That community is the People of God down through the ages. Christians lived out their faith for well over a millennium before the printing press was invented. For centuries, few believers owned copies of the Gospels, and few people could read anyway. Yet they absorbed the gospel—through the sermons of their bishops and clergy, through prayer and meditation, through Christian art, through liturgical celebrations, and through oral tradition. These were expressions of the one "living tradition", a culture of living faith that stretches from ancient Israel to the contemporary Church. For the early Christians, the gospel could not be understood apart from that tradition. So it is with us. Reverence for the Church's tradition is what protects us from any sort of chronological or cultural provincialism, such as scholarly fads that arise and carry away a generation of interpreters before being dismissed by the next generation.

The third criterion places scriptural texts within the framework of faith. If we believe that the Scriptures are divinely inspired, we must also believe them to be internally coherent and consistent with all the doctrines that Christians believe. Remember, the Church's dogmas (such as the Real Presence, the papacy, the Immaculate Conception) are not something *added* to Scripture; rather, they are the Church's infallible interpretation *of* Scripture.

Using This Study Guide This volume is designed to lead the reader through Scripture according to the Church's guidelines—faithful to the canon, to the tradition, and to the creeds. The Church's interpretive principles have thus shaped the component parts of this book, and they are designed to make the reader's study as effective and rewarding as possible.

Introductions: We have introduced the biblical book with an essay covering issues such as authorship, date of composition, purpose, and leading themes. This background information will assist readers to approach and understand the text on its own terms.

Annotations: The basic notes at the bottom of every page help the user to read the Scriptures with understanding. They by no means exhaust the meaning of the sacred text but provide background material to help the reader make sense of what he reads. Often these notes make explicit what the sacred writers assumed or held to be implicit. They also provide a great deal of historical, cultural, geographical, and theological information pertinent to the inspired narratives—information that can help the reader bridge the distance between the biblical world and his own.

Cross-References: Between the biblical text at the top of each page and the annotations at the bottom, numerous references are listed to point readers to other scriptural passages related to the one being studied. This follow-up is an essential part of any serious study. It is also an excellent way to discover how the content of Scripture "hangs together" in a providential unity. Along with biblical cross-references, the annotations refer to select paragraphs from the *Catechism of the Catholic Church*. These are not doctrinal "proof texts" but are designed to help the reader interpret the Bible in accordance with the mind of the Church. The *Catechism* references listed either handle the biblical text directly or treat a broader doctrinal theme that sheds significant light on that text.

Topical Essays, Word Studies, Charts: These features bring readers to a deeper understanding of select details. The *topical essays* take up major themes and explain them more thoroughly and theologically than the annotations, often relating them to the doctrines of the Church. Occasionally the annotations are supplemented by *word studies* that put readers in touch with the ancient languages of Scripture. These should help readers to understand better and appreciate the inspired terminology that runs throughout the sacred books. Also included are various *charts* that summarize biblical information "at a glance".

Icon Annotations: Three distinctive icons are interspersed throughout the annotations, each one corresponding to one of the Church's three criteria for biblical interpretation. Bullets indicate the passage or passages to which these icons apply.

📖 Notes marked by the book icon relate to the "content and unity" of Scripture, showing how particular passages of the Old Testament illuminate the mysteries of the New. Much of the information in these notes explains the original context of the citations and indicates how and why this has a direct bearing on Christ or the Church. Through these notes, the reader can develop a sensitivity to the beauty and unity of God's saving plan as it stretches across both Testaments.

🕊 Notes marked by the dove icon examine particular passages in light of the Church's "living tradition". Because the Holy Spirit both guides the Magisterium and inspires the spiritual senses of Scripture, these annotations supply information along both of these lines. On the one hand, they refer to the Church's doctrinal teaching as presented by various popes, creeds, and ecumenical councils; on the other, they draw from (and paraphrase) the spiritual interpretations of various Fathers, Doctors, and saints.

🗝 Notes marked by the keys icon pertain to the "analogy of faith". Here we spell out how the mysteries of our faith "unlock" and explain one another. This type of comparison between Christian beliefs displays the coherence and unity of defined dogmas, which are the Church's infallible interpretations of Scripture.

Putting It All in Perspective Perhaps the most important context of all we have saved for last: the interior life of the individual reader. What we get out of the Bible will largely depend on how we approach the Bible. Unless we are living a sustained and disciplined life of prayer, we will never have the reverence, the profound humility, or the grace we need to see the Scriptures for what they really are.

You are approaching the "word of God". But for thousands of years, since before he knit you in your mother's womb, the Word of God has been approaching you.

One Final Note. The volume you hold in your hands is only a small part of a much larger work still in production. Study helps similar to those printed in this booklet are being prepared for *all* the books of the Bible and will appear gradually as they are finished. Our ultimate goal is to publish a single, one-volume Study Bible that will include the entire text of Scripture, along with all the annotations, charts, cross-references, maps, and other features found in the following pages. Individual booklets will be published in the meantime, with the hope that God's people can begin to benefit from this labor before its full completion.

We have included a long list of Study Questions in the back to make this format as useful as possible, not only for individual study, but for group settings and discussions as well. The questions are designed to help readers both "understand" the Bible and "apply" it to their lives. We pray that God will make use of our efforts and yours to help renew the face of the earth! «

INTRODUCTION TO THE FIRST BOOK OF THE KINGS

Author and Date No one knows for certain who composed or compiled the Books of the Kings. One strand of rabbinic Judaism considered them the work of the prophet Jeremiah, based on similarities of perspective and the shared information in 2 Kings 24:18—25:30 and Jer 52:1–34 (Babylonian Talmud, *Baba Bathra* 15a), but the majority of modern scholars are unconvinced of this. Whatever his name, the anonymous compiler of Kings may be profiled as a historian and theologian who consulted several ancient sources to produce a narrative of the Israelite monarchy extending from the reign of Solomon in the tenth century B.C. up to the Babylonian Exile in the sixth century B.C. Three sources are identified by name in the work: "the book of the acts of Solomon" (1 Kings 11:41), "the Book of the Chronicles of the Kings of Israel" (1 Kings 14:19; 2 Kings 1:18, etc.), and "the Book of the Chronicles of the Kings of Judah" (1 Kings 14:29; 2 Kings 8:23, etc.). It is likely that these documents were royal administrative annals written close in time to the events they record and preserved in state archives. Other possible sources utilized in Kings include a "Succession Narrative" that details the transition from David's kingship to Solomon's rule (underlying 2 Sam 9–20 and 1 Kings 1–2) as well as stories about influential prophets who intervened in the affairs of Israel and Judah (e.g., the Elijah and Elisha cycles in 1 Kings 17—2 Kings 13).

Despite uncertainty of authorship, dating the Books of the Kings is straightforward. The final edition of the work must have appeared in the middle of the sixth century B.C., its last recorded event being the release of Jehoiachin from prison in 560 B.C. (2 Kings 25:27). At the same time, there are indications that an incomplete version of Kings existed in written form before the sixth century. For instance, several occurrences of the expression "to this day" appear in contexts that imply the narrator was writing in the land of Israel sometime before the Babylonian Exile (1 Kings 8:8; 9:13, 21). One can reasonably surmise, then, that a *first* edition of Kings existed before the sixth century B.C., even if the *final* edition can be dated to the middle of the sixth century B.C.

Modern scholarship often associates 1 and 2 Kings with a larger grouping of biblical writings that chronicles the fortunes of Israel living in the Promised Land. The conventional name for this corpus of texts, which extends from Joshua to 2 Kings, is the Deuteronomistic History. Advocates typically view these books (not including Ruth) as constituting a unified literary work that shares a common vocabulary and theological vision indebted to the Book of Deuteronomy. Initially, it was thought that Kings was produced by a single author, called the "Deuteronomist", who compiled his account during the Babylonian Exile. Subsequently, however, scholars began to argue that Kings (along with Joshua, Judges, and Samuel) was produced in stages by a school of theologians, called "Deuteronomists". One version of this hypothesis holds that the first edition of Kings was produced in the late seventh century, during the reign of King Josiah, and that an updated edition appeared in the middle of the sixth century, after the release of King Jehoiachin. Another hypothesis posits three editions of the book: the first consisting of the fundamental storyline, a second that added material about various prophets, and a third that showed great concern for observance of the Law. Given the lack of consensus on matters of detail and date, these and similar approaches to the compositional history of 1 and 2 Kings are best considered provisional, being subject to refinement or rejection as additional evidence comes to light in the future.

Title The Books of the Kings have borne different names over the centuries besides *Melakim*, the Hebrew word for "Kings". Though originally a single book, Kings was divided by the Greek Septuagint into two volumes in the second or third century B.C. and grouped together with the Books of Samuel under the heading "Kingdoms". First Kings was thus known in Greek as *Basileiōn Gamma*, "Third Kingdoms". Saint Jerome, in his translation of the Latin Vulgate, followed the Greek LXX tradition of dividing the work into two books but followed Hebrew tradition with the title *Libri Regum*, "Books of the Kings".

Place in the Canon First Kings stands after the Books of Samuel in the arrangement of the Old Testament because it continues the story of the Israelite monarchy after the kingship of David. In the Hebrew canon, it is the fifth of the "Former Prophets", a sequence of books that extends from Joshua to 2 Kings (minus Ruth) and evaluates the successes and failures of Israel from a prophetic perspective, which is to say, in direct relation to Israel's fidelity or infidelity to the Lord and his covenant. Christian tradition likewise accepts the prophetic perspective of 1 Kings but classifies it as one of the "Historical Books" of the Bible.

Structure First Kings divides neatly into two parts, with eleven chapters devoted to the united monarchy and eleven chapters devoted to the beginning of the divided monarchy. **(1)** Chapters 1–11 detail the rise and fall of the illustrious King Solomon. Attention is given to his succession, his wisdom, and his greatest architectural achievement—the building of the Jerusalem Temple. By the end of this section, however, the glory of Solomon begins to fade and his mighty empire begins to show signs of instability that forecast trouble for the future. **(2)** Chapters 12–22 open with the tragic division of the kingdom. Israel's northern tribes break away from Jerusalem to start their own kingdom (Israel), while two southern tribes remain loyal to the ruling house of David (Judah). Thereafter, the narrative is a back-and-forth report about the succession of kings in Israel and Judah in the years following Solomon's death. In the midst of these reports, several prophets appear on the scene to speak the word of the Lord. Elijah is singled out for prolonged attention since his ministry turns a spotlight on the spiritual crisis that prevailed in Israel during these troubled times.

Genre and Purpose First Kings is a work of theological history. It continues the running historical narrative that stretches from Israel's entrance into Canaan to its tragic exile from Canaan. The author's intention to write history is manifest through his interest in factual and statistical information connected with the kings of Israel and Judah as well as the scale of Solomon's monumental architecture. The chronology of the period is carefully outlined, and the tenures of Israel's northern and southern kings are capably synchronized. Utilizing a relatively fixed format, the historian records the accession of each king in relation to his royal counterpart in the neighboring kingdom, the length of his reign, his age when coming to power and the name of his mother (for the kings of Judah), and sometimes the location of his royal residence (for the kings of Israel). He also claims to have drawn his information from official sources that provide fuller documentation of the period (11:14; 14:19, 29, etc.). Archaeology has yet to confirm beyond dispute the discovery of artifacts from the kingdom of Solomon (but see note on 9:15); however, there have been numerous discoveries that verify the historicity of key figures and events from the period of the divided monarchy that are described in the Books of the Kings (see notes on 1 Kings 14:25; 16:16, 28; 2 Kings 3:5; 9:1—10:36; 15:17; 18:13; 20:20; 25:30).

That said, the Books of the Kings are not principally concerned with secular affairs and matters of state. Some attention is given to the political achievements of Israel's monarchs, but theological interests stand out as primary. The main objective of the Kings historian is to document the failure of Israel and its royal leaders to uphold their covenant commitment to Yahweh. Apostasy and idolatry are thereby exposed as the underlying causes of Israel's moral corruption, political decline, and societal troubles. Looking back from the experience of judgment and exile, Kings contends that God, far from forgetting his covenant with Israel, acted to enforce the terms of his covenant by sending the curses that disobedience triggers against his wayward people (see Deut 28:15–68).

Content and Themes First Kings begins as a national success story. Under the intelligent leadership of Solomon, Israel soars to spiritual and political greatness and enters a golden age of biblical history. It is a time of regional peace, a booming economy, and international prestige for the covenant people. For several decades, the tribes of Israel are united as one nation under God, and neighboring states are made part of the Solomonic empire (4:20–25). The secret behind this success: Solomon "loved" the Lord from the heart (3:3) and had the humility to ask God for wisdom in the ways of royal leadership (3:7–9). So generous is God's answer to this prayer that Solomon becomes the wisest man of his times, a teacher of Israel and other nations on a wide assortment of subjects (4:29–34; 10:23–24). The crown jewel of his achievements is the building of a temple for Yahweh, a national sanctuary to stand at the center of Israel's life and to shine out as a beacon to the world (chaps. 6–8). Love for God coupled with the use of the gifts that come from God for his glory—these, the book implies, are the keys that unlock the heavens and bring blessings upon the covenant people.

But the glory days of Solomon were not to last. Enamored by relentless success, the king oversteps the bounds of the Deuteronomic covenant, which forbids the king of Israel to pile up weapons, wives, and wealth for himself (compare 10:14–29 with Deut 17:14–17). From this point on, everything is downhill. Solomon quickly diverts his affection from the Lord to his royal ladies (11:1), and soon he is sponsoring their foreign religious cults in Jerusalem (11:4–8). Decisive proof that Solomon has broken the covenant comes after his death, when Israel itself breaks apart into two rival kingdoms (12:1–20). The rest of the story is a tale of ongoing religious and political rebellion. The Northern Kingdom that forms in opposition to Jerusalem and the Davidic kings of the south is idolatrous from the start (12:25–33), and certain northern kings, such as Ahab, continue to worsen the problem by promoting Canaanite religion throughout the land (16:30–33; 18:17–18). Corruption of faith and worship is also in evidence in the Southern Kingdom (14:22–24). Not a single king after Solomon, northern or southern, receives unqualified praise in the narrative of 1 Kings. Practically the only high point in the second half of the book comes when the prophet Elijah mounts a direct assault on Canaanite idolatry (Baal worship) and pleads for a return to Yahweh

(18:20–40). His efforts are successful but disappointingly short-lived. None of the spiritual crises that dominate the period of the divided monarchy are resolved by the end of the book.

Christian Perspective Christian reflection perceives many parallels between 1 Kings and the New Testament. The most important links concern King Solomon, who prefigures the Person of Jesus Christ. Both are anointed successors of David (1:33–34; Mt 1:1); both are renowned for wise teachings (4:29–34; Mt 12:42); both are proclaimed king while riding into Jerusalem on a donkey (1:38–40; Mt 21:6–11); and both come to reign over a vast multinational empire (4:21; Mt 28:18–20). For these and related reasons, the kingdom of Solomon stands as a historical prototype behind Jesus' proclamation of the kingdom of God. Moreover, Solomon's masterpiece, the Temple in Jerusalem, is a mystery that foreshadows both the Incarnation of God's Son (Mt 12:6; Jn 2:21) and the indwelling of God's Spirit in the Church (Eph 2:19–22). The prophet Elijah is likewise a typological figure. On the one hand, he anticipates John the Baptist as a preacher of repentance (18:20–21; Lk 1:17) and a fiery confronter of kings (21:17–24; Mk 6:14–18). On the other, Elijah prepares the way for Jesus as a miracle-working prophet. Both control the weather by their word (17:1; Mk 4:35–41); both multiply food for the hungry (17:8–16; Mt 14:13–21); both raise the dead (17:17–24; Jn 11:38–44); and both set out into the wilderness, where they fast for forty days and forty nights (19:8; Mt 4:1–2).

OUTLINE OF THE FIRST BOOK OF THE KINGS

1. Solomon and the United Monarchy (chaps. 1–11)
   A. Solomon Succeeds David (1:1—2:46)
   B. Solomon's Wisdom (3:1—4:34)
   C. Preparations for the Temple (5:1–18)
   D. Solomon Builds the Temple and Palace (6:1—7:51)
   E. Solomon Dedicates the Temple (8:1–66)
   F. Solomon's Reign, Reputation, and Riches (9:1—10:29)
   G. Solomon's Downfall and Death (11:1–43)

2. Rebellion and the Divided Monarchy (chaps. 12–22)
   A. Rehoboam, Jeroboam, and the Division of the Kingdom (12:1–33)
   B. Judgment against Jeroboam (13:1—14:20)
   C. Kingdom of Judah: Rehoboam, Abijam, Asa (14:21—15:15)
   D. Kingdom of Israel: Nadab, Baasha, Elah, Zimri, Omri, Ahab (15:16—16:34)
   E. Elijah the Prophet and King Ahab (17:1—21:29)
   F. Israel and Judah Allied in War (22:1–40)
   G. Kingdom of Judah: Jehoshaphat, Jehoram (22:41–50)
   H. Kingdom of Israel: Ahaziah (22:51–53)

THE FIRST BOOK OF THE
KINGS

The Struggle for Succession to the Throne

1 *Now King David was old and advanced in years; and although they covered him with clothes, he could not get warm. ²Therefore his servants said to him, "Let a young maiden be sought for my lord the king, and let her wait upon the king, and be his nurse; let her lie in your bosom, that my lord the king may be warm." ³So they sought for a beautiful maiden throughout all the territory of Israel, and found Ab'ishag the Shu'nammite, and brought her to the king. ⁴The maiden was very beautiful; and she became the king's nurse and ministered to him; but the king knew her not.

5 Now Adoni'jah the son of Haggith exalted himself, saying, "I will be king";† and he prepared for himself chariots and horsemen, and fifty men to run before him. ⁶His father had never at any time displeased him by asking, "Why have you done thus and so?" He was also a very handsome man; and he was born next after Ab'salom. ⁷He conferred with Jo'ab the son of Zeru'iah and with Abi'athar the priest; and they followed Adoni'jah and helped him. ⁸But Za'dok the priest, and Bena'iah the son of Jehoi'ada, and Nathan the prophet, and Shim'e-i, and Re'i, and David's mighty men were not with Adoni'jah.

9 Adoni'jah sacrificed sheep, oxen, and fatlings by the Serpent's Stone, which is beside En-ro'gel, and he invited all his brothers, the king's sons, and all the royal officials of Judah, ¹⁰but he did not invite Nathan the prophet or Bena'iah or the mighty men or Solomon his brother.

11 Then Nathan said to Bathshe'ba the mother of Solomon, "Have you not heard that Adoni'jah the son of Haggith has become king and David our lord does not know it? ¹²Now therefore come, let me give you counsel, that you may save your own life and the life of your son Solomon. ¹³Go in at once to King David, and say to him, 'Did you not, my lord the king, swear to your maidservant, saying, "Solomon your son shall reign after me, and he shall sit upon my throne"? Why then is Adoni'jah king?' ¹⁴Then while you are still speaking with the king, I also will come in after you and confirm your words."

15 So Bathshe'ba went to the king into his chamber (now the king was very old, and Ab'ishag the Shu'nammite was ministering to the king). ¹⁶Bathshe'ba bowed and did obeisance to the king, and the king said, "What do you desire?" ¹⁷She said to him, "My lord, you swore to your maidservant by the Lord your God, saying, 'Solomon your son shall reign after me, and he shall sit upon my throne.'

1:1–53 First Kings opens with a crisis of royal succession. David, old and nearing death, had sworn an oath to pass the crown to his tenth son, Solomon (1:13); however, since no official announcement had been made, the general public assumed that his oldest living son, Adonijah, was the heir apparent (2:15). The crisis is resolved with a public anointing of Solomon in full view of the people (1:38–40).

1:1 David was old: About 70 years old, judging from 2:11 and 2 Sam 5:4.

1:4 knew her not: The king did not have sexual relations with his nurse. See word study: *Know* at Judg 19:22.

📖 **1:5 Adonijah:** The fourth son born to David (2 Sam 3:4). He was widely expected to rule as his father's successor (2:15) since his three older brothers were already out of the running for David's throne: Amnon and Absalom had been killed by this point, and Chileab (2 Sam 3:2–4) seems to have died. In his attempt to gain power, Adonijah follows in the footsteps of Absalom, whose temporary coup is described in 2 Sam 15–18. Among parallels between the two, Adonijah, like Absalom, (1) assembles a small army with horses, chariots, and foot soldiers (1:5; 2 Sam 15:1), (2) stands out for his good looks (1:6; 2 Sam 14:25), (3) offers sacrifices like a priest (1:9; 2 Sam 15:12), and (4) invites the nobility of Jerusalem to his self-coronation banquet (1:9, 41; 2 Sam 15:11). The prominence of these parallels hints that Adonijah is destined for ruin (2:23–25), just as Absalom had been (2 Sam 18:9–15).

1:7 Joab: David's military commander (2 Sam 20:23). **Abiathar:** One of two chief priests in David's court, along with Zadok (2 Sam 20:25).

1:8 Zadok: One of two chief priests in David's court, along with Abiathar (2 Sam 20:25). **Benaiah:** The officer in charge of David's bodyguards, the Cherethites and Pelethites (2 Sam 20:23). **Nathan:** One of David's court prophets (2 Sam 7:2). **mighty men:** A corps of elite warriors who pledged their loyalty to David. See note on 2 Sam 23:8–39.

1:9 sacrificed: Either the priest Abiathar performed the cultic rites (1:7) or Adonijah acted illicitly, since he was neither a priest nor as yet a king. **En-rogel:** In the valley directly south of Jerusalem, within earshot of the Gihon spring (1:33), where proclamation of Solomon's kingship will be made (1:38–39).

1:11 Bathsheba: The widow of Uriah the Hittite, now married to David and the mother of his tenth son, Solomon (2 Sam 11:26–27; 12:24). Her name means "daughter of the oath".

1:13 swear: No record of this oath is preserved in 2 Samuel. Nevertheless, it is the decisive factor that prompts David to make his choice of a successor publicly known. Solomon's coronation will thus fulfill David's oath to Bathsheba (1:17) as well as God's earlier oath to David (2 Sam 7:8–16).

The First and Second Books of the Kings (the Third and Fourth Books of the Kings): the period covered in these books extends from the death of David to after the fall of Jerusalem in the year 586 B.C. The main theme is the steady decline of Israel dragged down by the monarchy, and her punishment by God for the worship of false gods, introduced by Solomon and actively promoted by many of his successors, especially in the Northern Kingdom.

*1:1: The story continues from 2 Sam 20:26.

†1:5: There was as yet no natural right of succession and David had already given the right to Solomon, a younger son; cf. verse 13.

¹⁸And now, behold, Adoni′jah is king, although you, my lord the king, do not know it. ¹⁹He has sacrificed oxen, fatlings, and sheep in abundance, and has invited all the sons of the king, Abi′athar the priest, and Jo′ab the commander of the army; but Solomon your servant he has not invited. ²⁰And now, my lord the king, the eyes of all Israel are upon you, to tell them who shall sit on the throne of my lord the king after him. ²¹Otherwise it will come to pass, when my lord the king sleeps with his fathers, that I and my son Solomon will be counted offenders."

22 While she was still speaking with the king, Nathan the prophet came in. ²³And they told the king, "Here is Nathan the prophet." And when he came in before the king, he bowed before the king, with his face to the ground. ²⁴And Nathan said, "My lord the king, have you said, 'Adoni′jah shall reign after me, and he shall sit upon my throne'? ²⁵For he has gone down this day, and has sacrificed oxen, fatlings, and sheep in abundance, and has invited all the king's sons, Jo′ab the commander ᵃ of the army, and Abi′athar the priest; and behold, they are eating and drinking before him, and saying, 'Long live King Adoni′jah!' ²⁶But me, your servant, and Za′dok the priest, and Bena′iah the son of Jehoi′ada, and your servant Solomon, he has not invited. ²⁷Has this thing been brought about by my lord the king and you have not told your servants who should sit on the throne of my lord the king after him?"

Solomon Is Made King

28 Then King David answered, "Call Bathshe′ba to me." So she came into the king's presence, and stood before the king. ²⁹And the king swore, saying, "As the Lᴏʀᴅ lives, who has redeemed my soul out of every adversity, ³⁰as I swore to you by the Lᴏʀᴅ, the God of Israel, saying, 'Solomon your son shall reign after me, and he shall sit upon my throne in my stead'; even so will I do this day." ³¹Then Bathshe′ba bowed with her face to the ground, and did obeisance to the king, and said, "May my lord King David live for ever!"

32 King David said, "Call to me Za′dok the priest, Nathan the prophet, and Bena′iah the son of Jehoi′ada." So they came before the king. ³³And the king said to them, "Take with you the servants of your lord, and cause Solomon my son to ride on my own mule, and bring him down to Gi′hon; ³⁴and let Za′dok the priest and Nathan the prophet there anoint him king over Israel; then blow the trumpet, and say, 'Long live King Solomon!' ³⁵You shall then come up after him, and he shall come and sit upon my throne; for he shall be king in my stead; and I have appointed him to be ruler over Israel and over Judah." ³⁶And Bena′iah the son of Jehoi′ada answered the king, "Amen! May the Lᴏʀᴅ, the God of my lord the king, say so. ³⁷As the Lᴏʀᴅ has been with my lord the king, even so may he be with Solomon, and make his throne greater than the throne of my lord King David."

38 So Za′dok the priest, Nathan the prophet, and Bena′iah the son of Jehoi′ada, and the Cher′ethites and the Pel′ethites, went down and caused Solomon to ride on King David's mule, and brought him to Gi′hon. ³⁹There Za′dok the priest took the horn of oil from the tent, and anointed Solomon. Then they blew the trumpet; and all the people said, "Long live King Solomon!" ⁴⁰And all the people went up after him, playing on pipes, and rejoicing with great joy, so that the earth was split by their noise.

41 Adoni′jah and all the guests who were with him heard it as they finished feasting. And when Jo′ab heard the sound of the trumpet, he said, "What does this uproar in the city mean?" ⁴²While he was still speaking, behold, Jonathan the son of Abi′athar the priest came; and Adoni′jah said, "Come in, for you are a worthy man and bring good news." ⁴³Jonathan answered Adoni′jah, "No, for our lord King David has made Solomon king; ⁴⁴and the king has sent with him Za′dok the priest, Nathan the prophet, and Bena′iah the son of Jehoi′ada, and the Cher′ethites and the Pel′ethites; and they have caused him to ride on the king's mule; ⁴⁵and Za′dok the priest and Nathan the prophet have anointed

---

1:21 sleeps with his fathers: An idiom for death, by which the deceased joins the company of his ancestors (Deut 31:16).

1:29 As the Lᴏʀᴅ lives: An oath formula. What follows is a second oath to Bathsheba that reinforces David's earlier pledge to make Solomon king (1:17).

1:33 Gihon: A natural spring on the eastern slope of Jerusalem.

1:34 anoint him: Anointing involves pouring oil upon the head of a candidate, whether a prophet (19:16), a priest (Lev 8:12), or a king (1 Sam 10:1). It is a sign of the Spirit pouring down upon the recipient (1 Sam 16:13; Is 61:1). Aside from this official rite of installation, the Bible also speaks of anointing for cosmetic and medicinal purposes (Ps 23:5; Song 1:3; Is 1:6; Mt 6:17; Lk 10:34) (CCC 436, 695).

1:35 over Israel ... Judah: I.e., over the northern and southern tribes of Israel. David was given this same dominion by a double anointing, one in 2 Sam 2:4 (over Judah) and another in 2 Sam 5:3 (over Israel).

1:37 the Lᴏʀᴅ ... my lord: Points to the close relationship between Yahweh and the kings of Israel. Its foundation is the Davidic covenant, which created a father-and-son bond between the Lord and his royal representative on earth (2 Sam 7:13–14). The same language is used in Ps 110:1.

1:38–40 Solomon's accession to the throne is made known to the public by a royal procession into the city. • The event foreshadows Jesus' triumphal entry into Jerusalem on Palm Sunday. Like Solomon, Jesus will mount a donkey (1:38; Jn 12:14) and ride into the city to the sound of cheering crowds (1:40, 45; Lk 19:37) hailing him as the heir to David's kingdom (1:39; Mk 11:10; Lk 19:38).

1:39 the tent: The tent that David pitched on Mt. Zion as a temporary shelter for the Ark of the Covenant. See notes on 2 Sam 6:17 and 1 Chron 16:1.

ᵃGk: Heb *commanders*.

him king at Gi′hon; and they have gone up from there rejoicing, so that the city is in an uproar. This is the noise that you have heard. ⁴⁶Solomon sits upon the royal throne. ⁴⁷Moreover the king's servants came to congratulate our lord King David, saying, 'Your God make the name of Solomon more famous than yours, and make his throne greater than your throne.' And the king bowed himself upon the bed. ⁴⁸And the king also said, 'Blessed be the Lord, the God of Israel, who has granted one of my offspring^b to sit on my throne this day, my own eyes seeing it.'"

49 Then all the guests of Adoni′jah trembled, and rose, and each went his own way. ⁵⁰And Adoni′jah feared Solomon; and he arose, and went, and caught hold of the horns of the altar. ⁵¹And it was told Solomon, "Behold, Adoni′jah fears King Solomon; for behold, he has laid hold of the horns of the altar, saying, 'Let King Solomon swear to me first that he will not slay his servant with the sword.'" ⁵²And Solomon said, "If he prove to be a worthy man, not one of his hairs shall fall to the earth; but if wickedness is found in him, he shall die." ⁵³So King Solomon sent, and they brought him down from the altar. And he came and did obeisance to King Solomon; and Solomon said to him, "Go to your house."

David's Instructions to Solomon

2 When David's time to die drew near, he charged Solomon his son, saying, ²"I am about to go the way of all the earth. Be strong, and show yourself a man, ³and keep the charge of the Lord your God, walking in his ways and keeping his statutes, his commandments, his ordinances, and his testimonies, as it is written in the law of Moses, that you may prosper in all that you do and wherever you turn;

⁴that the Lord may establish his word which he spoke concerning me, saying, 'If your sons take heed to their way, to walk before me in faithfulness with all their heart and with all their soul, there shall not fail you a man on the throne of Israel.'

5 "Moreover you know also what Jo′ab the son of Zeru′iah did to me, how he dealt with the two commanders of the armies of Israel, Abner the son of Ner, and Ama′sa the son of Je′ther, whom he murdered, avenging^c in time of peace blood which had been shed in war, and putting innocent blood^d upon the belt about my^e loins, and upon the sandals on my^e feet. ⁶Act therefore according to your wisdom, but do not let his gray head go down to Sheol in peace. ⁷But deal loyally with the sons of Barzil′lai the Gileadite, and let them be among those who eat at your table; for with such loyalty they met me when I fled from Ab′salom your brother. ⁸And there is also with you Shim′e-i the son of Gera, the Benjaminite from Bahu′rim, who cursed me with a grievous curse on the day when I went to Ma″hana′im; but when he came down to meet me at the Jordan, I swore to him by the Lord, saying, 'I will not put you to death with the sword.' ⁹Now therefore hold him not guiltless, for you are a wise man; you will know what you ought to do to him, and you shall bring his gray head down with blood to Sheol."

Death and Burial of David

10 Then David slept with his fathers, and was buried in the city of David. ¹¹And the time that David reigned over Israel was forty years; he reigned seven years in He′bron, and thirty-three years in Jerusalem. ¹²So Solomon sat upon the throne of David his father; and his kingdom was firmly established.

2:12: 1 Chron 29:23.

1:50 horns: Protruded from the top four corners of the sanctuary altar. This was a place of asylum for one seeking legal protection for his life (cf. Ex 21:12–14).

1:52 worthy ... wickedness: The question is whether Adonijah will acknowledge Solomon's kingship or continue to seek the crown for himself.

2:1–9 David's last will and testament delivered to Solomon, who is urged to follow the Law of God, to punish his father's opponents (Joab, Shimei), and to reward his loyal supporters (the sons of Barzillai). Similar farewell speeches are given by Moses (Deut 31:1–8), Joshua (Josh 23:1–16), and Samuel (1 Sam 12:1–25).

2:2 the way of all the earth: The road of human life that ends in death (Josh 23:14).

2:3 that you may prosper: Just as David prospered by the hand of the Lord (1 Sam 18:14).

2:4 his word: Yahweh's oath to establish an everlasting dynasty with David and his royal descendants (2 Sam 7:15–16). The Davidic covenant is conditional insofar as God promised to chastise the Davidic line should kings in the future turn away from him (see 2 Sam 7:14).

2:5 Joab: David's nephew, born to his sister Zeruiah (2 Sam 2:18). For years Joab served as David's chief military officer

(2 Sam 8:16), but on several occasions he defied the wishes of the king and murdered such rivals as Abner, the commander of Saul's army (2 Sam 3:26–30), and Amasa, the commander of Absalom's army (2 Sam 20:10). These assassinations dishonored David by making his administration guilty of shedding blood in peacetime. For Joab's violent temperament, see note on 2 Sam 18:14.

2:6 Sheol: Hebrew term for the realm of the dead. See word study: *Sheol* at Num 16:30.

2:7 sons of Barzillai: Sons of a wealthy benefactor who came to David's assistance during his temporary exile from Jerusalem (2 Sam 19:31–40). Solomon is to give them the benefits of living at the royal court (2 Sam 9:7).

2:8 Shimei: The scoundrel who cursed David on his harrowing flight from Jerusalem (2 Sam 16:5–8). David had sworn an oath to spare his life at the time (2 Sam 19:23), but there was nothing to prevent Solomon from repaying him for his treachery (2:36–46).

2:10 slept ... buried: David's obituary. • The NT points to the death and burial of David as indicating that God's promises *to* David are not ultimately fulfilled *in* David. The divine pledge of an everlasting Davidic kingdom (2 Sam 7:12–16) awaits an undying Davidic king: Jesus the Messiah, who was raised immortal (Acts 2:22–36; 13:32–37).

2:11 forty years: David reigned as king from ca. 1010 to 970 B.C. See chart: *Old Testament Chronology* at 1 Sam 13.

2:12 established: Alludes to the wording of the Davidic covenant in 2 Sam 7:12–13, 16.

---

^bGk: Heb *one.*
^cGk: Heb *placing.*
^dGk: Heb *blood of war.*
^eGk: Heb *his.*

Adonijah's Intrigue

13 Then Adoni′jah the son of Haggith came to Bathshe′ba the mother of Solomon. And she said, "Do you come peaceably?" He said, "Peaceably." ¹⁴Then he said, "I have something to say to you." She said, "Say on." ¹⁵He said, "You know that the kingdom was mine, and that all Israel fully expected me to reign; however the kingdom has turned about and become my brother's, for it was his from the LORD. ¹⁶And now I have one request to make of you; do not refuse me." She said to him, "Say on." ¹⁷And he said, "Please ask King Solomon—he will not refuse you—to give me Ab′ishag the Shu′nammite as my wife." ¹⁸Bathshe′ba said, "Very well; I will speak for you to the king."

19 So Bathshe′ba went to King Solomon, to speak to him on behalf of Adoni′jah. And the king rose to meet her, and bowed down to her; then he sat on his throne, and had a seat brought for the king's mother; and she sat on his right. ²⁰Then she said, "I have one small request to make of you; do not refuse me." And the king said to her, "Make your request, my mother; for I will not refuse you." ²¹She said, "Let Ab′ishag the Shu′nammite be given

---

2:13–46 Solomon begins his reign by settling accounts with opponents. He has his brother Adonijah slain (2:13–25), the priest Abiathar banished (2:26–27), the commander Joab put to death (2:28–35), and the reviling Shimei executed three years later for breaking his oath (2:36–46). Regrettably, bloodshed often accompanied transitions in power in the ruthless world of Near Eastern politics.

2:17 will not refuse you: An indication that the queen mother, in this instance Bathsheba, wielded considerable authority as an advocate on the Davidic royal court. See essay: *The Queen Mother.* **give me Abishag:** A subtle but sinister attempt to claim the Davidic throne. In Israel, as in the Near East, the harem of the king normally passed to his successor, and so possession of the royal women meant possession of royal authority (also implied in 2 Sam 16:21–22). Aware that Abishag appeared to be one of David's concubines (1:3–4), Solomon is quick to detect the political ambition that lurks behind this simple request (2:22–24).

2:19 seat: The Hebrew *kisse'* can also be translated as "throne", as in 1:13, 17, 20, 24, 27, 30, 35, 37, etc. **on his right:** A position of royal honor and authority (Ps 110:1; Mt 20:21).

The Queen Mother

Several times the Bible refers to a figure known in Hebrew as the *gebirah*, meaning "Great Lady". It is a title borne by the queens of the Israelite monarchy. Modern readers might expect this to be the king's wife. In Israel, however, the office of queenship was held by the king's mother, just as it was in many other royal courts of the ancient Near East. One reason for this is the near-universal practice of polygamy in biblical antiquity, most notably among rich and powerful monarchs capable of supporting a large harem of wives and concubines. Imagine the practical challenges of selecting only one wife from the harem to be the queen! The potential for conflict and power struggles is cleanly averted by this ancient institution, since regardless of how many royal women a king possessed, he had only one mother, and this made her the most suitable candidate to assume the office. So what do we know about the office of the queen mother in the Bible? And why is this important for Christians?

Royal Mothers in the Old Testament
Scripture presents the queen mother as a highly revered noblewoman who came to wield significant authority in the government affairs of Israel. Five considerations give shape and substance to our knowledge of this ancient institution. (1) The office of maternal queenship is inseparable from the office of Davidic kingship. That is, it belonged exclusively to the kingdom of Solomon and to the Southern Kingdom of Judah that descended from it. No parallel institution existed in the Northern Kingdom of Israel. There is one instance where Jezebel, the wife of the northern king, Ahab, is described as a queen mother, but this merely indicates that the southern delegates speaking these words perceived her in this way (2 Kings 10:13). The point stands that queen mothers are exclusively linked with the ruling family of David in Jerusalem. (2) Nearly every time the Bible introduces a new Davidic king, it also gives the name of the king's mother (1 Kings 14:21; 15:2, 10; 22:42; 2 Kings 8:26; 21:1, etc.). There would be no good reason to do this unless she held an official position at court and was part of the incoming administration for each successive king. In fact, there are times when the queen mother is not only numbered among the members of the court but even listed ahead of the king's princes and palace officials (2 Kings 24:12, 15; Jer 29:2). (3) Descriptions of the queen mother include all the pomp and ceremony one would expect for the royal "First Lady" of the kingdom. She wore a crown (Jer 13:18), was arrayed in the finest gold (Ps 45:9), and sat upon a throne at the right hand of the Davidic king (1 Kings 2:19). She was also the recipient of a stately reverence, for even the king was known to bow down in homage before his royal mother (1 Kings 2:19). (4) Parallel references to queen mothership in the ancient Near East indicate that she could be directly involved in the political life of the nation. There is some variation from kingdom to kingdom, but generally speaking she had a hand in domestic policymaking and played a pivotal role in securing the succession of the next king. The king's mother was also one of his most trusted counselors. One sees this, for instance, in Proverbs 31:1–9, which relays the advice of a queen mother who urges her son to administer justice to the poor and to avoid the perennial pitfalls of women and wine. The extent of her authority is made clear especially when her power is abused. A few queen mothers in Israel used their high-level position

to Adoni'jah your brother as his wife." ²²King Solomon answered his mother, "And why do you ask Ab'ishag the Shu'nammite for Adoni'jah? Ask for him the kingdom also; for he is my elder brother, and on his side are Abi'athar ᶠ the priest and Jo'ab the son of Zeru'iah." ²³Then King Solomon swore by the LORD, saying, "God do so to me and more also if this word does not cost Adoni'jah his life! ²⁴Now therefore as the LORD lives, who has established me, and placed me on the throne of David my father, and who has made me a house, as he promised,

Adoni'jah shall be put to death this day." ²⁵So King Solomon sent Bena'iah the son of Jehoi'ada; and he struck him down, and he died.

Solomon Consolidates His Reign

26 And to Abi'athar the priest the king said, "Go to An'athoth, to your estate; for you deserve death. But I will not at this time put you to death, because you bore the ark of the Lord GOD before David my father, and because you shared in all the affliction of my father." ²⁷So Solomon expelled Abi'athar from being priest to the LORD, thus fulfilling the word of

---

2:23 God do so to me: A conditional self-curse. See note on Ruth 1:17.

2:25 Benaiah: The officer formerly in charge of David's bodyguards, the Cherethites and Pelethites (2 Sam 20:23). In Solomon's administration, he is promoted to the rank of chief army commander (2:35) and serves as the king's royal executioner (slaying Adonijah, 2:25; Joab, 2:34; and Shimei, 2:46).

2:26 Abiathar: One of the two chief priests in David's court, the other being Zadok (2 Sam 20:25). Decades

earlier David had given Abiathar protection from Saul (1 Sam 22:20–23), and he seems to have remained loyal to David for many years thereafter (2 Sam 15:24–29). Now, however, Abiathar makes the fateful decision to side with Adonijah in his plan to seize the throne before Solomon's elevation (1:5–7). For this betrayal, Solomon strips him of priestly privileges and banishes him from Jerusalem (2:27). • Theologically, these actions are a fulfillment of the oracle of doom delivered in 1 Sam 2:31–36 that the priestly line of Eli would be punished and cut off. Eli was Abiathar's great-great-grandfather. **Anathoth:** A Levitical town, just north of Jerusalem, in the tribal territory of Benjamin (Josh 21:17–18; Jer 1:1).

ᶠ Gk Syr Vg: Heb *and for him and for Abiathar.*

---

to sponsor idolatry (1 Kings 15:13), to counsel their sons in doing wickedness (2 Chron 22:3), and even to seize control of the kingdom when the Davidic throne was temporarily vacant (2 Kings 11:1–3). (5) If the queen mother was a close advisor to the king, she was also a powerful advocate for the people. Her mediatory role is illustrated by Bathsheba, the mother of King Solomon, who is approached with a petition for the king and who intercedes on behalf of the petitioner (1 Kings 2:13–19). Though her request on this occasion is denied, due to the political treachery it entails, it is clear from Solomon's words that the king was accustomed to show exceptional deference to the queen: "Make your request, my mother; for I will not refuse you" (1 Kings 2:20).

Royal Mother in the New Testament

The role of the queen mother in the Old Testament lays the groundwork for Mary's role in the New Testament. This follows from her maternal relationship to Jesus, who is the royal Messiah from David's line (Mt 1:1–16), the one chosen by God to sit on David's throne (Lk 1:32–33). If Jesus reigns in heaven as the messianic Son of David, then Mary may be seen as the royal mother of the Son of David. Confirmation of this appears in the New Testament. For instance, at the visitation scene in Lk 1:43, Elizabeth humbles herself in the presence of Mary and calls her "the mother of my Lord". No doubt these words point to the mystery of her divine motherhood, since the infant Jesus is the Son of God. But they also point to her Davidic motherhood. The expression "my Lord" is a royal title used for the kings of Israel (2 Sam 24:21; 1 Kings 1:37; 3:17, etc.). Even clearer is the vision in Rev 12:1, where the mother of the Messiah appears in majesty with a crown of twelve stars upon her head. Many interpret this royal woman to be the reigning People of God—either Israel, a family of twelve tribes (Rev 7:4-8), or the Church, built upon the foundation of the twelve apostles (Rev 21:14). This level of symbolism need not be doubted, but a reference to Mary is also likely, for she is the one who actually gave birth to the Messiah, which is the primary focus of the vision. This is significant because the son who is born is a Davidic king who sits upon a "throne" and rules the nations "with a rod of iron" (Rev 12:5, alluding to Ps 2:9). Though modern readers might miss the logic of a queen giving birth to her king, this is precisely the logic of the queen mother tradition as it appears in the Old Testament.

More could be said about the queen mother theme in the Bible, for instance, how it appears in the Prophets (Jer 13:18, 29:2) and how it reappears elsewhere in the New Testament (see Lk 1:32–33). Suffice it to say that the mothers of the Davidic kings were both highly esteemed and politically powerful. Kings looked to them as counselors, and the people looked to them as advocates. In moving from the Old Testament to the New, we move forward and upward, from figures of the messianic kingdom to their fulfillment. We see that the political office in ancient Israel has become a spiritual office in the person of Mary. The queen mother is no longer a cabinet member in Israel's national government but a counselor and advocate in the messianic order of grace.

the LORD which he had spoken concerning the house of Eli in Shi'loh.

28 When the news came to Jo'ab—for Joab had supported Adoni'jah although he had not supported Ab'salom—Joab fled to the tent of the LORD and caught hold of the horns of the altar. ²⁹And when it was told King Solomon, "Jo'ab has fled to the tent of the LORD, and behold, he is beside the altar," Solomon sent Bena'iah the son of Jehoi'ada, saying, "Go, strike him down." ³⁰So Bena'iah came to the tent of the LORD, and said to him, "The king commands, 'Come forth.'" But he said, "No, I will die here." Then Benaiah brought the king word again, saying, "Thus said Jo'ab, and thus he answered me." ³¹The king replied to him, "Do as he has said, strike him down and bury him; and thus take away from me and from my father's house the guilt for the blood which Jo'ab shed without cause. ³²The LORD will bring back his bloody deeds upon his own head, because, without the knowledge of my father David, he attacked and slew with the sword two men more righteous and better than himself, Abner the son of Ner, commander of the army of Israel, and Ama'sa the son of Je'ther, commander of the army of Judah. ³³So shall their blood come back upon the head of Jo'ab and upon the head of his descendants for ever; but to David, and to his descendants, and to his house, and to his throne, there shall be peace from the LORD for evermore." ³⁴Then Bena'iah the son of Jehoi'ada went up, and struck him down and killed him; and he was buried in his own house in the wilderness. ³⁵The king put Bena'iah the son of Jehoi'ada over the army in place of Jo'ab, and the king put Za'dok the priest in the place of Abi'athar.

36 Then the king sent and summoned Shim'e-i, and said to him, "Build yourself a house in Jerusalem, and dwell there, and do not go forth from there to any place whatever. ³⁷For on the day you go forth, and cross the brook Kidron, know for certain that you shall die; your blood shall be upon your own head." ³⁸And Shim'e-i said to the king, "What you say is good; as my lord the king has said, so

will your servant do." So Shime-i dwelt in Jerusalem many days.

39 But it happened at the end of three years that two of Shim'e-i's slaves ran away to A'chish, son of Ma'acah, king of Gath. And when it was told Shime-i, "Behold, your slaves are in Gath," ⁴⁰Shim'e-i arose and saddled a donkey, and went to Gath to A'chish, to seek his slaves; Shime-i went and brought his slaves from Gath. ⁴¹And when Solomon was told that Shim'e-i had gone from Jerusalem to Gath and returned, ⁴²the king sent and summoned Shim'e-i, and said to him, "Did I not make you swear by the LORD, and solemnly admonish you, saying, 'Know for certain that on the day you go forth and go to any place whatever, you shall die'? And you said to me, 'What you say is good; I obey.' ⁴³Why then have you not kept your oath to the LORD and the commandment with which I charged you?" ⁴⁴The king also said to Shim'e-i, "You know in your own heart all the evil that you did to David my father; so the LORD will bring back your evil upon your own head. ⁴⁵But King Solomon shall be blessed, and the throne of David shall be established before the LORD for ever." ⁴⁶Then the king commanded Bena'iah the son of Jehoi'ada; and he went out and struck him down, and he died.

So the kingdom was established in the hand of Solomon.

Solomon Prays for Wisdom

3 *Solomon made a marriage alliance with Pharaoh king of Egypt; he took Pharaoh's daughter, and brought her into the city of David, until he had finished building his own house and the house of the LORD and the wall around Jerusalem. ²The people were sacrificing at the high places, however, because no house had yet been built for the name of the LORD.

3 Solomon loved the LORD, walking in the statutes of David his father; only, he sacrificed and burnt incense at the high places. ⁴And the king went to Gib'eon to sacrifice there, for that was the great high place; Solomon used to offer a thousand burnt

---

3:4–15: 2 Chron 1:3–13.

2:28 **horns of the altar:** A place of temporary asylum. According to Ex 21:12–14, no such protection can be guaranteed for Joab, since he is guilty of murder rather than accidental manslaughter (2:32). See note on 1:50.

2:32 **Abner ... Amasa:** Both were assassinated in cold blood. See note on 2:5.

2:35 **in place of:** Solomon appoints both an army commander (**Benaiah**) and a high priest (**Zadok**) to fill the offices made vacant by the banishment of Abiathar (2:26–27) and the execution of Joab (2:28–34).

2:36–46 The execution of Shimei, long prevented by David's oath to spare his life (2 Sam 19:23), is now made possible by Shimei's violation of an oath sworn to Solomon (2:43–44).

2:39 **Gath:** A Philistine city in southwest Canaan.

3:1 **Pharaoh:** Unnamed but likely Pharaoh Siamun of the 21st dynasty. Solomon's alliance with Egypt shows that Israel is a rising power on the international stage of Near Eastern politics. **Pharaoh's daughter:** Name unknown. She is mentioned again in 7:8 and 9:16, 24.

3:2 **high places:** Canaanite idol sanctuaries. Israel was commanded to demolish them upon entering the Promised Land (Deut 12:2–3). Instead, many were allowed to remain, with some being converted into worship sites dedicated to Yahweh. This compromise over the strict demands of the Mosaic Law paves the way for Israel's tragic descent into idolatry (2 Kings 17:7–18). See word study: *High Places* at 2 Kings 23:5.

3:4 **Gibeon:** Approximately six miles northwest of Jerusalem (located at el-Jib). The Mosaic Tabernacle was located there at this time (1 Chron 21:29). **a thousand burnt offerings:** An instance of hyperbole, meant to heighten the reader's appreciation for Solomon and his commitment to worship.

---

*3:1: Chapters 3–11 give the history of Solomon. The *Pharaoh* of 3:1 and 9:16 (?) was of the twenty-first dynasty, possibly Psusennes II.

offerings upon that altar. ⁵At Gib′eon the LORD appeared to Solomon in a dream* by night; and God said, "Ask what I shall give you." ⁶And Solomon said, "You have shown great and merciful love to your servant David my father, because he walked before you in faithfulness, in righteousness, and in uprightness of heart toward you; and you have kept for him this great and merciful love, and have given him a son to sit on his throne this day. ⁷And now, O LORD my God, you have made your servant king in place of David my father, although I am but a little child; I do not know how to go out or come in. ⁸And your servant is in the midst of your people whom you have chosen, a great people, that cannot be numbered or counted for multitude. ⁹Give your servant therefore an understanding mind to govern your people, that I may discern between good and evil; for who is able to govern this great people of yours?"

10 It pleased the LORD that Solomon had asked this. ¹¹And God said to him, "Because you have asked this, and have not asked for yourself long life or riches or the life of your enemies, but have asked for yourself understanding to discern what is right, ¹²behold, I now do according to your word. Behold, I give you a wise and discerning mind, so that none like you has been before you and none like you shall arise after you. ¹³I give you also what you have not asked, both riches and honor, so that no other king shall compare with you, all your days. ¹⁴And if you will walk in my ways, keeping my statutes and my commandments, as your father David walked, then I will lengthen your days."

15 And Solomon awoke, and behold, it was a dream. Then he came to Jerusalem, and stood before the ark of the covenant of the LORD, and offered up burnt offerings and peace offerings, and made a feast for all his servants.

Solomon's Wisdom in Judgment

16 Then two harlots came to the king, and stood before him. ¹⁷The one woman said, "Oh, my lord, this woman and I dwell in the same house; and I gave birth to a child while she was in the house.

Comparative studies show that exaggeration was often employed as a rhetorical device in Near Eastern royal histories, where scribes tended to depict kings as larger-than-life figures who brought times of unprecedented prosperity to their realms. If the account of Solomon follows this ancient convention, it is to enhance the perception of his greatness and to stress that the size and scale of his empire were unmatched by any other in Israel's history. This does not mean that all the details of the story are legendary, lacking a basis in history. Rather, it means that allowance must be made for occasional instances of inflated language and statistics in assessing the particulars of Solomon's reign (and that of subsequent kings). Other possible instances of hyperbole include expressions of incomparability (4:25, 34; 10:20, 24, 27; etc.) and unusually large numbers (8:63; 10:14; 11:3; etc.).

3:5 dream: Sometimes a channel of divine revelation. See word study: *Dream* at Gen 37:5.

3:7 a little child: Not in age, but in wisdom and life experience. Solomon humbly recognizes his inability to govern the Lord's people without the Lord's help.

3:9 an understanding mind: Literally "a listening heart", that is, one that is teachable and open to the Lord's guidance. For the connection between heart and mind in the Bible, see word study: *Heart* at Deut 30:6. **good and evil:** Solomon desires the wisdom of moral and juridical discernment, to know right from wrong and justice from injustice.

3:11 have not asked: Kings of the biblical world typically desired longevity, wealth, and the annihilation of their enemies.

3:13 riches and honor: In seeking first the good of the kingdom, and not personal gain or wealth, Solomon has his priorities in line with God's. This is why he receives blessings far in excess of his request (3:9). For Jesus' teaching on this principle, see Mt 6:33 and Lk 12:31.

3:15 ark of the covenant: Installed in the tent that David pitched for it on Mt. Zion (2 Sam 6:17). Worship at the Ark may indicate that Solomon, growing in spiritual maturity, is pulling away from the illicit "high places" (3:3). **offered up:** Like his father, David, Solomon assumes the role of a priest-king who offers sacrifice for Israel (8:62–64; 9:25). See note on 2 Chron 1:6.

3:16–28 Solomon's brilliant solution to the case of the two harlots. It confirms his well-known reputation as the quintessential "wise man" of Israel (10:24; Sir 47:13–17).
• The dead child, signifying dead works, belongs to the earthly Jerusalem, while the living child, signifying spiritual works, belongs to the heavenly Jerusalem. Enlightened by the break of dawn and spiritual graces, the Church pushes away the fleshly works of the Law, like the other woman's dead baby, and claims for herself a living faith (St. Augustine, *Sermons* 10).

WORD STUDY

Wisdom (3:28)

ḥokmah (Heb.): "wisdom" or "skill". In reference to men, wisdom can be the technical skills of a craftsman (1 Kings 7:14), the tactical skills of a military commander (Is 10:13), or the leadership skills of a national figurehead (Deut 34:9). In the moral and spiritual realm, wisdom belongs to the righteous (Ps 37:30). It is the fear of the Lord that leads them to make right choices in following God's plan for their lives (Job 28:28). Ultimately, wisdom belongs to God (Job 11:6; 12:13) and is only possessed by men as a gift that comes from God (Prov 2:6; Sir 1:1). Among those endowed with wisdom in the OT, none surpasses King Solomon (1 Kings 4:30–31; 10:23), who received from the Lord a superabundance of moral and spiritual understanding (1 Kings 4:29; 5:12). This enabled him to make wise judgments (1 Kings 3:28), to explain the mysteries of the natural world (1 Kings 4:33), and to draw the nations closer to the God of Israel (1 Kings 4:34; 10:1–10, 24). If Moses imparts wisdom to Israel through the Torah (Deut 4:6), Solomon imparts wisdom to the wider world through his instruction and inspiration in the Wisdom Books (Prov 1:1–2; cf. Eccles 1:1; Song 1:1).

---

*3:5, *a dream:* A common means of divine communication, especially before the age of the prophets.

[18]Then on the third day after I was delivered, this woman also gave birth; and we were alone; there was no one else with us in the house, only we two were in the house. [19]And this woman's son died in the night, because she lay on it. [20]And she arose at midnight, and took my son from beside me, while your maidservant slept, and laid it in her bosom, and laid her dead son in my bosom. [21]When I rose in the morning to nurse my child, behold, it was dead; but when I looked at it closely in the morning, behold, it was not the child that I had borne." [22]But the other woman said, "No, the living child is mine, and the dead child is yours." The first said, "No, the dead child is yours, and the living child is mine." Thus they spoke before the king.

23 Then the king said, "The one says, 'This is my son that is alive, and your son is dead'; and the other says, 'No; but your son is dead, and my son is the living one.'" [24]And the king said, "Bring me a sword." So a sword was brought before the king. [25]And the king said, "Divide the living child in two, and give half to the one, and half to the other." [26]Then the woman whose son was alive said to the king, because her heart yearned for her son, "Oh, my lord, give her the living child, and by no means slay it." But the other said, "It shall be neither mine nor yours; divide it." [27]Then the king answered and said, "Give the living child to the first woman, and by no means slay it; she is its mother." [28]And all Israel heard of the judgment which the king had rendered; and they stood in awe of the king, because they perceived that the wisdom of God was in him, to render justice.

Solomon's High Officials

4 King Solomon was king over all Israel, [2]and these were his high officials: Azari′ah the son of Za′dok was the priest; [3]Elihor′eph and Ahi′jah the sons of Shi′sha were secretaries; Jehosh′aphat the son of Ahi′lud was recorder; [4]Bena′iah the son of Jehoi′ada was in command of the army; Za′dok and Abi′athar were priests; [5]Azari′ah the son of Nathan was over the officers; Zabud the son of Nathan was priest and king's friend; [6]Ahi′shar was in charge of the palace; and Adoni′ram the son of Abda was in charge of the forced labor.

7 Solomon had twelve officers over all Israel, who provided food for the king and his household; each man had to make provision for one month in the year. [8]These were their names: Ben-hur, in the hill country of E′phraim; [9]Ben-de′ker, in Makaz, Sha-al′bim, Beth-she′mesh, and E′lonbethha′nan; [10]Ben-he′sed, in Arub′both (to him belonged Socoh and all the land of He′pher); [11]Ben-abin′adab, in all Na′phath-dor (he had Ta′phath the daughter of Solomon as his wife); [12]Ba′ana the son of Ahi′lud, in Ta′anach, Megid′do, and all Beth-she′an which is beside Zar′ethan below Jezre′el, and from Beth-shean to A′bel-meho′lah, as far as the other side of Jok′meam; [13]Ben-ge′ber, in Ra′moth-gil′ead (he had the villages of Ja′ir the son of Manas′seh, which are in Gilead, and he had the region of Argob, which is in Bashan, sixty great cities with walls and bronze bars); [14]Ahin′adab the son of Iddo, in Ma″hana′im; [15]Ahi′ma-az, in Naph′tali (he had taken Bas′emath the daughter of Solomon as his wife); [16]Ba′ana the son of Hu′shai, in Asher and Bea′loth; [17]Jehosh′aphat the son of Paru′ah, in Is′sachar; [18]Shim′e-i the son of E′la, in Benjamin; [19]Geber the son of U′ri, in the land of Gilead, the country of Si′hon king of the Am′orites and of Og king of Bashan. And there was one officer in the land of Judah.

20 Judah and Israel were as many as the sand by the sea; they ate and drank and were happy.

4:1–19 Solomon's royal court. It consists of 11 appointees in charge of religious, civil, and military affairs (4:1–6) and 12 revenue officers who oversee the administrative districts of the land (4:7–19). At least five of these individuals are senior ministers carried over from David's court (Jehoshaphat, Benaiah, Zadok, Abiathar, and Adoniram [Adoram], 2 Sam 20:23–25).

4:2 the priest: Azariah becomes high priest after Zadok, his grandfather (1 Chron 6:8–9).

4:3 secretaries: Scribes in charge of royal correspondence. **recorder:** Possibly in charge of state documents and archives.

4:4 Zadok and Abiathar: The chief priests of David's court (2 Sam 20:25). They retained these positions in the earliest days of Solomon's reign, but Abiathar was soon banished (2:26–27) and Zadok was succeeded by Azariah (4:2).

4:5 the officers: The provincial tax officials mentioned in 4:7–19. **king's friend:** A title for the king's personal confidant and advisor (2 Sam 15:37).

4:6 charge of the palace: Or "charge over the house". Ahishar seems to have served as the chief royal steward (= prime minister) over Solomon's kingdom. This would make him the highest government official in the land under the king. For the Hebrew expression used here, see word study: *Over the Household* at 16:9. **forced labor:** Labor gangs conscripted

by the government for public works projects. See note on 5:13–16.

4:7–19 Solomon organizes 12 administrative districts to supply the royal household with food each month and the royal cavalry and chariot corps with provisions (4:27–28). The districts do not align with the tribal territories in Josh 13–21, perhaps because some of the tribes were unable to meet the agricultural quotas of the tax system.
• *Allegorically*, the officials selected by Solomon point to those whom Christ appointed as rulers of his people. Twelve officers were chosen to oversee the house of the king, and so the apostles are made stewards of the divine mysteries in order to nourish the Israel of God and administer the household of the King of Peace (St. Ephraem the Syrian, *On First Kings* 4, 1).

4:19 one officer: Azariah, the head overseer of the district revenue officers (4:5).

4:20–34 Solomon's glory is summarized. It is a time when the OT story of Israel reaches its spiritual high point, a time when key promises of God's covenant with Abraham are fulfilled. See notes on 4:20 and 4:21.

4:20 as the sand: Israel's vast numbers are a fulfillment of Yahweh's oath to multiply the descendants of Abraham (Gen 22:17).

²¹ᵍSolomon ruled over all the kingdoms from the Euphrates to the land of the Philis′tines and to the border of Egypt; they brought tribute and served Solomon all the days of his life.

22 Solomon's provision for one day was thirty cors of fine flour, and sixty cors of meal, ²³ten fat oxen, and twenty pasturefed cattle, a hundred sheep, besides deer, gazelles, roebucks, and fatted fowl. ²⁴For he had dominion over all the region west of the Euphra′tes from Tiphsah to Gaza, over all the kings west of the Euphrates; and he had peace on all sides round about him. ²⁵And Judah

---

4:21 over all the kingdoms: Solomon sits enthroned over an empire that embraces all Israel (4:1) and further extends over several neighboring states in the region (4:24). • Its geographical reach, from the **Euphrates** River to the eastern **border of Egypt**, represents the full extent of the Promised Land that God pledged to Israel in the Abrahamic covenant (Gen 15:18; Deut 1:7–8). For David's role in expanding the kingdom to these proportions, see note on 2 Sam 8:1–14.

ᵍCh 5:1 in Heb.

4:22 cors: A cor equals roughly 6.5 bushels (dry measure).
4:24 Tiphsah: On the western bank of the upper Euphrates (modern Syria, east of Aleppo). **Gaza:** A Philistine coastal city in southwest Canaan. **peace on all sides:** Solomon is mainly a peacetime king, thanks to the conquests of his father, David, who was mainly a wartime king (5:3–4).
4:25 from Dan even to Beer-sheba: The extent of the Israelite homeland measured from north to south. **under his fig tree:** Points to a time of national peace and security when life is untroubled by war (Mic 4:4).

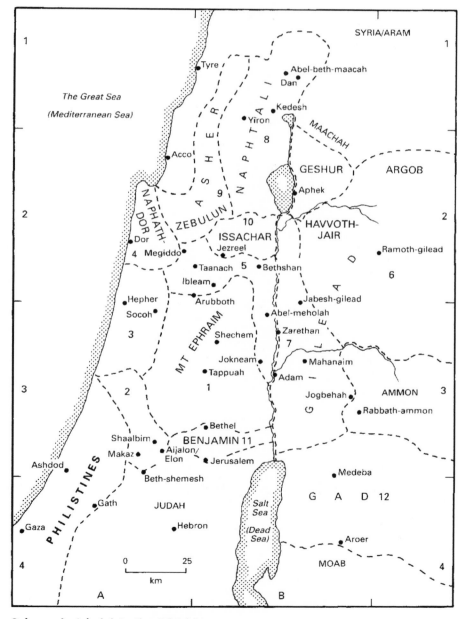

Solomon's Administrative Districts

and Israel dwelt in safety, from Dan even to Be'er-she'ba, every man under his vine and under his fig tree, all the days of Solomon. ²⁶Solomon also had forty thousand stalls of horses for his chariots, and twelve thousand horsemen. ²⁷And those officers supplied provisions for King Solomon, and for all who came to King Solomon's table, each one in his month; they let nothing be lacking. ²⁸Barley also and straw for the horses and swift steeds they brought to the place where it was required, each according to his charge.

Fame of Solomon's Wisdom

29 And God gave Solomon wisdom and understanding beyond measure, and largeness of mind like the sand on the seashore, ³⁰so that Solomon's wisdom surpassed the wisdom of all the people of the east, and all the wisdom of Egypt. ³¹For he was wiser than all other men, wiser than Ethan the Ez'rahite, and He'man, Calcol, and Darda, the sons of Mahol; and his fame was in all the nations round about. ³²He also uttered three thousand proverbs;* and his songs were a thousand and five. ³³He spoke of trees, from the cedar that is in Lebanon to the hyssop that grows out of the wall; he spoke also of beasts, and of birds, and of reptiles, and of fish. ³⁴And men came from all peoples to hear the wisdom of Solomon, and from all the kings of the earth, who had heard of his wisdom.

Preparations and Materials for the Temple

5 ʰNow Hiram king of Tyre sent his servants to Solomon, when he heard that they had anointed him king in place of his father; for Hiram always loved David. ²And Solomon sent word to Hiram, ³"You know that David my father could not build a house for the name of the LORD his God because of the warfare with which his enemies surrounded him, until the LORD put them under the soles of his feet. ⁴But now the LORD my God has given me rest on every side; there is neither adversary nor misfortune. ⁵And so I purpose to build a house for the name of the LORD my God, as the LORD said to David my father, 'Your son, whom I will set upon your throne in your place, shall build the house for my name.' ⁶Now therefore command that cedars of Lebanon be cut for me; and my servants will join your servants, and I will pay you for your servants such wages as you set; for you know that there is no one among us who knows how to cut timber like the Sido'nians."

7 When Hiram heard the words of Solomon, he rejoiced greatly, and said, "Blessed be the LORD this day, who has given to David a wise son to be over this great people." ⁸And Hiram sent to Solomon, saying, "I have heard the message which you have sent to me; I am ready to do all you desire in the matter of cedar and cypress timber. ⁹My servants

---

5:2–11: 2 Chron 2:3–16.   **5:5:** 2 Chron 2:1.

4:26 forty thousand: The parallel passage in 2 Chron 9:25 reads "four thousand", which is more likely the original number. Evidently the number in Kings is the result of an ancient copying error. In any case, the statement points to a significant military buildup during Solomon's reign.

4:30 people of the east: Arabian tribes. The cultivation of practical wisdom was popular throughout the Near East at this time.

4:31 Ethan ... Darda: Grandsons of the patriarch Judah according to 1 Chron 2:6.

4:32 proverbs ... songs: Solomon manifests his wisdom in literary and lyrical compositions in addition to showing himself brilliant in juridical rulings (3:16–28), economic initiatives (9:26–28), and problem-solving ability (10:1–5). No doubt some of his wise teachings are preserved in the Bible. His name is attached to several biblical writings (Ps 72 and 127; Prov 1–9, 10–22, 25–29; Song of Solomon), while others promote his wisdom without invoking his name (Ecclesiastes, Wisdom of Solomon). The proliferation of wisdom teaching in Israel is characteristic of the Solomonic era. See word study: *Wisdom* at 3:28.

4:33 trees ... beasts ... fish: Suggests that Solomon possessed an encyclopedic knowledge of the natural world, the observation of which supplied lessons for human conduct (Job 12:7–12; Prov 6:6–11; 30:24–28).

4:34 came from all peoples: Anticipates the visit of the queen of Sheba (10:1–13) as well as other foreign dignitaries (10:23–25).

5:1–18 Preparations are made for Solomon's main building projects: the Temple and royal palace of Jerusalem (chaps. 6–7). This is achieved through a peace accord with the king of Tyre, who agrees to supply lumber and skilled labor to Israel in return for food and wages (5:6–11).

5:1 Hiram: Hiram I, ruler of Phoenicia (modern Lebanon) from ca. 980 to 946 B.C. In saying that Hiram **loved David**, the author indicates that he had established a covenant or treaty relationship with David (2 Sam 5:11), just as he will with Solomon (5:12). See word study: *Loved* at Deut 4:37.

5:3 warfare: Bloodied the hands of David, making him unsuitable for the task of building the Temple (1 Chron 22:8). **under ... his feet:** Recalls how a warrior pressed his foot upon the neck of a subdued enemy (Josh 10:24).

5:4 rest on every side: Deuteronomy makes regional peace a necessary precondition for constructing Israel's national sanctuary (Deut 12:10–11).

5:5 Your son: Paraphrases the words of the Davidic covenant in 2 Sam 7:12–13. **my name:** An idiom for the localized presence of Yahweh (Ex 20:24; Deut 12:5). It can also mean "my reputation", meaning that God chooses the place where his greatness will be made known to the world.

5:6 cedars of Lebanon: Notoriously tall, straight, and strong. Lebanon cedar was high-quality lumber, ideally suited for monumental construction projects. **Sidonians:** Peoples of the Phoenician port of Sidon, known for being expert loggers. • *Allegorically*, the Tabernacle of Moses signifies the state of the Old Law, whereas the Temple of Solomon signifies the state of the New Law. For only Jews erected the Tabernacle, but the Temple was built with the cooperation of Gentiles, namely, Tyrians and Sidonians (St. Thomas Aquinas, *Summa Theologiae* I-II, 102, 4).

5:9 to the place: Timber was floated down the Mediterranean coast to Joppa, from which point it was hauled overland to Jerusalem (2 Chron 2:16).

---

*4:32, *proverbs:* Doubtless some of those of the book of Proverbs are to be ascribed to Solomon. The book of Wisdom however (called in Greek The Wisdom of Solomon), is ascribed to him only because of his reputation for wisdom. It was actually written in the first century B.C.
ʰCh 5:15 in Heb.

shall bring it down to the sea from Lebanon; and I will make it into rafts to go by sea to the place you direct, and I will have them broken up there, and you shall receive it; and you shall meet my wishes by providing food for my household." [10]So Hiram supplied Solomon with all the timber of cedar and cypress that he desired, [11]while Solomon gave Hiram twenty thousand cors of wheat as food for his household, and twenty thousand[i] cors of beaten oil. Solomon gave this to Hiram year by year. [12]And the LORD gave Solomon wisdom, as he promised him; and there was peace between Hiram and Solomon; and the two of them made a treaty.

13 King Solomon raised a levy of forced labor out of all Israel; and the levy numbered thirty thousand men. [14]And he sent them to Lebanon, ten thousand a month in relays; they would be a month in Lebanon and two months at home; Adoni'ram was in charge of the levy. [15]Solomon also had seventy thousand burden-bearers and eighty thousand hewers of stone in the hill country, [16]besides Solomon's three thousand three hundred chief officers who were over the work, who had charge of the people who carried on the work. [17]At the king's command, they quarried out great, costly stones in order to lay the foundation of the house with dressed stones. [18]So Solomon's builders and Hiram's builders and the men of Ge'bal did the hewing and prepared the timber and the stone to build the house.

Solomon Builds the Temple

6 In the four hundred and eightieth year after the sons of Israel came out of the land of Egypt, in the fourth year of Solomon's reign over Israel, in the month of Ziv, which is the second month, he began to build the house of the LORD.* [2]The house which King Solomon built for the LORD was sixty cubits long, twenty cubits wide, and thirty cubits high. [3]The vestibule in front of the nave of the house was twenty cubits long, equal to the width of the house, and ten cubits deep in front of the house. [4]And he made for the house windows with recessed frames. [5]He also built a structure against the wall of the house, running round the walls of the house, both the nave and the inner sanctuary; and he made side chambers all around. [6]The lowest story[j] was five cubits broad, the middle one was six cubits broad,

---

5:15, 16: 2 Chron 2:2, 18.   **6:1–28:** 2 Chron 3:1–13; Acts 7:47.

5:11 cors: A cor equals roughly 6.5 bushels (dry measure) or 60 gallons (liquid measure).

5:13–16 Solomon conscripts a massive work force of Israelite laborers (11:28) and Canaanite slaves (9:20–21). • The prophet Samuel forewarned that if Israel sets a king over itself, he would press the people into hard service (1 Sam 8:17). Beyond that, Solomon's levy of state workers caused a buildup of resentment that would later explode into one of the major factors that divided the kingdom (12:4). On the enslavement of the Canaanites, see note on Josh 16:10.

5:17 dressed stones: Carefully cut and squared to provide a stable base for the edifice.

5:18 men of Gebal: Skilled artisans from the Phoenician port of Byblos.

6:1–38 Solomon's Temple, built north of the city of David on the crest of Mt. Moriah (2 Chron 3:1). Its main features are modeled on the Mosaic Tabernacle, which it supersedes as the earthly dwelling of Yahweh (6:11–13) and the focal point of Israelite worship (8:30–53). (1) *Architecturally*, the structural design of the Temple includes an outdoor courtyard (court, 6:36), an entry porch (vestibule, 7:19), a main hall or holy place (nave, 6:17), and a concealed chamber or most holy place (inner sanctuary, 6:19). (2) *Historically*, the Temple of Solomon (a.k.a. the First Temple) stood for nearly four centuries, until its destruction by the Babylonians in 586 B.C. (2 Kings 25:8–9). (3) *Archaeologically*, no material remains of Solomon's Temple have been discovered so far, and the prospect of future findings is slight, given the ravages of time and war as well as the continuous redevelopment of Jerusalem over the centuries. That said, the lack of artifactual confirmation is insufficient reason to question its historical existence. The biblical description of the Temple in Kings, especially its three-part floor plan, shows close affinities with temples discovered at multiple sites in Canaan and Syria that date back to the second millennium (shrines at Ebla, Alalakh, Hazor) and the early first millennium B.C. (shrines at Ain Dara, Tell Tayinat, Hamath) (CCC 2580). For its religious significance and symbolism, see essay: *Theology of the Temple* at 2 Chron 5.

6:1 four hundred and eightieth year: An important benchmark of biblical chronology. In general, it suggests that the founding of the Temple is an event of great historic importance, comparable to the founding of Israel as a nation at the Exodus. More specifically, it gives a fixed point of reference for dating the early history of Israel. Counting back 480 years from Solomon's fourth year as king (ca. 966 B.C.) yields a date for the Exodus ca. 1446 B.C. This figure also coheres with the chronology of the Book of Judges, which puts at least 300 years between Israel's conquest of the Transjordan and the rise of the Israelite monarchy (Judg 11:26). Nevertheless, perceived conflicts between the biblical timeline and archaeological findings lead many scholars to shorten this period by putting the Exodus in the 1200s B.C., in which case the present verse is said to represent 12 generations in a symbolic way (12 × 40 years = 480 years). For additional considerations, see essay: *The Date of the Exodus* at Ex 11. **month of Ziv:** Corresponds to April-May in the ancient Phoenician calendar.

6:2 sixty ... twenty ... thirty: The interior dimensions of the sanctuary. Assuming an 18-inch cubit, its two main rooms together measure roughly 90 feet long × 30 feet wide × 45 feet high. • *Allegorically*, the walls of the Temple are the nations of believers that make up the holy Catholic Church. Their width signifies their wide distribution across the world, and their height signifies the upward striving of the Church for heavenly things. The courses of stones show that the elect are built on the foundation of Christ, each following the other in the succession of ages and each supporting the other as they fulfill the law of Christ, which is charity (St. Bede, *On the Temple* 1, 8).

6:5 side chambers: Storerooms that wrap around the outside of the sanctuary building on three sides. They are divided into three levels and joined by internal staircases. Most likely these compartments served as "the treasuries of the house of the LORD" (7:51).

---

*6:1: The temple was built on the high ground to the north of Ophel, David's city.
[i] Gk: Heb *twenty.*
[j] Gk: Heb *structure.*

and the third was seven cubits broad; for around the outside of the house he made offsets on the wall in order that the supporting beams should not be inserted into the walls of the house.

7 When the house was built, it was with stone prepared at the quarry; so that neither hammer nor axe nor any tool of iron was heard in the temple, while it was being built.

8 The entrance for the lowest[k] story was on the south side of the house; and one went up by stairs to the middle story, and from the middle story to the third. [9]So he built the house, and finished it; and he made the ceiling of the house of beams and planks of cedar. [10]He built the structure against the whole house, each story[l] five cubits high, and it was joined to the house with timbers of cedar.

11 Now the word of the LORD came to Solomon, [12]"Concerning this house which you are building, if you will walk in my statutes and obey my ordinances and keep all my commandments and walk in them, then I will establish my word with you, which I spoke to David your father. [13]And I will dwell among the children of Israel, and will not forsake my people Israel."

14 So Solomon built the house, and finished it. [15]He lined the walls of the house on the inside with boards of cedar; from the floor of the house to the rafters[m] of the ceiling, he covered them on the inside with wood; and he covered the floor of the house with boards of cypress. [16]He built twenty cubits of the rear of the house with boards of cedar from the floor to the rafters,[m] and he built this within as an inner sanctuary, as the most holy place. [17]The house, that is, the nave in front of the inner sanctuary, was forty cubits long. [18]The cedar within the house was carved in the form of gourds and open flowers; all was cedar, no stone was seen. [19]The inner sanctuary he prepared in the innermost part of the house, to set there the ark of the covenant of the LORD. [20]The inner sanctuary[n] was twenty cubits long, twenty cubits wide, and twenty cubits high; and he overlaid it with pure gold. He also made[o] an altar of cedar. [21]And Solomon overlaid the inside of the house with pure gold, and he drew chains of gold across, in front of the inner sanctuary, and overlaid it with gold. [22]And he overlaid the whole house with gold, until all the house was finished. Also the whole altar that belonged to the inner sanctuary he overlaid with gold.

Furnishings of the Temple

23 In the inner sanctuary he made two cherubim of olivewood, each ten cubits high. [24]Five cubits was the length of one wing of the cherub, and five cubits the length of the other wing of the cherub; it was ten cubits from the tip of one wing to the tip of the other. [25]The other cherub also measured ten cubits; both cherubim had the same measure and the same form. [26]The height of one cherub was ten cubits, and so was that of the other cherub. [27]He put the cherubim in the innermost part of the house; and the wings of the cherubim were spread out so that a wing of one touched the one wall, and a wing of the other cherub touched the other wall; their other wings touched each other in the middle of the house. [28]And he overlaid the cherubim with gold.

29 He carved all the walls of the house round about with carved figures of cherubim and palm trees and open flowers, in the inner and outer rooms. [30]The floor of the house he overlaid with gold in the inner and outer rooms.

31 For the entrance to the inner sanctuary he made doors of olivewood; the lintel and the doorposts formed a pentagon.[p] [32]He covered the two doors of olivewood with carvings of cherubim, palm

---

6:7 at the quarry: All blocks are prefabricated before transport to the building site, so that no stonecutting is done on the Temple Mount. • *Anagogically,* the Tabernacle and the Temple signify two states of life. The Tabernacle, being changeable, signifies the constant changes of our present life, whereas the Temple, being fixed and immovable, signifies the permanence of our future life. This is why no hammer or saw could be heard during construction, for this signified that the future would be free of all disturbances (St. Thomas Aquinas, *Summa Theologiae* I-II, 102, 4). See note on 2 Cor 5:1.

6:13 I will dwell: Just as Yahweh promised to "dwell" in the Tabernacle (Ex 25:8).

6:14 Solomon ... finished it: Recalls how Moses finished work on the Tabernacle (Ex 40:33), which in turn recalls how the Lord finished the work of creation (Gen 2:2). See note on 6:38.

6:15–22 Both interior rooms of the Temple, the nave and inner chamber, are paneled with wood planks that are carved with decorative images and covered with gold overlay.

6:17 the nave: Corresponds to the "holy place" of the Tabernacle (Ex 26:33; Heb 9:2).

6:19 ark of the covenant: A representation of Yahweh's throne. See note on Ex 25:10.

6:20 twenty ... twenty ... twenty: The innermost chamber, or most holy place, is a 30-foot-square cube lined with gold. It is twice the dimensions of the fabric inner chamber of the Tabernacle. **altar of cedar:** The wooden frame of the altar of incense, which is also gilded with gold (7:48).

6:23 two cherubim: Large angelic images tower over the Ark of the Covenant with wings outstretched (8:6-7). In the view of most scholars, they resembled sphinxlike creatures that had a human face and head, a bovine or lion body, and wings like an eagle. This was a popular motif in the religious iconography of the ancient Near East. Here they stand as guardians of God's holy presence, as in Gen 3:24. These freestanding cherubim are distinct from the smaller cherubim mounted on the lid of the ark (CCC 2130). See note on Ex 25:18.

6:31 doors of olivewood: Plated with gold (6:32) and hung before the veil that curtains off the most holy place (2 Chron 3:14).

---

[k]Gk Tg: Heb *middle.*
[l]Heb lacks *each story.*
[m]Gk: Heb *walls.*
[n]Vg: Heb *and before the inner sanctuary.*
[o]Gk: Heb *covered.*
[p]Heb obscure.

trees, and open flowers; he overlaid them with gold, and spread gold upon the cherubim and upon the palm trees.

33 So also he made for the entrance to the nave doorposts of olivewood, in the form of a square, [34]and two doors of cypress wood; the two leaves of the one door were folding, and the two leaves of the other door were folding. [35]On them he carved cherubim and palm trees and open flowers; and he overlaid them with gold evenly applied upon the carved work. [36]He built the inner court with three courses of hewn stone and one course of cedar beams.

37 In the fourth year the foundation of the house of the LORD was laid, in the month of Ziv. [38]And in the eleventh year, in the month of Bul, which is the eighth month, the house was finished in all its parts, and according to all its specifications. He was seven years in building it.

Solomon's House and Other Buildings

7 Solomon was building his own house thirteen years, and he finished his entire house.

2 He built the House of the Forest of Lebanon; its length was a hundred cubits, and its breadth fifty cubits, and its height thirty cubits, and it was built upon three*q* rows of cedar pillars, with cedar beams upon the pillars. [3]And it was covered with cedar above the chambers that were upon the forty-five pillars, fifteen in each row. [4]There were window frames in three rows, and window

---

6:34 doors of cypress: Plated with gold (6:35) and hung before the veil that conceals the nave or holy place (Ex 26:36). In the days of Hezekiah, the gold will be stripped from these doors and used to pay tribute to the Assyrians (2 Kings 18:16).

6:36 court: The outdoor pavement that surrounds the main Temple building. Its stone wall replaces the fabric fencing that once formed the perimeter of the Tabernacle courtyard (Ex 27:9–19).

6:38 month of Bul: The eighth month. It corresponds to October-November in the ancient Phoenician calendar. **seven years:** Temple construction lasted from ca. 966 to 958 B.C. Besides taking *seven* years to build the sanctuary, Solomon dedicates it (8:2) during the *seven*-day Feast of Booths (8:65). • Theologically, the prominence of seven time units recalls the creation of the world in seven days. See note on 6:14 and essay: *Theology of the Temple* at 2 Chron 5.

*q*Gk: Heb *four*.

7:1–12 Solomon constructs an administrative complex directly south of the Temple. Public buildings include a royal armory (House of the Forest of Lebanon, 7:2; 10:16–17; Is 22:8), a colonnade entrance hall (Hall of Pillars, 7:6), and a government chamber for royal decisions and audiences (Hall of the Throne, 7:7). Private buildings include palace residences for Solomon and his Egyptian wife (7:8). It is implied in several later passages that the Temple sat at a higher elevation than the royal buildings adjacent to it (see 2 Kings 11:19; 22:4; Jer 26:10).

7:1 thirteen years: Palace construction took almost twice as long as Temple construction, due to its vastly larger scale (6:38). The House of the Forest alone is roughly twice the size of the sanctuary building (compare the dimensions of 7:2 with 6:2). It is implied in 9:10 that work on these structures did not begin until after the Temple was finished.

7:2 House of the Forest: Its interior is dominated by towering cedar uprights and visible cedar crossbeams, thus resembling a forest. **hundred ... fifty ... thirty:** Roughly 150 feet long x 75 feet wide x 45 feet high, measured according to an 18-inch cubit.

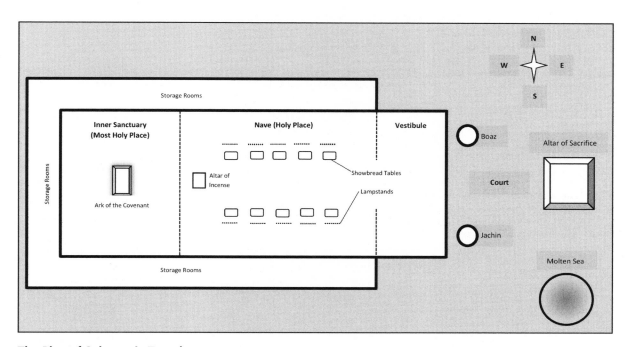

The Plan of Solomon's Temple

opposite window in three tiers. [5]All the doorways and windows[r] had square frames, and window was opposite window in three tiers.

6 And he made the Hall of Pillars; its length was fifty cubits, and its breadth thirty cubits; there was a porch in front with pillars, and a canopy before them.

7 And he made the Hall of the Throne where he was to pronounce judgment, even the Hall of Judgment; it was finished with cedar from floor to rafters. [s]

8 His own house where he was to dwell, in the other court back of the hall, was of like workmanship. Solomon also made a house like this hall for Pharaoh's daughter whom he had taken in marriage.

9 All these were made of costly stones, hewn according to measure, sawed with saws, back and front, even from the foundation to the coping, and from the court of the house of the LORD[t] to the great court. [10]The foundation was of costly stones, huge stones, stones of eight and ten cubits. [11]And above were costly stones, hewn according to measurement, and cedar. [12]The great court had three courses of hewn stone round about, and a course of cedar beams; so had the inner court of the house of the LORD, and the vestibule of the house.

Works of Hiram the Bronzeworker

13 And King Solomon sent and brought Hiram from Tyre. [14]He was the son of a widow of the tribe of Naph'tali, and his father was a man of Tyre, a worker in bronze; and he was full of wisdom, understanding, and skill, for making any work in bronze. He came to King Solomon, and did all his work.

15 He cast two pillars of bronze. Eighteen cubits was the height of one pillar, and a line of twelve cubits measured its circumference; it was hollow, and its thickness was four fingers; the second pillar was the same.[u] [16]He also made two capitals of molten bronze, to set upon the tops of the pillars; the height of the one capital was five cubits, and the height of the other capital was five cubits. [17]Then he made two[v] nets of checker work with wreaths of chain work for the capitals upon the tops of the pillars; a net[w] for the one capital, and a net[w] for the other capital. [18]Likewise he made pomegranates;[x] in two rows round about upon the one network, to cover the capital that was upon the top of the pillar; and he did the same with the other capital. [19]Now the capitals that were upon the tops of the pillars in the vestibule were of lily-work, four cubits. [20]The capitals were upon the two pillars and also above the rounded projection which was beside the network; there were two hundred pomegranates, in two rows round about; and so with the other capital. [21]He set up the pillars at the vestibule of the temple; he set up the pillar on the south and called its name Ja'chin; and he set up the pillar on the north and called its name Boaz. [22]And upon the tops of the pillars was lily-work. Thus the work of the pillars was finished.

23 Then he made the molten sea; it was round, ten cubits from brim to brim, and five cubits high, and a line of thirty cubits measured its circumference. [24]Under its brim were gourds, for thirty[y] cubits, compassing the sea round about; the gourds were in two rows, cast with it when it was cast. [25]It stood upon twelve oxen, three facing north, three facing west, three facing south, and three facing east; the

---

7:15-21: 2 Chron 3:15–17.   **7:23-26:** 2 Chron 4:2–5.

7:8 Pharaoh's daughter: Wedded to Solomon as part of a political alliance between Israel and Egypt (3:1). She evidently received preferential treatment among the numerous wives of the king (11:3).

7:9 sawed: A technique used to create a smooth surface on stone blocks (ashlar masonry).

7:12 The great court: Appears to encompass the entire building complex, the Temple and the royal palaces.

7:13 Hiram from Tyre: Not the king of Tyre, who shares the same name (5:1), but a skilled artisan and metallurgist (7:14). His name appears as "Huramabi" in 2 Chron 2:13.

7:14 wisdom, understanding, and skill: The same gifts of the Spirit bestowed on Bezalel of Judah, the head craftsman entrusted with fabricating the Mosaic Tabernacle (Ex 31:3, translated "ability … intelligence … knowledge").

7:15 pillars of bronze: Freestanding columns over 30 feet high. They stand on either side of the Temple entrance and appear to have a decorative rather than a structural function. Their names are given in 7:21 as Jachin ("he establishes") and Boaz ("in him is strength"), which may be the first word of a dedicatory inscription that appeared on each pillar. The symbolism of these uprights is debated, though evidence favors a *creational* significance. It seems they represent (1) the pillars that uphold the earth in Semitic cosmology (1 Sam 2:8; Ps 75:3), or else (2) the two trees of paradise, the tree of life and the tree of knowledge, that stood in the garden of Eden (Gen 2:9). Some scholars, noting that the twin columns are topped with hundreds of pomegranates, have called them stylized trees. That the sanctuary in Jerusalem was viewed as a representation of Eden, see essay: *Theology of the Temple* at 2 Chron 5.

7:23 the molten sea: A giant water basin set in the southeast corner of the Temple's outer court (7:39). Its full capacity is 12,000 gallons, and it rests on a pedestal of 12 bronze oxen facing out in all directions. Priests used the sea for ritual purification (2 Chron 4:6). • *Allegorically*, the molten sea prefigures the baptismal font that cleanses us by a remission of sins. And just as priests washed in it, so the elect are called priests insofar as they are members of Jesus Christ the high priest (St. Bede, *On the Temple* 2, 19).

---

[r]Gk: Heb *posts*.

[s]Syr Vg: Heb *floor*.

[t]With 7:12: Heb *from the outside*.

[u]Tg Syr Compare Gk and Jer 52:21: Heb *and a line of twelve cubits measured the circumference of the second pillar*.

[v]Gk: Heb lacks *he made two*.

[w]Gk: Heb *seven*.

[x]With 2 Mss Compare Gk: Heb *pillars*.

[y]Heb *ten*.

sea was set upon them, and all their posterior parts were inward. [26]Its thickness was a handbreadth; and its brim was made like the brim of a cup, like the flower of a lily; it held two thousand baths.

27 He also made the ten stands of bronze; each stand was four cubits long, four cubits wide, and three cubits high. [28]This was the construction of the stands: they had panels, and the panels were set in the frames [29]and on the panels that were set in the frames were lions, oxen, and cherubim. Upon the frames, both above and below the lions and oxen, there were wreaths of beveled work. [30]Moreover each stand had four bronze wheels and axles of bronze; and at the four corners were supports for a laver. The supports were cast, with wreaths at the side of each. [31]Its opening was within a crown which projected upward one cubit; its opening was round, as a pedestal is made, a cubit and a half deep. At its opening there were carvings; and its panels were square, not round. [32]And the four wheels were underneath the panels; the axles of the wheels were of one piece with the stands; and the height of a wheel was a cubit and a half. [33]The wheels were made like a chariot wheel; their axles, their rims, their spokes, and their hubs, were all cast. [34]There were four supports at the four corners of each stand; the supports were of one piece with the stands. [35]And on the top of the stand there was a round band half a cubit high; and on the top of the stand its stays and its panels were of one piece with it. [36]And on the surfaces of its stays and on its panels, he carved cherubim, lions, and palm trees, according to the space of each, with wreaths round about. [37]After this manner he made the ten stands; all of them were cast alike, of the same measure and the same form.

38 And he made ten lavers of bronze; each laver held forty baths, each laver measured four cubits, and there was a laver for each of the ten stands. [39]And he set the stands, five on the south side of the house, and five on the north side of the house; and he set the sea at the southeast corner of the house.

40 Hiram also made the pots, the shovels, and the basins. So Hiram finished all the work that he did for King Solomon on the house of the LORD: [41]the two pillars, the two bowls of the capitals that were on the tops of the pillars, and the two networks to cover the two bowls of the capitals that were on the tops of the pillars; [42]and the four hundred pomegranates for the two networks, two rows of pomegranates for each network, to cover the two bowls of the capitals that were upon the pillars; [43]the ten stands, and the ten lavers upon the stands; [44]and the one sea, and the twelve oxen underneath the sea.

45 Now the pots, the shovels, and the basins, all these vessels in the house of the LORD, which Hiram made for King Solomon, were of burnished bronze. [46]In the plain of the Jordan the king cast them, in the clay ground between Succoth and Zar′ethan. [47]And Solomon left all the vessels unweighed, because there were so many of them; the weight of the bronze was not found out.

48 So Solomon made all the vessels that were in the house of the LORD: the golden altar, the golden table for the bread of the Presence, [49]the lampstands of pure gold, five on the south side and five on the north, before the inner sanctuary; the flowers, the lamps, and the tongs, of gold; [50]the cups, snuffers, basins, dishes for incense, and firepans, of pure gold; and the sockets of gold, for the doors of the innermost part of the house, the most holy place, and for the doors of the nave of the temple.

51 Thus all the work that King Solomon did on the house of the LORD was finished. And Solomon brought in the things which David his father had dedicated, the silver, the gold, and the vessels, and stored them in the treasuries of the house of the LORD.

Dedication of the Temple

8 Then Solomon assembled the elders of Israel and all the heads of the tribes, the leaders of the fathers' houses of the sons of Israel, before King Solomon in Jerusalem, to bring up the ark of the covenant of the LORD out of the city of David, which

---

7:38–51: 2 Chron 4:6, 5:1.   **8:1–6:** Rev 11:19.

7:27 ten stands: Wheeled stands having decorated frames and panels. They are positioned in two rows in the Temple courtyard and support ten water basins that the priests use to rinse off various parts of sacrificial animals (Lev 1:9, 13; 2 Chron 4:6).

7:38 forty baths: A bath equals about six gallons (liquid measure).

7:40 pots ... shovels ... basins: Bronze utensils used in connection with the altar of sacrifice (Ex 38:3), which was also cast in bronze (2 Chron 4:1).

7:46 Succoth ... Zarethan: East of the Jordan near the Jabbok River.

7:48 golden altar: The altar of incense, which stands just outside the most holy place (Ex 30:1–10). **golden table:** A display table for the 12 loaves of showbread stands in the nave or holy place (Ex 25:23–30; Lev 24:5–9).

7:49 lampstands: Ten candelabras light up the nave or holy place of the Temple. Only one flickered in the Tabernacle.

Presumably each lampstand, like its predecessor, branched out into seven actual lamps (Ex 25:31–39).

7:50 cups ... firepans: Cultic implements for such rites as wine libations, tending the lamps, incense offerings, etc.

7:51 dedicated: David consecrated spoil from military campaigns as well as tribute from vassal states subject to Israel (see 2 Sam 8:10–11). **treasuries:** Presumably the sacred storerooms wrapped around the main Temple building (6:5; 1 Chron 28:12).

8:1–66 The dedication of the Temple. Solomon stages the event during a weeklong festival (8:65) almost a year after construction is complete (compare 8:2 with 6:38). Highlights of the ceremony include (1) the installation of the Ark of the Covenant in the inner sanctuary (8:1–8), (2) the visible infusion of Yahweh's glory into his dwelling place (8:10–11), and (3) the petitions of Solomon for those who worship at the Temple (8:22–53) (CCC 2580).

8:1 Zion: The southeast ridge of Jerusalem, site of the city of David. See note on 2 Sam 5:7.

is Zion. ²And all the men of Israel assembled to King Solomon at the feast in the month Eth′anim, which is the seventh month. ³And all the elders of Israel came, and the priests took up the ark. ⁴And they brought up the ark of the Lord, the tent of meeting, and all the holy vessels that were in the tent; the priests and the Le-vites brought them up. ⁵And King Solomon and all the congregation of Israel, who had assembled before him, were with him before the ark, sacrificing so many sheep and oxen that they could not be counted or numbered. ⁶Then the priests brought the ark of the covenant of the Lord to its place, in the inner sanctuary of the house, in the most holy place, underneath the wings of the cherubim. ⁷For the cherubim spread out their wings over the place of the ark, so that the cherubim made a covering above the ark and its poles. ⁸And the poles were so long that the ends of the poles were seen from the holy place before the inner sanctuary; but they could not be seen from outside; and they are there to this day. ⁹There was nothing in the ark except the two tables of stone which Moses put there at Horeb, where the Lord made a covenant with the sons of Israel, when they came out of the land of Egypt. ¹⁰And when the priests came out of the holy place, a cloud* filled the house of the Lord, ¹¹so that the priests could not stand to minister because of the cloud; for the glory of the Lord filled the house of the Lord.

Solomon's Speech

12 Then Solomon said,

"The Lord has set the sun in the heavens,
but ᶻ has said that he would dwell in thick darkness.

¹³I have built you an exalted house,
a place for you to dwell in for ever."

¹⁴Then the king faced about, and blessed all the assembly of Israel, while all the assembly of Israel stood. ¹⁵And he said, "Blessed be the Lord, the God of Israel, who with his hand has fulfilled what he promised with his mouth to David my father, saying, ¹⁶'Since the day that I brought my people Israel out of Egypt, I chose no city in all the tribes of Israel in which to build a house, that my name might be there; but I chose David to be over my people Israel.' ¹⁷Now it was in the heart of David my father to build a house for the name of the Lord, the God of Israel. ¹⁸But the Lord said to David my father, 'Whereas it was in your heart to build a house for my name, you did well that it was in your heart; ¹⁹nevertheless you shall not build the house, but your son who shall be born to you shall build the house for my name.' ²⁰Now the Lord has fulfilled his promise which he made; for I have risen in the place of David my father, and sit on the throne of Israel, as the Lord promised, and I have built the house for the name of the Lord, the God of Israel. ²¹And there I have provided a place for the ark, in which is the covenant of the Lord which he made with our fathers, when he brought them out of the land of Egypt."

Solomon's Prayer of Dedication

22 Then Solomon stood before the altar of the Lord in the presence of all the assembly of Israel, and spread forth his hands toward heaven; ²³and said,† "O Lord, God of Israel, there is no God like you, in heaven above or on earth beneath, keeping covenant and showing mercy to your servants who

---

8:10, 11: 2 Chron 5:13, 14; Rev 15:8.   8:12-50: 2 Chron 6:1–39.

8:2 the month Ethanim: Corresponds to September-October in the ancient Phoenician calendar. **seventh month:** The holiest month of the Israelite liturgical year. See note on Lev 23:24.

8:4 the ark: Taken from the provisional tent that David had pitched for it on Zion, directly south of Solomon's Temple (2 Sam 6:17). **the tent of meeting:** The Mosaic Tabernacle. It is brought to Jerusalem from Gibeon, roughly six miles northwest of the city, where it stood for many years during David's reign (1 Chron 16:39). Storage of the tent inside Solomon's sanctuary indicates that the Jerusalem Temple is the successor to the desert Tabernacle as the liturgical center of Mosaic religion.

8:5 before the ark: Recalls the liturgical procession of the ark to Mt. Zion conducted by David in 2 Sam 6:12-17. **sacrificing:** A priestly action. See note on 8:63.

8:7 the cherubim: The angelic images manufactured in 6:23-28.

8:8 poles: Used to lift and transport the ark so as to avoid direct human contact (Ex 25:13-15). **to this day:** Indicates that the original author of this account must have written before the disappearance of the ark and the destruction of the Temple in 586 B.C.

8:9 tables of stone: The two tablets inscribed with the Decalogue (Ex 34:27-28). The ark, having the form of a lidded chest, was a place of sacred storage for these witnesses to the Sinai covenant (Ex 25:16). **Horeb:** Mt. Sinai, or possibly the range of peaks associated with it. See note on Ex 3:1.

8:10 cloud: The visible sign of God's glory takes possession of the Temple. The cloud that manifests Yahweh's presence was called the "Shekinah" in rabbinic Judaism (CCC 697). • The event recalls how the Lord settled in a firecloud on the Mosaic Tabernacle (Ex 40:34-38).

8:12 thick darkness: The dense cloud that envelops and conceals God's presence (Ex 20:21; Dt 5:22; 2 Sam 22:10; Ps 97:2).

8:14-26 Solomon's opening address celebrates the fulfillment of God's word (8:15, 20, 24). On the one hand, the Lord has begun to fulfill the Davidic covenant, specifically his pledge to give David a "son" who will build him a "house" in which to dwell (8:18, referencing the promise in 2 Sam 7:12-13). On the other, Solomon looks to the future and prays that God will honor his adjoining pledge to establish David's "throne" for all time (8:25, referencing the promise in 2 Sam 7:16).

8:14 blessed all: Solomon assumes the role of a priest, invoking a divine blessing upon the people (Lev 9:22; Num 6:22-27). See note on 8:63.

8:22 the altar: The bronze altar of sacrifice that stands in the outdoor court of the Temple (8:64). **spread ... hands:** A gesture of prayer and praise (8:38; Is 1:15) (CCC 2702).

---

*8:10, *cloud:* The visible sign of the presence of Yahweh taking possession of his sanctuary; later called the shekinah by the rabbis.
†8:23-53: This eloquent prayer admirably sums up the relation of God to his people.
ᶻGk: Heb lacks *has set the sun in the heavens, but.*

walk before you with all their heart; ²⁴who have kept with your servant David my father what you declared to him; yes, you spoke with your mouth, and with your hand have fulfilled it this day. ²⁵Now therefore, O Lᴏʀᴅ, God of Israel, keep with your servant David my father what you have promised him, saying, 'There shall never fail you a man before me to sit upon the throne of Israel, if only your sons take heed to their way, to walk before me as you have walked before me.' ²⁶Now therefore, O God of Israel, let your word be confirmed, which you have spoken to your servant David my father.

27 "But will God indeed dwell on the earth? Behold, heaven and the highest heaven cannot contain you; how much less this house which I have built! * ²⁸Yet have regard to the prayer of your servant and to his supplication, O Lᴏʀᴅ my God, listening to the cry and to the prayer which your servant prays before you this day; ²⁹that your eyes may be open night and day toward this house, the place of which you have said, 'My name shall be there,' that you may listen to the prayer which your servant offers toward this place. ³⁰And hear the supplication of your servant and of your people Israel, when they pray toward this place; yes, hear in heaven your dwelling place; and when you hear, forgive.

31 "If a man sins against his neighbor and is made to take an oath, and comes and swears his oath before your altar in this house, ³²then hear in heaven, and act, and judge your servants, condemning the guilty by bringing his conduct upon his own head, and vindicating the righteous by rewarding him according to his righteousness.

33 "When your people Israel are defeated before the enemy because they have sinned against you, if they turn again to you, and acknowledge your name, and pray and make supplication to you in this house; ³⁴then hear in heaven, and forgive the sin of your people Israel, and bring them again to the land which you gave to their fathers.

35 "When heaven is shut up and there is no rain because they have sinned against you, if they pray toward this place, and acknowledge your name, and turn from their sin, when you afflict them, ³⁶then hear in heaven, and forgive the sin of your servants, your people Israel, when you teach them the good way in which they should walk; and grant rain upon your land, which you have given to your people as an inheritance.

37 "If there is famine in the land, if there is pestilence or blight or mildew or locust or caterpillar; if their enemy besieges them in any ᵃ of their cities; whatever plague, whatever sickness there is; ³⁸whatever prayer, whatever supplication is made by any man or by all your people Israel, each knowing the affliction of his own heart and stretching out his hands toward this house; ³⁹then hear in heaven your dwelling place, and forgive, and act, and render to each whose heart you know, according to all his ways (for you, you only, know the hearts of all the children of men); ⁴⁰that they may fear you all the days that they live in the land which you gave to our fathers.

41 "Likewise when a foreigner, who is not of your people Israel, comes from a far country for your name's sake ⁴²(for they shall hear of your great name, and your mighty hand, and of your outstretched arm), when he comes and prays toward this house, ⁴³hear in heaven your dwelling place, and do according to all for which the foreigner calls to you; in order that all the peoples of the earth may know your name and fear you, as do your people Israel, and that they may know that this house which I have built is called by your name.

44 "If your people go out to battle against their enemy, by whatever way you shall send them, and they pray to the Lᴏʀᴅ toward the city which you

---

8:25–53 Solomon's dedication prayer. Following two general appeals (8:25–30), he makes seven specific petitions, asking the Lord (1) to enforce oaths of innocence that are sworn at the sanctuary (8:31–32), (2) to forgive and restore penitent exiles (8:33–34), (3) to end droughts occasioned by sin (8:35–36), (4) to rescue sinners besieged by hardships (8:37–40), (5) to grant the requests of Gentiles praying toward the Temple (8:41–43), (6) to give Israel victory in war (8:44–45), and (7) to show mercy to penitent captives (8:46–53). In several cases, Solomon requests deliverance for Israel from the curses of the Deuteronomic covenant (military defeat, drought, famine, pestilence, siege, plague, sickness, captivity, Deut 28:21–25, 36–41, 52, 58–61, 64–68) (CCC 2629).

8:27 cannot contain you: Solomon articulates the theology of divine transcendence. The Lord dwells in a special way within the sacred space marked out by the Temple, and yet he is not confined to that space, since his presence fills heaven and earth to overflowing (Ps 139:7–10; Acts 17:24). The presence of God encompasses the world rather than vice versa (CCC 300).

📖 **8:29 My name shall be there:** The promise was made in these terms by Moses in the law of the central sanctuary (Deut 12:5, 10–11). **toward this place:** Begins a long tradition of prayer directed to the Lord's Temple (Ps 5:7; 138:2; Dan 6:10). As the king's own prayer unfolds, the definition of "this place" expands concentrically to include the holy sanctuary of Yahweh (8:42), the holy city of Jerusalem (8:44), and the holy land of Israel (8:48).

8:30 your dwelling place: Solomon is aware that the Temple building, though grand and glorious by human standards, is only an image of Yahweh's eternal sanctuary in heaven (Ps 11:4). See essay: *Theology of the Temple* at 2 Chron 5.

8:41 a foreigner ... comes: Envisions individual Gentiles making a pilgrimage to Jerusalem, as happens during Solomon's reign (10:1–10, 24). Theologically, the Temple embodies the missionary spirit of the Davidic covenant, with its aim to extend the wisdom and blessings of God to other nations beyond Israel (Is 55:3–5; 56:3–8). Here Yahweh is asked to heed the prayers of the Gentiles and thus begin the process of spreading the "knowledge" and "fear" of the Lord throughout the world (8:43, 60). See essay: *The Davidic Covenant* at 2 Sam 7.

---

*8:27: A reminder that Yahweh was very different from the gods of other nations, who dwelt in their temples.
ᵃGk Syr: Heb *the land.*

have chosen and the house which I have built for your name, [45]then hear in heaven their prayer and their supplication, and maintain their cause.

46 "If they sin against you—for there is no man who does not sin—and you are angry with them, and give them to an enemy, so that they are carried away captive to the land of the enemy, far off or near; [47]yet if they lay it to heart in the land to which they have been carried captive, and repent, and make supplication to you in the land of their captors, saying, 'We have sinned, and have acted perversely and wickedly'; [48]if they repent with all their mind and with all their heart in the land of their enemies, who carried them captive, and pray to you toward their land, which you gave to their fathers, the city which you have chosen, and the house which I have built for your name; [49]then hear in heaven your dwelling place their prayer and their supplication, and maintain their cause [50]and forgive your people who have sinned against you, and all their transgressions which they have committed against you; and grant them compassion in the sight of those who carried them captive, that they may have compassion on them [51](for they are your people, and your heritage, which you brought out of Egypt, from the midst of the iron furnace). [52]Let your eyes be open to the supplication of your servant, and to the supplication of your people Israel, giving ear to them whenever they call to you. [53]For you separated them from among all the peoples of the earth, to be your heritage, as you declared through Moses, your servant, when you brought our fathers out of Egypt, O Lord God."

Solomon Blesses the Assembly

54 Now as Solomon finished offering all this prayer and supplication to the LORD, he arose from before the altar of the LORD, where he had knelt with hands outstretched toward heaven; [55]and he stood, and blessed all the assembly of Israel with a loud voice, saying, [56]"Blessed be the LORD who has given rest to his people Israel, according to all that he promised; not one word has failed of all his good promise, which he uttered by Moses his servant. [57]The LORD our God be with us, as he was with our fathers; may he not leave us or forsake us; [58]that he may incline our hearts to him, to walk in all his ways, and to keep his commandments, his statutes, and his ordinances, which he commanded our fathers. [59]Let these words of mine, wherewith I have made supplication before the LORD, be near to the LORD our God day and night, and may he maintain the cause of his servant, and the cause of his people Israel, as each day requires; [60]that all the peoples of the earth may know that the LORD is God; there is no other. [61]Let your heart therefore be wholly true to the LORD our God, walking in his statutes and keeping his commandments, as at this day."

Solomon Offers Sacrifices

62 Then the king, and all Israel with him, offered sacrifice before the LORD. [63]Solomon offered as peace offerings to the LORD twenty-two thousand oxen and a hundred and twenty thousand sheep. So the king and all the sons of Israel dedicated the house of the LORD. [64]The same day the king consecrated the middle of the court that was before the house of the LORD; for there he offered the burnt offering and the cereal offering and the fat pieces of the peace offerings, because the bronze altar that was before the LORD was too small to receive the burnt offering and the cereal offering and the fat pieces of the peace offerings.

65 So Solomon held the feast at that time, and all Israel with him, a great assembly, from the entrance of Ha′math to the Brook of Egypt, before the LORD our God, seven days.[b] [66]On the eighth day he sent the people away; and they blessed the king, and

---

8:62–66: 2 Chron 7:4–10.

8:55 blessed all: In the manner of a priest. See note on 8:63.

8:58 incline our hearts: An appeal for God's grace, i.e., for the divine assistance needed to walk faithfully in the Lord's commandments. See word study: *Heart* at Deut 30:6.

📖 **8:60 there is no other:** Restates the Mosaic doctrine that Yahweh alone is God (Deut 4:35, 39; 32:39). This implies that the multitude of other gods and goddesses worshiped in the ancient world are not really divinities at all. In some instances, at least, Scripture defines worship of pagan deities as service to demons (see Deut 32:17; 1 Cor 10:20–21; Rev 9:20). The monotheistic faith of Israel is thus squarely at odds with the polytheistic faith that prevailed throughout the ancient Near East and beyond.

📖 **8:63 offered ... oxen ... sheep:** Solomon plays the part of a royal priest, just as his father, David, had done (2 Sam 6:12–14). His priestly actions include blessing the assembly (8:14), interceding on behalf of the people (8:27–30), and sacrificing animals before the Lord (8:5, 62–64). This is in stark contrast to King Saul, who was sternly rebuked and even deprived of a royal dynasty for presuming to sacrifice burnt offerings like a priest (see 1 Sam 13:8–15). The difference is rooted in the Davidic covenant, specifically in Yahweh's oath to the royal son of David: "You are a priest for ever according to the order of Melchizedek" (Ps 110:4). The Bible only hints at some of the details of this arrangement, which invested the Davidic monarch with kingly and cultic prerogatives. This same combination is visible in the figure of Melchizedek, onetime ruler of ancient Jerusalem, in whom the two offices of kingship and priesthood converged (Gen 14:18–20). See note on 8:14 and 2 Sam 6:12–19.

8:65 the feast: The seven-day Feast of Booths (later called Tabernacles), held each year in the seventh month (Deut 16:13–15). **entrance of Hamath:** Marks the northernmost extent of Israelite territory (Num 34:8). **Brook of Egypt:** Flows into the Mediterranean across the land bridge between Egypt and Canaan. It marks the southern border of Israelite territory (Num 34:5).

---

[b]Gk: Heb *seven days and seven days, fourteen days.*

went to their homes joyful and glad of heart for all the goodness that the Lord had shown to David his servant and to Israel his people.

The Lord's Second Appearance to Solomon

9 When Solomon had finished building the house of the Lord and the king's house and all that Solomon desired to build, ²the Lord appeared to Solomon a second time, as he had appeared to him at Gib'eon. ³And the Lord said to him,* "I have heard your prayer and your supplication, which you have made before me; I have consecrated this house which you have built, and put my name there for ever; my eyes and my heart will be there for all time. ⁴And as for you, if you will walk before me, as David your father walked, with integrity of heart and uprightness, doing according to all that I have commanded you, and keeping my statutes and my ordinances, ⁵then I will establish your royal throne over Israel for ever, as I promised David your father, saying, 'There shall not fail you a man upon the throne of Israel.' ⁶But if you turn aside from following me, you or your children, and do not keep my commandments and my statutes which I have set before you, but go and serve other gods and worship them, ⁷then I will cut off Israel from the land which I have given them; and the house which I have consecrated for my name I will cast out of my sight; and Israel will become a proverb and a byword among all peoples. ⁸And this house will become a heap of ruins;ᶜ every one passing by it will be astonished, and will hiss; and they will say, 'Why has the Lord done thus to this land and to this house?' ⁹Then they will say, 'Because they forsook the Lord their God who brought their fathers out of the land of Egypt, and laid hold on other gods, and worshiped them and served them; therefore the Lord has brought all this evil upon them.'"

10 At the end of twenty years, in which Solomon had built the two houses, the house of the Lord and the king's house, ¹¹and Hiram king of Tyre had supplied Solomon with cedar and cypress timber and gold, as much as he desired, King Solomon gave to Hiram twenty cities in the land of Galilee. ¹²But when Hiram came from Tyre to see the cities which Solomon had given him, they did not please him. ¹³Therefore he said, "What kind of cities are these which you have given me, my brother?" So they are called the land of Ca'bul to this day. ¹⁴Hiram had sent to the king one hundred and twenty talents of gold.

Other Works of Solomon

15 And this is the account of the forced labor which King Solomon levied to build the house of the Lord and his own house and the Millo and the wall of Jerusalem and Ha'zor and Megid'do and Gezer ¹⁶(Pharaoh king of Egypt had gone up and captured Gezer and burnt it with fire, and had slain the Canaanites who dwelt in the city, and had given it as dowry to his daughter, Solomon's

---

9:1–9: 2 Chron 7:11–22.   **9:10–28:** 2 Chron 8:8–18.

9:2 a second time: The first vision came in a dream in 3:5–15.

9:3 I have consecrated: The sanctuary is "made holy" by the glorious presence of Yahweh filling its courts (8:1–11).

9:4–9 In this second divine encounter, the Lord reminds Solomon of the "two ways" of the covenant (Deut 30:15–20). Faithfulness will bring the *blessing* of a stable dynasty (9:5), but apostasy and idolatry will bring the *curse* of exile and reduce the Temple to a smoldering heap of destruction (9:7–8). Both threats become realities at the conclusion of the Books of the Kings. Theologically, the Davidic covenant is unconditional insofar as Yahweh pledges to grant David a perpetual dynasty (2 Sam 23:5; Ps 89:3–4); however, the covenant is conditional in the sense that God pledges to chastise the kings of the Davidic line for their iniquities (2 Sam 7:14; Ps 89:30–32; 132:11–12).

9:8 heap of ruins: A frightful possibility that becomes history when the Babylonians sack Jerusalem in 586 B.C. (2 Kings 25:8–9).

9:10–28 Solomon strengthens his empire with a series of economic and defense initiatives.

9:10 end of twenty years: About 946 B.C., following seven years of sanctuary construction (6:38) and thirteen years of palace construction (7:1).

9:11 twenty cities: Presumably towns in northwest Israel, close to Phoenicia. It is unclear whether this transaction completed Solomon's payments to Hiram and his laborers (noted in 5:6, 11) or whether Solomon sold the towns for 120 talents of gold (mentioned in 9:14). Whatever the case, it is taken as a meager gesture that stands in sharp contrast to Hiram's abundant contributions to Solomon's building projects. Hiram, not surprisingly, found the exchange disagreeable (9:12–13).

9:13 my brother: Diplomatic language for a covenant partner of equal rank. Recall that the two kings forged a treaty covenant in 5:12. **Cabul:** Meaning uncertain, possibly "nothing" or "worthless".

9:14 one hundred and twenty talents: A talent is estimated to weigh around 75 pounds. The same quantity of gold is brought to Solomon by the queen of Sheba (10:10).

9:15 the Millo: The name points to some type of earthen fill. Most identify the Millo with a terrace structure designed to support building expansion on the crest of the Ophel ridge, where the city of David stood (see 2 Sam 5:9). Others envision an artificial land bridge that filled the depression between the city of David and the Temple Mount. **wall of Jerusalem:** Solomon repaired a breach in the defenses of the city of David (11:27). **Hazor ... Megiddo ... Gezer:** Cities that Solomon refounded and fortified. Each commanded a strategic position near trade routes in northern Israel (Hazor), the central plain (Megiddo), and the western foothills (Gezer). Archaeology has revealed similar construction designs and techniques at these sites (e.g., multi-chambered gates, public buildings, casemate walls) that appear to date back to Solomonic times.

9:16 captured Gezer: Probably the work of Pharaoh Siamun of the 21st dynasty. **Solomon's wife:** The Egyptian princess introduced in 3:1.

*9:3–9: God's response to Solomon's prayer.
ᶜSyr Old Latin: Heb *high*.

wife; [17]so Solomon rebuilt Gezer) and Lower Beth-ho'ron [18]and Ba'alath and Ta'mar in the wilderness, in the land of Judah,[d] [19]and all the store-cities that Solomon had, and the cities for his chariots, and the cities for his horsemen, and whatever Solomon desired to build in Jerusalem, in Lebanon, and in all the land of his dominion. [20]All the people who were left of the Am'orites, the Hittites, the Per'izzites, the Hi'vites, and the Jeb'usites, who were not of the sons of Israel—[21]their descendants who were left after them in the land, whom the sons of Israel were unable to destroy utterly—these Solomon made a forced levy of slaves, and so they are to this day. [22]But of the sons of Israel Solomon made no slaves; they were the soldiers, they were his officials, his commanders, his captains, his chariot commanders and his horsemen.

23 These were the chief officers who were over Solomon's work: five hundred and fifty, who had charge of the people who carried on the work.

24 But Pharaoh's daughter went up from the city of David to her own house which Solomon had built for her; then he built the Millo.

25 Three times a year Solomon used to offer up burnt offerings and peace offerings upon the altar which he built to the Lord, burning incense[e] before the Lord. So he finished the house.

Solomon's Fleet

26 King Solomon built a fleet of ships at E'zion-ge'ber, which is near E'loth on the shore of the Red Sea, in the land of E'dom. [27]And Hiram sent with the fleet his servants, seamen who were familiar with the sea, together with the servants of Solomon; [28]and they went to O'phir, and brought from there gold, to the amount of four hundred and twenty talents; and they brought it to King Solomon.

Visit of the Queen of Sheba

10 Now when the queen of Sheba* heard of the fame of Solomon concerning the name of the Lord, she came to test him with hard questions. [2]She came to Jerusalem with a very great retinue, with camels bearing spices, and very much gold, and precious stones; and when she came to Solomon, she told him all that was on her mind. [3]And Solomon answered all her questions; there was nothing hidden from the king which he could not explain to her. [4]And when the queen of Sheba had seen all the wisdom of Solomon, the house that he had built, [5]the food of his table, the seating of his officials, and the attendance of his servants, their clothing, his cupbearers, and his burnt offerings which he offered at the house of the Lord, there was no more spirit in her.

6 And she said to the king, "The report was true which I heard in my own land of your affairs and of your wisdom, [7]but I did not believe the reports until I came and my own eyes had seen it; and behold, the half was not told me; your wisdom and prosperity surpass the report which I heard. [8]Happy are your wives![f] Happy are these your servants, who continually stand before you and hear your wisdom! [9]Blessed be the Lord your God, who has delighted in you and set you on the throne of Israel! Because

---

10:1–29: 2 Chron 9:1–28.

9:17 Lower Beth-horon: Northwest of Jerusalem. It flanks one of the main routes leading from the Mediterranean coast into the central highlands of Israel.

9:18 Baalath: Exact location uncertain, but probably the Danite coastal town mentioned in Josh 19:44. **Tamar:** In the eastern Negev, south of Judah.

9:21 forced levy of slaves: Canaanites living among the Israelites are sentenced to hard labor on royal construction projects. See note on 5:13–16.

9:25 Three times a year: At the three pilgrim festivals mandated by the Torah: the Feasts of Passover, Weeks, and Booths (Deut 16:1–17; 2 Chron 8:13). **used to offer up:** The sacred actions of a priest. See note on 8:63. **burning incense:** The Hebrew expression is "sending up smoke with it", which the Greek LXX takes to mean incense offerings that accompanied the blood offerings. The verb can also designate the burning of animals and their sacrificial parts (Ex 29:13; Lev 4:26; Num 18:17; 2 Kings 16:15).

9:26 Ezion-geber: A shipping port at the northern tip of the Gulf of Aqaba (an inlet of the Red Sea). Solomon initiates a business venture in maritime trade to expand the economy of Israel. He was also an arms merchant, according to 2 Chron 1:15–17.

9:28 Ophir: In southwest Arabia (or possibly along the eastern coast of Africa). Ophir was renowned in biblical times

for its high-quality gold (1 Chron 29:4; Job 28:16; Ps 45:9; Is 13:12).

10:1–29 Solomon stands at the pinnacle of his royal career. He has become internationally famous for his wisdom, and now travelers and treasures are pouring into his kingdom from afar. Nevertheless, the height of Solomon's glory in chap. 10 will only accentuate the depth of his fall in chap. 11.

10:1 queen of Sheba: Sheba was probably located at the southern tip of the Arabian Peninsula (modern Yemen). It was a major trading empire in biblical times (Jer 6:20; Ezek 27:22). The queen's historic visit, perhaps in the interest of forging a trade agreement with Israel, magnifies the extent of Solomon's reputation throughout the Near Eastern world. It also serves as a paradigm of Israel's hopes for the future. This is especially clear in Isaiah, where the prophet envisions Yahweh's glory and wisdom radiating forth from Zion while the nations stream in to offer bountiful gifts to the Davidic ruler (see Is 2:1–3; 51:4; 55:3–5; 60:1–6). • In the teaching of Jesus, the acceptance of wisdom is exemplified by the queen of Sheba, and the proclamation of wisdom by Solomon foreshadows the teaching of a greater wisdom by the Messiah (Mt 12:42; Lk 11:31).

10:5 his burnt offerings: For Solomon's priestly actions, see note on 8:63. **no more spirit:** The queen is overwhelmed by all that she sees and hears. In modern idiom, they "took her breath away".

10:9 Blessed be the Lord: An exclamation of praise, similar to that of Hiram king of Tyre in 5:7. The queen is moved to this when she perceives the glory of the God of Israel shining forth in the brilliance of Solomon and the splendors of his court.

---

*10:1, *Sheba:* A kingdom in southwestern Arabia.
[d]Heb lacks *of Judah.*
[e]Gk: Heb *burning incense with it which.*
[f]Gk Syr: Heb *men.*

the Lord loved Israel for ever, he has made you king, that you may execute justice and righteousness." ¹⁰Then she gave the king a hundred and twenty talents of gold, and a very great quantity of spices, and precious stones; never again came such an abundance of spices as these which the queen of Sheba gave to King Solomon.

11 Moreover the fleet of Hiram, which brought gold from O'phir, brought from Ophir a very great amount of almug wood and precious stones. ¹²And the king made of the almug wood supports for the house of the Lord, and for the king's house, lyres also and harps for the singers; no such almug wood has come or been seen, to this day.

13 And King Solomon gave to the queen of Sheba all that she desired, whatever she asked besides what was given her by the bounty of King Solomon. So she turned and went back to her own land, with her servants.

14 Now the weight of gold that came to Solomon in one year was six hundred and sixty-six talents of gold, ¹⁵besides that which came from the traders and from the traffic of the merchants, and from all the kings of Arabia and from the governors of the land. ¹⁶King Solomon made two hundred large shields of beaten gold; six hundred shekels of gold went into each shield. ¹⁷And he made three hundred shields of beaten gold; three minas of gold went into each shield; and the king put them in the House of the Forest of Lebanon. ¹⁸The king also made a great ivory throne, and overlaid it with the finest gold. ¹⁹The throne had six steps, and at the back of the throne was a calf's head, and on each side of the seat

were arm rests and two lions standing beside the arm rests, ²⁰while twelve lions stood there, one on each end of a step on the six steps. The like of it was never made in any kingdom. ²¹All King Solomon's drinking vessels were of gold, and all the vessels of the House of the Forest of Lebanon were of pure gold; none were of silver, it was not considered as anything in the days of Solomon. ²²For the king had a fleet of ships of Tar'shish at sea with the fleet of Hiram. Once every three years the fleet of ships of Tarshish* used to come bringing gold, silver, ivory, apes, and peacocks.ᵍ

23 Thus King Solomon excelled all the kings of the earth in riches and in wisdom. ²⁴And the whole earth sought the presence of Solomon to hear his wisdom, which God had put into his mind. ²⁵Every one of them brought his present, articles of silver and gold, garments, myrrh, spices, horses, and mules, so much year by year.

26 And Solomon gathered together chariots and horsemen; he had fourteen hundred chariots and twelve thousand horsemen, whom he stationed in the chariot cities and with the king in Jerusalem. ²⁷And the king made silver as common in Jerusalem as stone, and he made cedar as plentiful as the sycamore of the Shephe'lah. ²⁸And Solomon's import of horses was from Egypt and Ku'e, and the king's traders received them from Kue at a price. ²⁹A chariot could be imported from Egypt for six hundred shekels of silver, and a horse for a hundred and fifty; and so through the king's traders they were exported to all the kings of the Hittites and the kings of Syria.

10:11 fleet of Hiram: Merchant ships jointly manned by Phoenician and Israelite seamen (9:27–28). **almug wood:** Not identified with certainty (possibly "red sandalwood").

10:12 lyres ... harps ... singers: Elements of the Temple's liturgical music. This dimension of Israel's worship receives minimal attention in the Books of the Kings but is a major focus of the Books of the Chronicles. See essay: *David's New Liturgy* at 1 Chron 16.

10:14–11:8 A turning point in the Solomon story. Politically and economically, the king stands at the height of his reign, having an empire unmatched by any in the region. But morally, he has transgressed the three limits placed on kingship by Deuteronomy, namely, that Israel's kings must not indulge in selfish extravagance by multiplying wealth, weapons, and wives (Deut 17:16–17). Solomon does precisely this as he piles up unbelievable riches (10:14–22), imports mass numbers of warhorses and chariots from Egypt (10:26–29), and surrounds himself with a harem of a thousand women (11:1–8).

10:14 six hundred and sixty-six: Each talent weighs roughly 75 pounds, and so the annual influx of 666 talents equals more than 20 tons of gold. Remarkably, this figure does not include tariffs from merchant sales, tribute

from Arabian monarchs, or taxes from the king's provinces (10:15). See note on 3:4. • The number 666 appears also in Rev 13:18 as the number of the beast, a cryptic reference to an agent of evil opposed to the Messiah and his people. An allusion to Solomon and his gold seems likely, since the number represents the corruption of Solomon's kingship by an idolatrous drive to amass superabundant wealth. Note, too, that Revelation connects this number with "wisdom" (Rev 13:18), a classic Solomonic trait, and with the economic activity of buying and selling (Rev 13:17).

10:16 large shields: Elongated shields giving soldiers full frontal protection. These are faced with gold overlay and intended for ceremonial display.

10:17 shields: Small round shields or bucklers. **House of the Forest:** The royal armory in Jerusalem (7:2; Is 22:8).

10:18 great ivory throne: Placed in the Hall of the Throne, where the king makes his royal judgments (7:7). The seat is set on a stepped platform, overlaid with gold, ornamented with animal images, and presumably inlaid with large ivory panels.

10:22 ships of Tarshish: Merchant vessels built for sea voyages as far away as "Tartessos" in southern Spain. Others identify Tarshish with "Tarsus" in Asia Minor.

10:26 the chariot cities: Mentioned but not named in 9:17.

10:27 Shephelah: The low hills of western Palestine.

10:28 Kue: Cilicia in southeast Asia Minor (modern Turkey).

10:29 imported ... exported: Solomon was both a buyer and a seller in the regional horse-trading business. **Hittites:** Anatolian peoples of ancient Asia Minor.

---

*10:22, *ships of Tarshish*: i.e., ships that could sail to Tarshish (usually located in Spain). The word then came to be applied to ocean-going vessels.
ᵍOr *baboons*.

Solomon's Errors

11 *Now King Solomon loved many foreign women: the daughter of Pharaoh, and Moabite, Am'monite, E'domite, Sido'nian, and Hittite women, ²from the nations concerning which the Lord had said to the sons of Israel, "You shall not enter into marriage with them, neither shall they with you, for surely they will turn away your heart after their gods"; Solomon clung to these in love. ³He had seven hundred wives, princesses, and three hundred concubines; and his wives turned away his heart. ⁴For when Solomon was old his wives turned away his heart after other gods; and his heart was not wholly true to the Lord his God, as was the heart of David his father. ⁵For Solomon went after Ash'toreth the goddess of the Sido'nians, and after Milcom the abomination of the Am'monites. ⁶So Solomon did what was evil in the sight of the Lord, and did not wholly follow the Lord, as David his father had done. ⁷Then Solomon built a high place for Che'mosh the abomination of Moab, and for Mo'lech the abomination of the Am'monites, on the mountain east of Jerusalem. ⁸And so he did for all his foreign wives, who burned incense and sacrificed to their gods.

⁹ And the Lord was angry with Solomon, because his heart had turned away from the Lord, the God of Israel, who had appeared to him twice, ¹⁰and had commanded him concerning this thing, that he should not go after other gods; but he did not keep what the Lord commanded. ¹¹Therefore the Lord said to Solomon, "Since this has been your mind and you have not kept my covenant and my statutes which I have commanded you, I will surely tear the kingdom from you and will give it to your servant. ¹²Yet for the sake of David your father I will not do it in your days, but I will tear it out of the hand of your son. ¹³However I will not tear away all the kingdom; but I will give one tribe to your son, for the sake of David my servant and for the sake of Jerusalem which I have chosen."

Adversaries of Solomon

14 † And the Lord raised up an adversary against Solomon, Ha'dad the E'domite; he was of the royal house in E'dom. ¹⁵For when David was in E'dom, and Jo'ab the commander of the army went up to bury the slain, he slew every male in Edom ¹⁶(for Jo'ab and all Israel remained there six months, until he had cut off every male in E'dom); ¹⁷but Ha'dad fled to Egypt, together with certain E'domites of

---

11:1 loved: Solomon's fascination with women overpowers his love for the Lord (compare 11:1 with 3:3).

11:2 You shall not: Refers to the prohibition of mixed marriages between Israelites and Gentiles in Deut 7:3–4. The rationale for this law is the expectation that pagan wives will corrupt Israel with pagan ways and contaminate the purity of Mosaic faith. Solomon is the foremost example of this danger: his disregard for the law against intermarriage ends with his heart ensnared in idolatry (11:4–8).

11:3 seven hundred ... three hundred: A harem of royal women enlarged beyond all reasonable limits. The numbers are likely inflated for rhetorical effect (see Song 6:8, which counts 60 queens and 80 concubines). Presumably many of these unions were diplomatic marriages made to seal political alliances between Israel and neighboring states (as in 3:1). Along the path of salvation history, polygamy is a deviation from God's original design for marriage as a union between one man and one woman (Gen 2:18–24). Yet a departure from this monogamous standard is visible in the aftermath of Adam's fall (Gen 4:23) and became a tolerated practice for much of the Old Testament period (Gen 29:21—30:23; 1 Sam 1:1–2; 2 Sam 3:2–5; 2 Chron 11:21, etc.). Even so, Moses forbade the kings of Israel to multiply their wives (Deut 17:17). The original plan for marriage was finally restored by the Lord Jesus (Mk 10:2–12). See note on 3:4. • Lust was no temporary guest in Solomon, for it took over his entire kingdom. Scripture refuses to keep silent about the matter and so condemns him as a womanizer. In his early days, the king greatly desired wisdom; but after gaining it through spiritual love, he lost it through carnal love (St. Augustine, *On Christian Doctrine* 3, 22).

11:4 the heart of David: Not sinless or free from selfishness, but uncorrupted by the evil of idolatry. Undivided commitment to Yahweh—and not any other deity—is what makes David the model king of Israel and the standard by which all subsequent kings are judged (15:3, 11).

11:5–7 Foreign gods venerated by Solomon. **Ashtoreth** is a goddess of fertility and love, also known as Ishtar or Astarte. She boasted numerous devotees in the Phoenician port of Sidon, northwest of Israel (Judg 10:6). **Milcom** is a god of the Ammonites, who dwelt east of Israel near the edge of the Arabian Desert (Jer 49:1). **Chemosh** is the national god of the Moabites, who were settled east of the Dead Sea (Num 21:29). **Molech** is the name of an Ammonite deity worshiped by child sacrifice (2 Kings 23:10).

11:7 the mountain east: The Mount of Olives.

11:8 for all his foreign wives: Honoring the wishes of a wife while dishonoring the Lord is the most ancient sin in the Bible (Gen 3:6, 17).

11:9 twice: Once in 3:5–14 and again in 9:1–9.

11:11 your servant: Jeroboam (11:26).

11:12 your son: Rehoboam (11:43).

11:13 one tribe: The royal tribe of Judah (12:20), to which the small tribe of Benjamin also attached itself (12:21). Ten of the 12 tribes will break away from Solomon's successor (11:31).

11:14–40 The Lord disciplines Solomon for idolatry by raising up three adversaries who cause him trouble. One gains strength in the south (Hadad of Edom, 11:14–22), a second in the north (Rezon of Syria, 11:23–25), and a third within Israel itself (Jeroboam of Ephraim, 11:26–40).

11:14 Hadad: The name of a Semitic storm god. It was also borne by an Edomite king in Gen 36:35.

11:15 David was in Edom: His military campaign is noted in 2 Sam 8:13–14. **slew every male:** An instance of hyperbole, as 11:17 makes clear.

11:17 fled to Egypt: In order to escape the wrath of David. Jeroboam will also flee to Egypt from the wrath of Solomon (11:40).

---

*11:1–8: This account of Solomon's moral decline stresses the connection between apostasy and sexual excess—a theme often met with in the Old Testament.

†11:14: Because of Solomon's idolatry, God raised up enemies, to the south (Edom), to the north (Damascus), and within the kingdom (Jeroboam).

his father's servants, Hadad being yet a little child. ¹⁸They set out from Mid'ian and came to Par'an, and took men with them from Paran and came to Egypt, to Pharaoh king of Egypt, who gave him a house, and assigned him an allowance of food, and gave him land. ¹⁹And Ha'dad found great favor in the sight of Pharaoh, so that he gave him in marriage the sister of his own wife, the sister of Tah'penes the queen. ²⁰And the sister of Tah'penes bore him Genu'bath his son, whom Tahpenes weaned in Pharaoh's house; and Genubath was in Pharaoh's house among the sons of Pharaoh. ²¹But when Ha'dad heard in Egypt that David slept with his fathers and that Jo'ab the commander of the army was dead, Hadad said to Pharaoh, "Let me depart, that I may go to my own country." ²²But Pharaoh said to him, "What have you lacked with me that you are now seeking to go to your own country?" And he said to him, "Only let me go."

23 God also raised up as an adversary to him, Re'zon the son of Eli'ada, who had fled from his master Ha'dad-e'zer king of Zobah. ²⁴And he gathered men about him and became leader of a marauding band, after the slaughter by David; and they went to Damascus, and dwelt there, and made him king in Damascus. ²⁵He was an adversary of Israel all the days of Solomon, doing mischief as Ha'dad did; and he abhorred Israel, and reigned over Syria.

Jeroboam's Rebellion

26 Jerobo'am the son of Ne'bat, an E'phraimite of Zer'edah, a servant of Solomon, whose mother's name was Zeru'ah, a widow, also lifted up his hand against the king. ²⁷And this was the reason why he lifted up his hand against the king. Solomon built the Millo, and closed up the breach of the city of David his father. ²⁸The man Jerobo'am was very able,

and when Solomon saw that the young man was industrious he gave him charge over all the forced labor of the house of Joseph. ²⁹And at that time, when Jerobo'am went out of Jerusalem, the prophet Ahi'jah the Shi'lonite found him on the road. Now Ahijah had clad himself with a new garment; and the two of them were alone in the open country. ³⁰Then Ahi'jah laid hold of the new garment that was on him, and tore it into twelve pieces. ³¹And he said to Jerobo'am, "Take for yourself ten pieces; for thus says the Lord, the God of Israel, 'Behold, I am about to tear the kingdom from the hand of Solomon, and will give you ten tribes ³²(but he shall have one tribe, for the sake of my servant David and for the sake of Jerusalem, the city which I have chosen out of all the tribes of Israel), ³³because he hasʰ forsaken me, and worshiped Ash'toreth the goddess of the Sido'nians, Che'mosh the god of Moab, and Milcom the god of the Am'monites, and hasʰ not walked in my ways, doing what is right in my sight and keeping my statutes and my ordinances, as David his father did. ³⁴Nevertheless I will not take the whole kingdom out of his hand; but I will make him ruler all the days of his life, for the sake of David my servant whom I chose, who kept my commandments and my statutes; ³⁵but I will take the kingdom out of his son's hand, and will give it to you, ten tribes. ³⁶Yet to his son I will give one tribe, that David my servant may always have a lamp before me in Jerusalem, the city where I have chosen to put my name. ³⁷And I will take you, and you shall reign over all that your soul desires, and you shall be king over Israel. ³⁸And if you will listen to all that I command you, and will walk in my ways, and do what is right in my eyes by keeping my statutes and my commandments, as David my servant did, I will be with you, and will build you a sure house, as I

11:18 Midian: East of the Gulf of Aqaba. **Paran:** On the Sinai Peninsula. **Pharaoh:** Probably it was Amenemope who gave asylum to Hadad and furnished him with an estate and royal allowance.

11:20 Genubath: His upbringing as a foreigner at the Egyptian royal court is reminiscent of Moses' early years (Ex 2:5–10; Acts 7:22).

11:23 Rezon: The name means "ruler".

11:24 the slaughter by David: The subjugation of Zobah and Damascus are mentioned in 2 Sam 8:3–6.

11:26 Jeroboam: An official in Solomon's government (11:28) and destined to become the first ruler of the Northern Kingdom of Israel (12:20). **Ephraimite:** I.e., belonging to the tribe of Ephraim, settled in the central highlands of Israel.

11:27 the Millo: An earthen foundation of some sort. See note on 9:15.

11:28 house of Joseph: The tribes of Ephraim and Manasseh, both of whom are descended from the patriarch Joseph (Gen 46:20).

11:29 Ahijah: The name means "Yahweh is my brother." **Shilonite:** A resident of the town of Shiloh, about 20 miles north of Jerusalem (modern Khirbet Seilun).

11:30 twelve pieces: Ahijah tears his cloak into an image of Israel, tribe by tribe. Prophets often performed dramatic and symbolic actions in order to press their message deep into the hearts and minds of the people (see Is 20:2–4; Jer 19:1–13; Ezek 4–5). • The tribes of Israel were torn apart, for the prophet Ahijah rent his garment. In contrast, the people of Christ cannot be torn apart, for his tunic, woven as one piece throughout, was not divided (cf. Jn 19:23–24). By the sign of his garment, Christ declared the unity of the Church (St. Cyprian, *Unity of the Church* 7).

11:36 lamp: Symbolizes the Davidic covenant. God's pledge to preserve the royal line of David means that his lamp will never be extinguished despite the sins of individual Davidic kings and the fluctuating historical fortunes of Israel (2 Sam 7:14–16). The motif of keeping "a lamp" in Jerusalem, the sight where God has chosen "to put his name", is repeated in 15:4; 2 Kings 8:19; 2 Chron 21:7. An association with the Davidic line and a lamp is also given earlier in 2 Sam 21:17.

11:38 a sure house: A stable dynasty. See word study: *Sure House* at 1 Sam 25:28.

ʰGk Syr Vg: Heb *they have.*

built for David, and I will give Israel to you. ³⁹And I will for this afflict the descendants of David, but not for ever.'" ⁴⁰Solomon sought therefore to kill Jerobo'am; but Jeroboam arose, and fled into Egypt, to Shi'shak king of Egypt, and was in Egypt until the death of Solomon.

Death of Solomon

41 Now the rest of the acts of Solomon, and all that he did, and his wisdom, are they not written in the book of the acts of Solomon? ⁴²And the time that Solomon reigned in Jerusalem over all Israel was forty years. ⁴³And Solomon slept with his fathers, and was buried in the city of David his father; and Rehobo'am his son reigned in his stead.

The Northern Tribes Secede

12 Rehobo'am went to She'chem,* for all Israel had come to Shechem to make him king. ²And when Jerobo'am the son of Ne'bat heard of it (for he was still in Egypt, whither he had fled from King Solomon), then Jeroboam returned from¹ Egypt. ³And they sent and called him; and Jerobo'am and all the assembly of Israel came and said to Rehobo'am, ⁴"Your father made our yoke heavy. Now therefore lighten the hard service of your father and his heavy yoke upon us, and we will serve you." ⁵He said to them, "Depart for three days, then come again to me." So the people went away.

6 Then King Rehobo'am took counsel with the old men, who had stood before Solomon his father while he was yet alive, saying, "How do you advise me to answer this people?" ⁷And they said to him, "If you will be a servant to this people today and serve them, and speak good words to them when you answer them, then they will be your servants for ever." ⁸But he forsook the counsel which the old men gave him, and took counsel with the young men who had grown up with him and stood before him. ⁹And he said to them, "What do you advise that we answer this people who have said to me, 'Lighten the yoke that your father put upon us'?" ¹⁰And the young men who had grown up with him said to him, "Thus shall you speak to this people who said to you, 'Your father made our yoke heavy, but please lighten it for us'; thus shall you say to them, 'My little finger is thicker than my father's loins. ¹¹And now, whereas my father laid upon you a heavy yoke, I will add to your yoke. My father chastised you with whips, but I will chastise you with scorpions.'"

12 So Jerobo'am and all the people came to Rehobo'am the third day, as the king said, "Come to me again the third day." ¹³And the king answered the people harshly, and forsaking the counsel which the old men had given him, ¹⁴he spoke to them according to the counsel of the young men, saying, "My father made your yoke heavy, but I will add to your yoke; my father chastised you with whips, but I will chastise you with scorpions."

11:42–43: 2 Chron 9:30, 31.   **12:1–19:** 2 Chron 10:1–19.

11:39 not for ever: The sundering of Israel into two states will be a tragic consequence of Solomon's apostasy but not a permanent one. Several prophets announce the reunification of the 12 tribes, along with the restoration of the Davidic kingdom, as among the great hopes for the messianic future (see Jer 3:18; 50:17–20; Ezek 37:15–28; Hos 1:10–11). For the fulfillment of these expectations in the NT, see essays: *Kingdom Restoration* at Acts 15 and *The Salvation of All Israel* at Rom 11.

11:40 Shishak: A Hebrew spelling for Shoshenq I, king of Egypt from ca. 945 to 924 B.C. and the founder of its 22nd dynasty. The Pharaoh's decision to harbor an enemy of Solomon is suspicious, since Egypt is supposed to be an ally of Israel (3:1).

11:41 book of the acts of Solomon: Historical annals consulted and utilized by the author of Kings. It was standard practice in the courts of the Near East to compose administrative daybooks that kept a running record of a king's activities, along with dates and statistics.

11:42 forty years: Solomon's reign lasted from ca. 970 to 930 B.C.

11:43 buried in the city of David: The same place his father, David, was buried (2:10). The royal tombs for most of the kings of Judah were located in the southeast corner of ancient Jerusalem (Neh 3:16). **Rehoboam:** The first king of Judah after the breakup of Solomon's empire (ca. 930 to 913 B.C.). He is Solomon's first-born son (1 Chron 3:10) by an Ammonite princess (14:21).

12:1–33 The division of Solomon's kingdom ca. 930 B.C. The northern tribes of Israel break away from the southern tribes of Judah and Benjamin to form their own kingdom, severing all political and religious ties with Jerusalem and the royal house of David. The era of the united monarchy thus gives way to the era of the divided monarchy, with Israel forming two independent states that will never again reunite in OT times. Historically, the Northern Kingdom of Israel will survive until the Assyrian conquest of Samaria in 722 B.C. (2 Kings 17), and the Southern Kingdom of Judah will last until the Babylonian conquest of Jerusalem in 586 B.C. (2 Kings 25).

12:1 Shechem: About 30 miles north of Jerusalem between Mt. Ebal and Mt. Gerizim in central Palestine. This is where the 12 tribes first ratified (Josh 8:30–35) and later renewed the Deuteronomic covenant (Josh 24:1–28). Shechem will become the site of Jeroboam's royal residence and serve as the first capital of the Northern Kingdom (12:25). **all Israel:** Representatives from the northern tribes gather to pledge allegiance to David's grandson, Rehoboam, just as they had done for David himself in 2 Sam 5:1–3.

12:4 our yoke: Made heavy by Solomon's policies of forced labor and onerous taxation.

12:6 the old men: Elder statesmen whose experienced counsel is rejected.

12:8 the young men: Peers of the king whose reckless advice is followed.

12:10 My little finger: Inflammatory words that destroy all hope of holding Solomon's empire together any longer. The Hebrew expression is literally "my little thing" and may, in fact, be a crude sexual innuendo.

12:11 whips . . . scorpions: The difference between a lashing and a severe flogging with barbed scourges.

---

*12:1, *Shechem* was the old religious center of the northern tribes. The alliance between these and Judah was never very strong, even during the united monarchy.
¹Gk Vg Compare 2 Chron 10:2: Heb *dwelt in.*

¹⁵So the king did not listen to the people; for it was a turn of affairs brought about by the Lᴏʀᴅ that he might fulfil his word, which the Lᴏʀᴅ spoke by Ahi'jah the Shi'lonite to Jerobo'am the son of Ne'bat.

Jeroboam Reigns over Israel

16 And when all Israel saw that the king did not listen to them, the people answered the king,

"What portion have we in David?

We have no inheritance in the son of Jesse.

To your tents, O Israel!

Look now to your own house, David."

So Israel departed to their tents. ¹⁷But Rehobo'am reigned over the sons of Israel who dwelt in the cities of Judah. ¹⁸Then King Rehobo'am sent Ador'am, who was taskmaster over the forced labor, and all Israel stoned him to death with stones. And King Rehoboam made haste to mount his chariot, to flee to Jerusalem. ¹⁹So Israel has been in rebellion against the house of David to this day. ²⁰And when all Israel heard that Jerobo'am had returned, they sent and called him to the assembly and made him king over all Israel. There was none that followed the house of David, but the tribe of Judah only.

21 When Rehobo'am came to Jerusalem, he assembled all the house of Judah, and the tribe of Benjamin, a hundred and eighty thousand chosen warriors, to fight against the house of Israel, to restore the kingdom to Rehoboam the son of Solomon. ²²But the word of God came to Shemai'ah the man of God: ²³"Say to Rehobo'am the son of Solomon, king of Judah, and to all the house of Judah and Benjamin, and to the rest of the people, ²⁴'Thus says the Lᴏʀᴅ, You shall not go up or fight against your kinsmen the sons of Israel. Return every man to his home, for this thing is from me.'" So they listened to the word of the Lᴏʀᴅ, and went home again, according to the word of the Lᴏʀᴅ.

Jeroboam's Golden Calves

25 Then Jerobo'am built She'chem in the hill country of E'phraim, and dwelt there; and he went out from there and built Penu'el. ²⁶And Jerobo'am said in his heart, "Now the kingdom will turn back to the house of David; ²⁷if this people go up to offer sacrifices in the house of the Lᴏʀᴅ at Jerusalem, then the heart of this people will turn again to their lord, to Rehobo'am king of Judah, and they will kill me and return to Rehoboam king of Judah." ²⁸So the king took counsel, and made two calves of gold. And he said to the people, "You have gone up to Jerusalem long enough. Behold your gods,* O Israel, who brought you up out of the land of Egypt." ²⁹And he set one in Bethel, and the other he

---

12:22-24: 2 Chron 11:1-4.

12:15 by the Lᴏʀᴅ: The division of Solomon's kingdom is a historical disaster, but one that takes place in accord with divine Providence. Yahweh is the helmsman of history, steering the course of events to fulfill Ahijah's prophecy (11:29–39) and chastise the house of David for Solomon's apostasy (11:9–13). The remark indicates that God *allowed* events to unfold in this direction, but not that God *inspired* the harsh words of Rehoboam or the senseless counsel of his advisors.

12:16 What portion have we ...?: An old rebel cry against the house of David, first attested in 2 Sam 20:1. It is basically a declaration of independence by the northern tribes.

12:18 Adoram: The overseer of forced labor under David (2 Sam 20:24) and again under Solomon (called Adoniram in 4:6).

12:19 to this day: Indicates these words were penned before the demise of the Northern Kingdom of Israel in 722 ʙ.ᴄ.

12:20 Judah: The primary tribe still loyal to the house of David in Jerusalem. Its neighbor, the small tribe of Benjamin, also formed part of the Southern Kingdom of Judah (12:21, 23).

12:21 house of Judah: The Davidic kingdom of Rehoboam. It is centered in Jerusalem and encompasses most of southern Palestine. **house of Israel:** The breakaway kingdom of Jeroboam. It is centered initially in Shechem and encompasses northern Palestine as well as lands east of the Jordan.

12:25-33 Jeroboam devises a new state religion for the Northern Kingdom. His efforts are guided by politics, not piety, especially the fear that religious unity with Jerusalem will lead again to political unity between north and south. He establishes a rival cult (12:28), rival sanctuaries (12:29), a rival clergy (12:31), and a rival feast day (12:32), all in opposition to the rites of Mosaic worship conducted in the Jerusalem Temple. Ironically, Jeroboam bows to a secular philosophy that believes religion should be subordinate to the State and geared to serve its political goals of creating a unified and stable society.

12:25 Shechem: The first capital city of the Northern Kingdom, to be succeeded by Tirzah (15:33; 16:8) and eventually Samaria (16:23-24). See note on 12:1. **Penuel:** East of the Jordan River on the banks of the Jabbok.

📖 **12:28-33** Jeroboam reenacts the apostasy of Aaron on Mt. Sinai. Notice how (1) both men recently left Egypt (12:2; Ex 6:13), (2) both manufacture golden calves (12:28; Ex 32:4), (3) both hail the calves as gods and deliverers (12:28; Ex 32:4), (4) both proclaim a new feast day (12:33; Ex 32:5), (5) both offer sacrifice to the calves (12:32; Ex 32:6, 8); (6) both lead Israel into sin (12:30; 14:16; Ex 32:21), and (7) in both cases, the Levites have no official involvement in the calf worship (12:31; Ex 32:25-29). The point of the parallels is to show that the Northern Kingdom of Israel was idolatrous from the start.

12:28 calves of gold: Idols worshiped as "other gods" (14:9). Perhaps they are images of the Egyptian bull god, Apis, since Jeroboam has just recently returned from Egypt (11:40; 12:2). Some scholars, noting parallels with other bovine imagery of the Near East, interpret the calves either as animal representations of Yahweh or as cultic pedestals where Yahweh was thought to sit invisibly enthroned. But even on these readings, Jeroboam would still be faulted for sponsoring a corrupted, syncretistic worship of Israel's God.

12:29 Bethel ... Dan: Prominent towns that mark the southern and northern boundaries of Jeroboam's new kingdom. Both are ancient cult centers with a history of mixed religious associations. Bethel was revered as a worship site by the early patriarchs (Gen 12:8; 28:10-22; 35:1-8), while Dan became a haven of deviant religion in the time of the judges (Judg 18:29-31). See notes on Judg 1:23 and Judg 18:7.

---

*12:28, *Behold your gods:* Jeroboam seems to have had no intention of introducing false gods. These were to be images of Yahweh. But in doing this he debased the whole idea of true worship and made it more like pagan religion, to which it was bound to lead in the end; cf. 16:31. Judah, with all its advantages of temple and dynasty, was no better at this time, but reforms were instituted at intervals.

put in Dan. ³⁰And this thing became a sin, for the people went to the one at Bethel and to the other as far as Dan.ʲ ³¹He also made houses on high places, and appointed priests from among all the people, who were not of the Levites. ³²And Jerobo'am appointed a feast on the fifteenth day of the eighth month like the feast that was in Judah, and he offered sacrifices upon the altar; so he did in Bethel, sacrificing to the calves that he had made. And he placed in Bethel the priests of the high places that he had made. ³³He went up to the altar which he had made in Bethel on the fifteenth day in the eighth month, in the month which he had devised of his own heart; and he ordained a feast for the sons of Israel, and went up to the altar to burn incense.

A Man of God from Judah

13 And behold, a man of God came out of Judah by the word of the LORD to Bethel. Jerobo'am

---

12:31 high places: Cultic sanctuaries. See word study: *High Places* at 2 Kings 23:5. **not of the Levites:** Ordaining non-Levites is a rebellion against the Torah, which confines the priesthood to Levites descended from Aaron (Ex 40:12–15; Num 18:7).

12:32 a feast: Observed exactly one month after the annual Feast of Booths is celebrated in Solomon's Temple (Lev 23:34). The festival is a pure invention of Jeroboam and is meant to discourage northern Israelites from making the annual pilgrimages to Jerusalem mandated in the Torah (Deut 16:1–17).

ʲGk: Heb *went to the one as far as Dan.*

12:33 went up to the altar: Jeroboam assumes the role of a priest-king at the inauguration ceremonies in Bethel, just as Solomon did at the dedication of the Jerusalem Temple, which was likewise timed to fall in the midst of a festival (8:62–65).

13:1–32 A tale of two prophets, one from Judah (13:1) and the other from Bethel (13:11). Both deliver oracles that are validated by miraculous signs (13:5, 26). These signs, in turn, give assurance that the prediction in 13:2 will come to pass (13:32). Prophetic narratives will punctuate the rest of 1 Kings from this point forward.

13:1 man of God: A prophet or inspired messenger who bears the word of the Lord to his people. As the following

---

Kings of the Divided Monarchy

The chronology of the kings of Israel and Judah is difficult to reconstruct. Its complexity is due to many factors. One is that several kingships overlap during periods of co-regency, so the reigns of the kings cannot always be lined up end to end. Another is that different methods of calculation were used at different times in the two rival kingdoms. Sometimes the accession year of the king is *counted* in the total years of his reign, as was customary in Egypt, and sometimes the accession year is *omitted* from the final reckoning, as was typical in Mesopotamia. Thirdly, there is some evidence that calendar years were counted differently in the period of the divided monarchy, with Judah beginning each New Year in the spring month of Nisan and Israel beginning each New Year in the fall month of Tishri. Despite these complicating factors, the dates appearing below are reasonably well established.

What is most obvious from the data below is the stark difference between the two kingdoms. The Southern Kingdom of Judah was clearly the more stable one: it produced 19 kings, all from the dynastic line of David, and it lasted three and a half centuries. The Northern Kingdom of Israel, by contrast, was unstable for much of its history: it, too, produced 19 kings, but these came from nine different dynastic families (marked below with superscript numerals), and it lasted little more than two centuries.

HOUSE OF JUDAH (south)		HOUSE OF ISRAEL (north)	
Rehoboam	930–913 B.C.	Jeroboam I[1]	930–910 B.C.
Abijam	913–911	Nadab	910–909
Asa	911–870	Baasha[2]	909–886
Jehoshaphat	873–848	Elah	886–885
Jehoram	848–841	Zimri[3]	885
Ahaziah	841	Omri[4]	885–874
(Athaliah, queen)	841–835	Ahab	874–853
Joash	835–796	Ahaziah	853–852
Amaziah	796–767	Jehoram	852–841
Azariah/Uzziah	792–740	Jehu[5]	841–814
Jotham	750–731	Jehoahaz	814–798
Ahaz	735–715	Joash	798–782
Hezekiah	729–686	Jeroboam II	793–753
Manasseh	696–642	Zechariah	753
Amon	642–640	Shallum[6]	752
Josiah	640–609	Menahem[7]	752–742
Jehoahaz	609	Pekahiah	742–740
Jehoiakim	609–598	Pekah[8]	740–732
Jehoiachin	598–597	Hoshea[9]	732–722
Zedekiah	597–586	**ASSYRIAN CONQUEST OF ISRAEL: 722 B.C.**	
BABYLONIAN CONQUEST OF JUDAH: 586 B.C.			

was standing by the altar to burn incense. ²And the man cried against the altar by the word of the Lord, and said, "O altar, altar, thus says the Lord: 'Behold, a son shall be born to the house of David, Josi'ah by name; and he shall sacrifice upon you the priests of the high places who burn incense upon you, and men's bones shall be burned upon you.'" ³And he gave a sign the same day, saying, "This is the sign that the Lord has spoken: 'Behold, the altar shall be torn down, and the ashes that are upon it shall be poured out.'" ⁴And when the king heard the saying of the man of God, which he cried against the altar at Bethel, Jerobo'am stretched out his hand from the altar, saying, "Lay hold of him." And his hand, which he stretched out against him, dried up, so that he could not draw it back to himself. ⁵The altar also was torn down, and the ashes poured out from the altar, according to the sign which the man of God had given by the word of the Lord. ⁶And the king said to the man of God, "Entreat now the favor of the Lord your God, and pray for me, that my hand may be restored to me." And the man of God entreated the Lord; and the king's hand was restored to him, and became as it was before. ⁷And the king said to the man of God, "Come home with me, and refresh yourself, and I will give you a reward." ⁸And the man of God said to the king, "If you give me half your house, I will not go in with you. And I will not eat bread or drink water in this place; ⁹for so was it commanded me by the word of the Lord, saying, 'You shall neither eat bread, nor drink water, nor return by the way that you came.'" ¹⁰So he went another way, and did not return by the way that he came to Bethel.

11 Now there dwelt an old prophet in Bethel. And his sons ᵏ came and told him all that the man of God had done that day in Bethel; the words also which he had spoken to the king, they told to their father. ¹²And their father said to them, "Which way did he go?" And his sons showed him the way which the man of God who came from Judah had gone. ¹³And he said to his sons, "Saddle the donkey for me." So they saddled the donkey for him and he mounted it. ¹⁴And he went after the man of God, and found him sitting under an oak; and he said to him, "Are you the man of God who came from Judah?" And he said, "I am." ¹⁵Then he said to him, "Come home with me and eat bread." ¹⁶And he said, "I may not return with you, or go in with you; neither will I eat bread nor drink water with you in this place; ¹⁷for it was said to me by the word of the Lord, 'You shall neither eat bread nor drink water there, nor return by the way that you came.'" ¹⁸And he said to him, "I also am a prophet as you are, and an angel spoke to me by the word of the Lord, saying, 'Bring him back with you into your house that he may eat bread and drink water.'" But he lied to him. ¹⁹So he went back with him, and ate bread in his house, and drank water.

20 And as they sat at the table, the word of the Lord came to the prophet who had brought him back; ²¹and he cried to the man of God who came from Judah, "Thus says the Lord, 'Because you have disobeyed the word of the Lord, and have not kept the commandment which the Lord your God commanded you, ²²but have come back, and have eaten bread and drunk water in the place of which he said to you, "Eat no bread, and drink no water"; your body shall not come to the tomb of your fathers.'" ²³And after he had eaten bread and drunk, he saddled the donkey for the prophet whom he had brought back. ²⁴And as he went away a lion met him on the road and killed him. And his body was thrown in the road, and the donkey stood beside it; the lion also stood beside the body. ²⁵And behold, men passed by, and saw the body thrown in the road, and the lion standing by the body. And they came and told it in the city where the old prophet dwelt.

26 And when the prophet who had brought him back from the way heard of it, he said, "It is the

---

account shows, a prophet is also responsible for obeying the divine word (13:20-24).

13:2 Josiah: A Davidic king who will come to power three centuries later (640 B.C.). Among his many actions aimed at cleansing Israel of idolatry, Josiah will destroy the altar of Bethel and defile it with human bones (2 Kings 23:15-16).

13:4 dried up: I.e., became lifeless and immovable.

13:5 was torn down: Or "broke apart", an anticipatory fulfillment of 13:3.

📖 **13:6 the king's hand was restored:** The divine authority of the prophet is revealed through the power of his intercessory prayer. • Restoring the withered hand of Jeroboam anticipates a similar healing miracle performed by Jesus as a sign of his messianic authority (Mt 12:9-14; Lk 6:6-11).

13:8 I will not eat: Acceptance of Jeroboam's hospitality would imply an endorsement of his heretical religion (12:25-33).

13:11 his sons: Either biological children or perhaps junior members of a prophetic guild, known as "sons of the prophets" (20:35; 2 Kings 4:1). One such school of prophets resided in the aged man's hometown of Bethel (2 Kings 2:3).

13:18 an angel spoke to me: Lying words. Apparently the deception is meant to test the claims of the prophet from Judah regarding the demise of the Bethel altar (13:3).

13:19 he went back: The prophet fails his test of obedience. Having delivered the word of God faithfully, he transgresses it with fatal consequences (13:24). He was mistaken to think that the message of an angel outranks a direct word from the Lord (13:17; cf. Gal 1:8).

13:21 you have disobeyed: Similar language is used in Num 20:24 to describe how Moses and Aaron rebelled against the Lord's command at Meribah (Num 20:10-13).

13:24 the lion: Mauls the prophet to death but makes no attempt to feast on his corpse, his donkey, or any passers-by. Clearly the Lord is behind the incident (13:26). For similar cases of divine judgment by lions, see 20:36 and 2 Kings 17:25.

ᵏGk Syr Vg: Heb *son*.

man of God, who disobeyed the word of the Lord; therefore the Lord has given him to the lion, which has torn him and slain him, according to the word which the Lord spoke to him." 27And he said to his sons, "Saddle the donkey for me." And they saddled it. 28And he went and found his body thrown in the road, and the donkey and the lion standing beside the body. The lion had not eaten the body or torn the donkey. 29And the prophet took up the body of the man of God and laid it upon the donkey, and brought it back to the city,[1] to mourn and to bury him. 30And he laid the body in his own grave; and they mourned over him, saying, "Alas, my brother!" 31And after he had buried him, he said to his sons, "When I die, bury me in the grave in which the man of God is buried; lay my bones beside his bones. 32For the saying which he cried by the word of the Lord against the altar in Bethel, and against all the houses of the high places which are in the cities of Samar′ia, shall surely come to pass."

33 After this incident Jerobo′-am did not turn from his evil way, but made priests for the high places again from among all the people; any who would, he consecrated to be priests of the high places. 34And this thing became sin to the house of Jerobo′am, so as to cut it off and to destroy it from the face of the earth.

Judgment on the House of Jeroboam

14 At that time Abi′jah the son of Jerobo′am fell sick. 2And Jerobo′am said to his wife, "Arise, and disguise yourself, that it be not known that you are the wife of Jeroboam, and go to Shiloh; behold, Ahi′jah the prophet is there, who said of me that I should be king over this people. 3Take with you ten loaves, some cakes, and a jar of honey, and go to him; he will tell you what shall happen to the child."

4 Jerobo′am's wife did so; she arose, and went to Shiloh, and came to the house of Ahi′jah. Now Ahijah could not see, for his eyes were dim because of his age. 5And the Lord said to Ahi′jah, "Behold, the wife of Jerobo′am is coming to inquire of you concerning her son; for he is sick. Thus and thus shall you say to her."

When she came, she pretended to be another woman. 6But when Ahi′jah heard the sound of her feet, as she came in at the door, he said, "Come in, wife of Jerobo′am; why do you pretend to be another? For I am charged with heavy tidings for you. 7Go, tell Jerobo′am, 'Thus says the Lord, the God of Israel: "Because I exalted you from among the people, and made you leader over my people Israel, 8and tore the kingdom away from the house of David and gave it to you; and yet you have not been like my servant David, who kept my commandments, and followed me with all his heart, doing only that which was right in my eyes, 9but you have done evil above all that were before you and have gone and made for yourself other gods, and molten images, provoking me to anger, and have cast me behind your back; 10therefore behold, I will bring evil upon the house of Jerobo′am, and will cut off from Jeroboam every male, both bond and free in Israel, and will utterly consume the house of Jeroboam, as a man burns up dung until it is all gone. 11Any one belonging to Jerobo′am who dies in the city the dogs shall eat; and any one who dies in the open country the birds of the air shall eat; for the Lord has spoken it."' 12Arise therefore, go to your house. When your feet enter the city, the child shall die. 13And all Israel shall mourn for him, and bury him; for he only of Jerobo′am shall come to the grave, because in him there is found something pleasing to the Lord, the God of Israel, in the house of Jeroboam. 14Moreover the Lord will raise up for himself a king over Israel, who shall cut off the house of Jerobo′am today. And henceforth[m] 15the Lord will strike Israel, as a reed is shaken in the water, and root up Israel out of this good land which he gave to their fathers, and scatter them beyond the Euphrates, because they have made their Ashe′rim, provoking the Lord to

---

13:30 his own grave: Burial away from home and family fulfills the oracle in 13:22.

13:32 Samaria: The central hill country of Israel, named after the capital city later founded by King Omri (16:24).

13:33 made priests: Jeroboam continues to defy the Mosaic Law by recruiting ineligible laypeople for his sham priesthood. See note on 12:31.

13:34 the house of Jeroboam: A short-lived dynasty of two kings, Jeroboam and his son Nadab (15:25-28).

14:2 Shiloh: About 20 miles north of Jerusalem. **Ahijah:** Foretold both the rise of Jeroboam to kingship as well as the division of Solomon's kingdom in 11:29-39.

14:3 loaves ... cakes ... honey: Patrons typically offered gifts to the prophets in exchange for their services (1 Sam 9:5-10; 2 Kings 8:7-9).

14:7-16 Ahijah's oracle of judgment. The Lord's punishment will take three forms: (1) the son of Jeroboam will not recover from sickness but die; (2) the prospect of a lasting dynasty offered to Jeroboam in 11:38 is forfeit; and (3) the northern tribes of Israel will be exiled from their lands. All of this will take place because Jeroboam led the Israelites to worship "other gods" (14:9). For the king's religious apostasy, see note on 12:25-33.

14:9 other gods: The manufacture of idols is prohibited by the first commandment of the Decalogue (Ex 20:2-6). **molten images:** The golden calves in Dan and Bethel (12:28-29).

14:11 dogs ... birds ... eat: One of the curses of the Deuteronomic covenant (Deut 28:26).

14:14 cut off the house: Fulfilled in Baasha, who will massacre Jeroboam's royal family and claim the kingship for himself (15:27-29).

14:15 root up ... scatter: The language of conquest and exile, which is the ultimate curse of the Deuternomic covenant (Deut 29:28). The prophet foresees the Assyrian overthrow of the Northern Kingdom and the deportation of the northern tribes to Mesopotamian lands east of the **Euphrates**, an event 200 years in the future (2 Kings 17:1-23). **Asherim:** Sacred poles or trees dedicated to Asherah, a fertility goddess of Canaanite religion.

---

[1] Gk: Heb *he came to the city of the old prophet.*
[m] Heb obscure.

anger. ¹⁶And he will give Israel up because of the sins of Jerobo'am, which he sinned and which he made Israel to sin."

Death of Jeroboam

17 Then Jerobo'am's wife arose, and departed, and came to Tirzah. And as she came to the threshold of the house, the child died. ¹⁸And all Israel buried him and mourned for him, according to the word of the LORD, which he spoke by his servant Ahi'jah the prophet. ¹⁹Now the rest of the acts of Jerobo'am, how he warred and how he reigned, behold, they are written in the Book of the Chronicles of the Kings of Israel. ²⁰And the time that Jerobo'am reigned was twenty-two years; and he slept with his fathers, and Na'dab his son reigned in his stead.

Rehoboam Reigns over Judah

21 Now Rehobo'am the son of Solomon reigned in Judah. Rehoboam was forty-one years old when he began to reign, and he reigned seventeen years in Jerusalem, the city which the LORD had chosen out of all the tribes of Israel, to put his name there. His mother's name was Na'amah the Am'monitess. ²²And Judah did what was evil in the sight of the LORD, and they provoked him to jealousy with their sins which they committed, more than all that their fathers had done. ²³For they also built for themselves high places, and pillars, and Ashe'rim on every high hill and under every green tree; ²⁴and there were also male cult prostitutes in the land. They did according to all the abominations of the nations which the LORD drove out before the sons of Israel.

25 In the fifth year of King Rehobo'am, Shi'shak king of Egypt came up against Jerusalem; ²⁶he took away the treasures of the house of the LORD and the treasures of the king's house; he took away everything. He also took away all the shields of gold which Solomon had made; ²⁷and King Rehobo'am made in their stead shields of bronze, and committed them to the hands of the officers of the guard, who kept the door of the king's house. ²⁸And as often as the king went into the house of the LORD, the guard bore them and brought them back to the guardroom.

29 Now the rest of the acts of Rehobo'am, and all that he did, are they not written in the Book of the Chronicles of the Kings of Judah? ³⁰And there was war between Rehobo'am and Jerobo'am continually. ³¹And Rehobo'am slept with his fathers and was buried with his fathers in the city of David. His mother's name was Na'amah the Am'monitess. And Abi'jam his son reigned in his stead.

Abijam Reigns over Judah

15 Now in the eighteenth year of King Jerobo'am the son of Ne'bat, Abi'jam began to reign over Judah. ²He reigned for three years in Jerusalem. His mother's name was Ma'acah the daughter of Abish'alom. ³And he walked in all the sins which his father did before him; and his heart was not wholly true to the LORD his God, as the heart of David his father. ⁴Nevertheless for David's sake the LORD his God gave him a lamp in Jerusalem, setting up his son after him, and establishing Jerusalem; ⁵because David did what

---

14:25–31: 2 Chron 12:1–16.   **15:1, 2, 7:** 2 Chron 13:1, 2.

14:17 Tirzah: Successor to Shechem (12:25) as the royal residence and capital city of the Northern Kingdom of Israel (15:33). Tirzah lies seven miles northeast of Shechem.

14:19 how he warred: I.e., against the southern kings of Judah (14:30; 15:6–7). **Book of the Chronicles:** One of two archival documents that are referenced repeatedly in 1 and 2 Kings. Presumably these were administrative scrolls in which scribes kept a record of the political, economic, military, and religious policies of the two kingdoms of Israel and Judah, respectively. Neither of these books survives today.

14:20 Nadab: The second king of Israel (ca. 910 to 909 B.C.). He is the sole descendant of Jeroboam to reign as king after him; as such, he represents both the beginning and the end of his father's dynasty.

14:21 Rehoboam: The first king of Judah. See note on 11:43. **forty-one years old:** Part of a standardized formula that is used for introducing the kings of Judah. It notes (1) the king's age at the beginning of his reign, (2) the length of his reign, and (3) the name of his mother, who was the Davidic queen (15:1, 9, 22:41–42). See essay: *The Queen Mother* at 1 Kings 2.

14:22 provoked him to jealousy: The Lord's response to idolatry, according to the Song of Moses (Deut 32:16, 21).

14:23–24 The degeneration of religious practice in Judah. Pagan shrines called **high places** are dotting the landscape; stones are being turned on end as **pillars** dedicated to the Canaanite storm and fertility god, Baal; trees or wooden polls called **Asherim** are being raised in honor of the Canaanite fertility goddess, Asherah; and **male cult prostitutes** are using religion as a cover for sexual impurity. Deuteronomy calls for

the total eradication of these forms of deviant worship (Deut 7:5; 12:2–3; 23:17).

14:25 Shishak: Pharaoh Shoshenq I, who plundered the treasuries of Jerusalem ca. 925 B.C. A wall inscription in the Egyptian temple of Amun at Karnak commemorates his campaign in Palestine. See note on 11:40.

14:26 shields of gold: See note on 10:16.

14:27 shields of bronze: Bucklers made to arm the king's personal guard unit.

14:29 Book of the Chronicles: See note on 14:19.

14:31 Abijam: The second king of Judah (ca. 913 to 911 B.C.). He is faulted for an ungodly reign, specifically for tolerating the Canaanite abominations that established themselves in Judah on his father's watch (14:21–24). The name Abijam appears as "Abijah" in Chronicles (2 Chron 13:1).

15:3 the heart of David: The standard by which all other kings of Judah are measured. The point is not that David was sinless, but that David was single-minded in his commitment to the Lord. At no point did he compromise his faith in Yahweh by dabbling in foreign idolatry or sponsoring it in Israel. For the author of Kings, then, cultic fidelity—rather than flawless character—is what made David the model king by which his successors are judged.

15:4 a lamp: A sign of the Davidic covenant. See note on 11:36.

15:5 except in the matter: A frank acknowledgment that David was not a man of spotless moral character. **Uriah the Hittite:** Wronged by David when the king committed adultery with his wife and then arranged for his death (2 Sam 11:1–21).

was right in the eyes of the Lord, and did not turn aside from anything that he commanded him all the days of his life, except in the matter of Uri'ah the Hittite. ⁶Now there was war between Rehobo'am and Jerobo'am all the days of his life. ⁷The rest of the acts of Abi'jam, and all that he did, are they not written in the Book of the Chronicles of the Kings of Judah? And there was war between Abijam and Jerobo'am. ⁸And Abi'jam slept with his fathers; and they buried him in the city of David. And Asa his son reigned in his stead.

Asa Reigns over Judah

9 In the twentieth year of Jerobo'am king of Israel Asa began to reign over Judah, ¹⁰and he reigned forty-one years in Jerusalem. His mother's name was Ma'acah the daughter of Abish'alom. ¹¹And Asa did what was right in the eyes of the Lord, as David his father had done. ¹²He put away the male cult prostitutes out of the land, and removed all the idols that his fathers had made. ¹³He also removed Ma'acah his mother from being queen mother because she had an abominable image made for Ashe'rah; and Asa cut down her image and burned it at the brook Kidron. ¹⁴But the high places were not taken away. Nevertheless the heart of Asa was wholly true to the Lord all his days. ¹⁵And he brought into the house of the Lord the votive gifts of his father and his own votive gifts, silver, and gold, and vessels.

War between Asa and Baasha

16 And there was war between Asa and Ba'asha king of Israel all their days. ¹⁷Ba'asha king of Israel went up against Judah, and built Ra'mah, that he might permit no one to go out or come in to Asa king of Judah. ¹⁸Then Asa took all the silver and the gold that were left in the treasures of the house of the Lord and the treasures of the king's house, and gave them into the hands of his servants; and King Asa sent them to Ben-ha'dad the son of Tabrim'mon, the son of He'zi-on, king of Syria, who dwelt in Damascus, saying, ¹⁹"Let there be a league between me and you, as between my father and your father: behold, I am sending to you a present of silver and gold; go, break your league with Ba'asha king of Israel, that he may withdraw from me." ²⁰And Ben-ha'dad listened to King Asa, and sent the commanders of his armies against the cities of Israel, and conquered I'jon, Dan, A'bel-beth-ma'acah, and all Chin'neroth, with all the land of Naph'tali. ²¹And when Ba'asha heard of it, he stopped building Ra'mah, and he dwelt in Tirzah. ²²Then King Asa made a proclamation to all Judah, none was exempt, and they carried away the stones of Ra'mah and its timber, with which Ba'asha had been building; and with them King Asa built Ge'ba of Benjamin and Mizpah. ²³Now the rest of all the acts of Asa, all his might, and all that he did, and the cities which he built, are they not written in the Book of the Chronicles of the Kings of Judah? But in his old age he was diseased in his feet. ²⁴And Asa slept with his fathers, and was buried with his fathers in the city of David his father; and Jehosh'aphat his son reigned in his stead.

Nadab Reigns over Israel

25 Nadab the son of Jerobo'am began to reign over Israel in the second year of Asa king of Judah; and he reigned over Israel two years. ²⁶He did what

---

15:8–12: 2 Chron 14:1–5. **15:13–22:** 2 Chron 15:16—16:6. **15:23, 24:** 2 Chron 16:12–14. **15:24:** 2 Chron 17:1.

15:7 Book of the Chronicles: See note on 14:19.

15:8 Asa: The third king of Judah (ca. 911 to 870 B.C.). Asa is admired for being a religious reformer (15:11–15) and a shrewd politician (15:16–22).

15:10 Maacah: Appears to be Asa's grandmother (15:2). She is deposed from her position as queen mother for the crime of idolatry (15:13).

15:13 Asherah: The name of a Canaanite fertility goddess. **the brook Kidron:** A seasonal watercourse that runs through the ravine directly east of Jerusalem. Asa's burning of the cult object at this location anticipates the reforms of Josiah (2 Kings 23:6).

15:14 high places: Cultic sanctuaries. See note on 3:2.

15:15 votive gifts: To be stored in the Temple treasury (7:51).

15:16 Baasha: Formally introduced in 15:33–34.

15:17 Ramah: Six miles north of Jerusalem in the territory of Benjamin. Baasha reasons that a fortified Ramah will block his Israelite subjects from traveling south into Judah. The effort to block southbound traffic hints that some northerners remained loyal to Jerusalem and its worship of Yahweh in the Temple (confirmed in 2 Chron 11:13–17 and 15:9).

15:18 Ben-hadad: Ben-hadad I, son of Tabrimmon, ruler of the Aramean kingdom of Syria in Damascus. His name declares him "the son" of the Semitic storm god "Hadad". Here is is bribed to form an alliance with Judah while turning his back on an earlier treaty with the house of Israel (15:19). Judging from 1–2 Kings, it appears that Ben-hadad is a dynastic title

shared by two—or possibly three—Syrian monarchs. It is clear that "Ben-hadad" in 15:18 is distinguished from "Ben-hadad the son of Hazael" in 2 Kings 13:3. The question remains, however, whether the "Ben-hadad" in 20:1 (also 2 Kings 6:24; 8:7, etc.) is the same as Ben-hadad I or whether he is an otherwise unknown Ben-hadad II, which is favored by 20:34.

15:19 league: The Hebrew refers to a "covenant" or "treaty".

15:20 Ijon ... Chinneroth: Localities in upper Galilee sacked by the Syrians. This region will be overrun again by the Assyrians a century and a half later (2 Kings 15:29).

15:21 Tirzah: Capital of the Northern Kingdom (15:33).

15:22 Geba ... Mizpah: Two towns north of Jerusalem, both in the territory of Benjamin, are fortified to protect the capital.

15:23 Book of the Chronicles: See note on 14:19.

15:24 Jehoshaphat: The fourth king of Judah (ca. 873 to 848 B.C.). The story of his reign is delayed until 22:41–50.

15:25 Nadab: Successor of Jeroboam. See note on 14:20.

15:26 the way of his father: The way of idolatry. Just as the southern kings of Judah are measured against David's cultic fidelity (see note on 15:3), so the northern kings of Israel are judged by their tolerance of Jeroboam's cultic aberrations (see 12:25–33). The author's chief interest is not in the political ability of each king but in his policies related to worship, whether he followed the stipulations of the Mosaic covenant or abandoned them in favor of idols. The latter is branded "evil in the sight of the Lord".

was evil in the sight of the Lord, and walked in the way of his father, and in his sin which he made Israel to sin.

27 Ba'asha the son of Ahi'jah, of the house of Is'sachar, conspired against him; and Baasha struck him down at Gib'bethon, which belonged to the Philis'tines; for Na'dab and all Israel were laying siege to Gibbethon. ²⁸So Ba'asha killed him in the third year of Asa king of Judah, and reigned in his stead. ²⁹And as soon as he was king, he killed all the house of Jerobo'am; he left to the house of Jeroboam not one that breathed, until he had destroyed it, according to the word of the Lord which he spoke by his servant Ahi'jah the Shi'lonite; ³⁰it was for the sins of Jerobo'am which he sinned and which he made Israel to sin, and because of the anger to which he provoked the Lord, the God of Israel.

31 Now the rest of the acts of Na'dab, and all that he did, are they not written in the Book of the Chronicles of the Kings of Israel? ³²And there was war between Asa and Ba'asha king of Israel all their days.

Baasha Reigns over Israel

33 In the third year of Asa king of Judah, Ba'asha the son of Ahi'jah began to reign over all Israel at Tirzah, and reigned twenty-four years. ³⁴He did what was evil in the sight of the Lord, and walked in the way of Jerobo'am and in his sin which he made Israel to sin.

16 And the word of the Lord came to Je'hu the son of Hana'ni against Ba'asha, saying, ²"Since I exalted you out of the dust and made you leader over my people Israel, and you have walked in the way of Jerobo'am, and have made my people Israel to sin, provoking me to anger with their sins, ³behold, I will utterly sweep away Ba'asha and his house, and I will make your house like the house of Jerobo'am the son of Ne'bat. ⁴Any one belonging to Ba'asha who dies in the city the dogs shall eat; and any one of his who dies in the field the birds of the air shall eat."

5 Now the rest of the acts of Ba'asha, and what he did, and his might, are they not written in the Book of the Chronicles of the Kings of Israel? ⁶And Ba'asha slept with his fathers, and was buried at Tirzah; and E'lah his son reigned in his stead. ⁷Moreover the word of the Lord came by the prophet Je'hu the son of Hana'ni against Ba'asha and his house, both because of all the evil that he did in the sight of the Lord, provoking him to anger with the work of his

---

15:27 Baasha: See note on 15:33. **Gibbethon:** About 25 miles west of Jerusalem. It was a Levitical city originally assigned to the tribe of Dan (Josh 19:44; 21:23). At this point in the story, Gibbethon is under Philistine control (16:15).

15:29 according to ... Ahijah: A reference to the prophetic words in 14:14.

15:31 Book of the Chronicles: See note on 14:19.

15:33 Baasha: The third king of Israel and the founder of its second dynasty (ca. 909 to 886 B.C.). To secure his rule, he massacred the last remnants of Jeroboam's royal line (15:29). Baasha is condemned for endorsing the idolatrous state religion of the north (15:34) and is denied the blessing of a long dynasty (16:2–3). He hails from the tribe of Issachar (15:27).

15:34 did what was evil: See note on 15:26.

16:1 Jehu: A prophet of the Lord (16:7). His oracle against Baasha (16:2–4) recalls Ahijah's oracle against Jeroboam (14:7–16). Jehu likewise addressed King Jehoshaphat of Judah (2 Chron 19:2-3) and chronicled his reign in writing (2 Chron 20:34). **son of Hanani:** The father of Jehu was likewise a "seer" or prophet (2 Chron 16:7).

16:2 the way of Jeroboam: See note on 15:26.

16:3 like the house of Jeroboam: Baasha's dynasty will be short-lived, limited to a single successor (Elah, 16:6). All other male descendants are struck down by Zimri (16:11).

16:4 dogs ... birds ... eat: A curse. See note on 14:11.

16:5 Book of the Chronicles: See note on 14:19.

16:6 Elah: The fourth king of Israel (ca. 886 to 885 B.C.). Practically nothing is known of his reign except that it ended with his assassination (16:8-10).

WORD STUDY

Over the Household (16:9)

'al habbayit (Heb.): a prepositional phrase meaning "over the house". It often occurs in the expression "one who is over the house", which is a title for the steward of a private estate (Gen 39:4; 43:19) or for the senior government official below the monarch, akin to a prime minister. Thus, when Joseph is installed over the house of Pharaoh, he becomes the highest-ranking authority in Egypt next to the king (Gen 41:40). Something similar appears in the monarchies of ancient Israel, beginning with Solomon, who appears to have introduced this position in the royal court (translated "charge of the palace" in 1 Kings 4:6). Thereafter, prime ministers play key administrative and diplomatic roles in both the Northern Kingdom of Israel (1 Kings 16:9; 18:3) and the Southern Kingdom of Judah (2 Kings 15:5; 18:18). It is possible this office was originally that of a palace administrator or perhaps an overseer of the royal estates, but over time the "one over the house" came to wield significant authority in government affairs. An instance of this can be seen in Isaiah, where one prime minister yields his position to a successor, who is entrusted with the "key" of the Davidic kingdom and who occupies a "throne of honor" (Is 22:15–23). Archaeology has turned up the names of several individuals (Gedalyahu, Adoniyahu, Natan) bearing the title "over the house"—one on a seal, one on a tomb inscription, and several more on clay seal-impressions (called *bullae*). In the NT, Jesus assigns Peter a role in the kingdom of God that is modeled on the OT office of the royal steward (Mt 16:17–19).

hands, in being like the house of Jerobo'am, and also because he destroyed it.

Elah Reigns over Israel

8 In the twenty-sixth year of Asa king of Judah, E'lah the son of Ba'asha began to reign over Israel in Tirzah, and he reigned two years. [9]But his servant Zimri, commander of half his chariots, conspired against him. When he was at Tirzah, drinking himself drunk in the house of Arza, who was over the household in Tirzah, [10]Zimri came in and struck him down and killed him, in the twenty-seventh year of Asa king of Judah, and reigned in his stead.

11 When he began to reign, as soon as he had seated himself on his throne, he killed all the house of Ba'asha; he did not leave him a single male of his kinsmen or his friends. [12]Thus Zimri destroyed all the house of Ba'asha, according to the word of the LORD, which he spoke against Baasha by Je'hu the prophet, [13]for all the sins of Ba'asha and the sins of E'lah his son which they sinned, and which they made Israel to sin, provoking the LORD God of Israel to anger with their idols. [14]Now the rest of the acts of E'lah, and all that he did, are they not written in the Book of the Chronicles of the Kings of Israel?

The Conspiracy and Death of Zimri

15 In the twenty-seventh year of Asa king of Judah, Zimri reigned seven days in Tirzah. Now the troops were encamped against Gib'bethon, which belonged to the Philis'tines, [16]and the troops who were encamped heard it said, "Zimri has conspired, and he has killed the king"; therefore all Israel made Omri, the commander of the army, king over Israel that day in the camp. [17]So Omri went up from Gib'bethon, and all Israel with him, and they besieged Tirzah. [18]And when Zimri saw that the city was taken, he went into the citadel of the king's house, and burned the king's house over

him with fire, and died, [19]because of his sins which he committed, doing evil in the sight of the LORD, walking in the way of Jerobo'am, and for his sin which he committed, making Israel to sin. [20]Now the rest of the acts of Zimri, and the conspiracy which he made, are they not written in the Book of the Chronicles of the Kings of Israel?

Omri Reigns over Israel and Builds Samaria

21 Then the sons of Israel were divided into two parts; half of the people followed Tibni the son of Ginath, to make him king, and half followed Omri. [22]But the people who followed Omri overcame the people who followed Tibni the son of Ginath; so Tibni died, and Omri became king. [23]In the thirty-first year of Asa king of Judah, Omri began to reign over Israel, and reigned for twelve years; six years he reigned in Tirzah. [24]He bought the hill of Samar'ia* from She'mer for two talents of silver; and he fortified the hill, and called the name of the city which he built, Samaria, after the name of Shemer, the owner of the hill.

25 Omri did what was evil in the sight of the LORD, and did more evil than all who were before him. [26]For he walked in all the way of Jerobo'am the son of Ne'bat, and in the sins which he made Israel to sin, provoking the LORD, the God of Israel, to anger by their idols. [27]Now the rest of the acts of Omri which he did, and the might that he showed, are they not written in the Book of the Chronicles of the Kings of Israel? [28]And Omri slept with his fathers, and was buried in Samar'ia; and A'hab his son reigned in his stead.

Ahab Reigns over Israel and Does Evil

29 In the thirty-eighth year of Asa king of Judah, A'hab the son of Omri began to reign over Israel, and Ahab the son of Omri reigned over Israel in Samar'ia twenty-two years. [30]And A'hab the son of Omri did evil in the sight of the LORD more than

---

16:10 Zimri: The fifth king of Israel and the would-be founder of a new northern dynasty (ca. 885 B.C.). Though Zimri staged a successful coup, he failed to win the support of the people (16:16). As a result, he occupied the throne for a mere seven days, produced no successor, and took his own life by setting fire to his royal residence (16:18).

16:14 Book of the Chronicles: See note on 14:19.

16:16 Omri: The sixth king of Israel and founder of its fourth dynasty (ca. 885 to 874 B.C.). He was politically astute and militarily strong but unusually wicked (16:25). The first years of his reign were marked by conflicts with the supporters of Tibni, a rival claimant for the throne of Israel (16:21-22). His memory is linked mainly with the founding of Samaria as the longtime capital of the Northern Kingdom (16:24). Outside the Bible, Omri is referenced by name as the king of Israel on a Moabite stele dating back to the ninth century B.C. (*Mesha Inscription*, lines 4-5). Likewise, several Assyrian

records speak of the Northern Kingdom of Israel as "the house of Omri". See note on 2 Kings 9:1-10:36.

16:19 the way of Jeroboam: See note on 15:26.

16:20 Book of the Chronicles: See note on 14:19.

16:21 Tibni ... Omri: The political struggle lasts several years before Omri finally wins out (16:22). The author of Kings does not consider Tibni to have reigned as king.

16:24 Samaria: Nearly 40 miles north of Jerusalem in the heart of central Canaan (later called Sebaste). It is the permanent successor to Tirzah as the capital of the Northern Kingdom (16:29). Samaria remained the seat of government until its overthrow by the Assyrians in 722 B.C. (2 Kings 17:5-6).

16:26 the way of Jeroboam: See note on 15:26.

16:27 Book of the Chronicles: See note on 14:19.

16:28 Ahab: The seventh king of Israel and the first of three successors of Omri forming the Omride dynasty (ca. 874 to 853 B.C.). Memories of Ahab are scarred by the corruptive influence of his wife, Jezebel, and by his efforts to make Samaria a center of Canaanite idol worship (16:31-32). Scripture judges him harshly for his failings (21:25-26), though a spark of repentance is visible in the end (21:27-29). Ahab is mentioned by name outside the Bible in a report of the battle of Qarqar (853 B.C.) by the Assyrian king Shalmaneser III (*The Kurkh Monolith*).

---

*16:24, *hill of Samaria:* One of the most splendid sites in the Middle East for a capital city. But even so, the northern kingdom never achieved stability.

all that were before him. ³¹And as if it had been a light thing for him to walk in the sins of Jerobo′am the son of Ne′bat, he took for his wife Jez′ebel the daughter of Ethba′al king of the Sido′nians, and went and served Ba′al, and worshiped him. ³²He erected an altar for Ba′al in the house of Baal, which he built in Samar′ia. ³³And A′hab made an Ashe′rah. Ahab did more to provoke the Lord, the God of Israel, to anger than all the kings of Israel who were before him. ³⁴In his days Hiel of Bethel built Jericho; he laid its foundation at the cost of Abi′ram his firstborn, and set up its gates at the cost of his youngest son Segub, according to the word of the Lord, which he spoke by Joshua the son of Nun.

Elijah's Prophecy of a Drought

17 Now Eli′jah the Tishbite, of Tishbeⁿ in Gilead, said to A′hab, "As the Lord the God of Israel lives, before whom I stand, there shall be neither dew nor rain these years, except by my word."* ²And the word of the Lord came to him, ³"Depart from here and turn eastward, and hide yourself by the brook Cherith, that is east of the Jordan. ⁴You shall drink from the brook, and I have commanded the ravens to feed you there." ⁵So he went and did according to the word of the Lord; he went and dwelt by the brook Cherith that is east of the Jordan. ⁶And the ravens brought him bread and meat in the morning, and bread and meat in the evening; and he drank from the brook. ⁷And after a while the brook dried up, because there was no rain in the land.

The Widow of Zarephath

8 Then the word of the Lord came to him. ⁹"Arise, go to Zar′ephath, which belongs to Si′don, and dwell there. Behold, I have commanded a widow there to feed you." ¹⁰So he arose and went to Zar′ephath; and when he came to the gate of the city, behold, a widow was there gathering sticks; and he called to her and said, "Bring me a little water in a vessel, that I may drink." ¹¹And as she was going to bring it, he called to her and said, "Bring me a morsel of bread in your hand." ¹²And she said, "As the Lord your God lives, I have nothing baked, only a handful of meal in a jar, and a little oil in a pitcher; and now, I am gathering a couple of sticks, that I may go in and prepare it for myself and my son, that we may eat it, and die." ¹³And Eli′jah said to her, "Fear not; go and do as you have said; but first make me a little cake of it and bring it to me, and afterward

---

16:34: Josh 6:26. **17:1:** Rev 11:6. **17:8–16:** Lk 4:25, 26.

16:31 Jezebel: The villainous princess of Phoenicia. Once married to King Ahab, she makes herself the official sponsor of the Baal cult in Israel (18:19), promoting all the "harlotries" and "sorceries" that this entails (2 Kings 9:22). She is likewise the official enemy of Yahweh, as evidenced by her campaign to seek and destroy the Lord's prophets (18:4), most notably Elijah (19:2). Jezebel's sinister influence over Ahab (21:5–16) is one of the main reasons for his downfall (21:25). **Ethbaal:** A pagan priest who violently seized the Phoenician kingdom of Tyre, northwest of Israel, about 887 B.C. His daughter's marriage to Ahab suggests that a political alliance had been forged between them. **Sidonians:** Phoenicians from the port city of Sidon. **Baal:** The storm and fertility god of Canaanite religion. Devotees believed Baal was responsible for sending the rains that made farmlands fertile. See note on Judg 2:11.

16:33 Asherah: A tree or wooden pole dedicated to Asherah, a Canaanite fertility goddess (cf. 2 Kings 13:6).

16:34 Jericho: Left in ruins since the triumphant days of the Conquest. No one before Hiel dared to rebuild it, since Joshua pronounced a curse upon the oldest and youngest son of any who would try (Josh 6:26).

17:1—21:29 Stories of the prophet Elijah, whose ministry of renewal aims at fighting against Baal worship in the Northern Kingdom and calling the people back to the Lord. The narrative is punctuated with food miracles (17:4–6, 8–16; 19:5–7) as well as confrontations with King Ahab (17:1; 18:1, 17–19; 21:17–24). High points occur on Mt. Horeb, where Elijah hears the voice of Yahweh (19:8–18), and on Mt. Carmel, where he stages a dramatic showdown with the prophets of Baal (18:20–40). Many scholars believe

these prophetic traditions circulated in northern Israel in oral and possibly written form long before their inclusion in the Bible. The finale of the Elijah cycle appears in 2 Kings 1–2 (CCC 2582–83). • Elijah foreshadows the coming Messiah. Anticipating the life and ministry of Jesus, he controls the weather by his word (17:1; Mt 8:23–27), ministers to a Phoenician woman outside of Israel (17:9–16; Mk 7:24–30), multiplies food (17:14–16; Jn 6:1–14), raises the dead son of a widow (17:21–22; Lk 7:11–17), fasts for forty days and nights (19:8; Mt 4:2), benefits from the ministry of angels (19:5–8; Mt 4:11), ascends visibly into heaven (2 Kings 2:11; Acts 1:9), and is promised to come again (Mal 4:5; Acts 1:11). Elijah is also a type of John the Baptist. See note on 2 Kings 1:8.

17:1 Elijah: The name translates "Yahweh is my God." **Tishbe:** East of the Jordan in Gilead. Its exact location is unknown. **As the Lord ... lives:** An oath formula (17:12). **nor rain:** Drought and famine will weigh heavy upon Israel as divine judgments for worshiping the Canaanite god Baal (16:32). Likewise, the drought will show that Baal, the god of storm and rain, is really no god at all; it is Yahweh, the God of Israel, who brings and withholds the rains (Deut 11:13–17).

17:3 brook Cherith: A seasonal watercourse not yet identified. It quickly dries up without normal rainfall (17:7).

17:6 bread and meat: Calls to mind how the Lord fed Israel with "bread" (manna) and "flesh" (quail) in the wilderness (Ex 16:8).

17:8 Zarephath: A Phoenician coastal city between the ports of Tyre and Sidon, northwest of Israel. The widow who is hostess for Elijah is thus a Gentile (Lk 4:25–26).

17:10 a widow: Widows typically depended on the charity of others for survival. Thus, under normal circumstances, they were not in a position to support traveling visitors for an extended stay.

17:12 As the Lord ... lives: An oath formula (17:1).

17:13 first make me a little: A test of faith.

---

*17:1: With this description of the drought begins the prophetic career of Elijah, the great opponent of the nature religion that flourished in the northern kingdom and that Ahab and his Phoenician wife, Jezebel, were so active in promoting.
ⁿGk: Heb *of the settlers.*

make for yourself and your son. ¹⁴For thus says the LORD the God of Israel, 'The jar of meal shall not be spent, and the pitcher of oil shall not fail, until the day that the LORD sends rain upon the earth.'" ¹⁵And she went and did as Eli'jah said; and she, and he, and her household ate for many days. ¹⁶The jar of meal was not spent, neither did the pitcher of oil fail, according to the word of the LORD which he spoke by Eli'jah.

Elijah Revives the Widow's Son

17 After this the son of the woman, the mistress of the house, became ill; and his illness was so severe that there was no breath left in him. ¹⁸And she said to Eli'jah, "What have you against me, O man of God? You have come to me to bring my sin to remembrance, and to cause the death of my son!" ¹⁹And he said to her, "Give me your son." And he took him from her bosom, and carried him up into the upper chamber, where he lodged, and laid him upon his own bed. ²⁰And he cried to the LORD, "O LORD my God, have you brought calamity even upon the widow with whom I sojourn, by slaying her son?" ²¹Then he stretched himself upon the child three times, and cried to the LORD, "O LORD my God, let this child's soul come into him again." ²²And the LORD listened to the voice of Eli'jah; and the soul of the child came into him again, and he revived. ²³And Eli'jah took the child, and brought him down from the upper chamber into the house, and delivered him to his mother; and Elijah said, "See, your son lives." ²⁴And the woman said to Eli'jah, "Now I know that you are a man of God, and that the word of the LORD in your mouth is truth."

Elijah's Message to Ahab

18 After many days the word of the LORD came to Eli'jah, in the third year, saying, "Go, show yourself to A'hab; and I will send rain upon the earth." ²So Eli'jah went to show himself to A'hab. Now the famine was severe in Samar'ia. ³And A'hab called Obadi'ah, who was over the

household. (Now Obadiah revered the LORD greatly; ⁴and when Jez'ebel cut off the prophets of the LORD, Obadi'ah took a hundred prophets and hid them by fifties in a cave, and fed them with bread and water.) ⁵And A'hab said to Obadi'ah, "Go through the land to all the springs of water and to all the valleys; perhaps we may find grass and save the horses and mules alive, and not lose some of the animals." ⁶So they divided the land between them to pass through it; A'hab went in one direction by himself, and Obadi'ah went in another direction by himself.

7 And as Obadi'ah was on the way, behold, Eli'jah met him; and Obadiah recognized him, and fell on his face, and said, "Is it you, my lord Elijah?" ⁸And he answered him, "It is I. Go, tell your lord, 'Behold, Eli'jah is here.'" ⁹And he said, "Wherein have I sinned, that you would give your servant into the hand of A'hab, to kill me? ¹⁰As the LORD your God lives, there is no nation or kingdom whither my lord has not sent to seek you; and when they would say, 'He is not here,' he would take an oath of the kingdom or nation, that they had not found you. ¹¹And now you say, 'Go, tell your lord, "Behold, Eli'jah is here."' ¹²And as soon as I have gone from you, the Spirit of the LORD will carry you I know not where; and so, when I come and tell A'hab and he cannot find you, he will kill me, although I your servant have revered the LORD from my youth. ¹³Has it not been told my lord what I did when Jez'ebel killed the prophets of the LORD, how I hid a hundred men of the LORD's prophets by fifties in a cave, and fed them with bread and water? ¹⁴And now you say, 'Go, tell your lord, "Behold, Eli'jah is here"'; and he will kill me." ¹⁵And Eli'jah said, "As the LORD of hosts lives, before whom I stand, I will surely show myself to him today." ¹⁶So Obadi'ah went to meet A'hab, and told him; and Ahab went to meet Eli'jah.

17 When A'hab saw Eli'jah, Ahab said to him, "Is it you, you troubler of Israel?" ¹⁸And he answered, "I have not troubled Israel; but you have,

---

17:18: Mt 8:29; Mk 1:24; Jn 2:4.

17:14 shall not fail: Elijah promises a miracle: a continuous food supply in a time of famine (17:16). • The miracle happened as a sign, not as the ultimate reward. What the widow received was only temporary; the flour did not run out nor did the oil diminish until God sent rain upon the land. This was a sign of the life to come, when God, our flour and our reward, will never run out (St. Augustine, *Sermons* 11).

17:18 my sin: The widow complains that her past sins are being punished by the visitation of the holy prophet. Little does she know that her son's death will occasion a blessing from the Lord.

17:21 stretched himself upon: Elijah performs the first resurrection miracle in the Bible. It combines symbolic action (warming the body) with intense prayer (petitioning the Lord to summon back the spirit). The Greek LXX says that Elijah "breathed upon" the boy (CCC 2583). • Nearly identical miracles are performed by the prophet Elisha (2 Kings 4:32–37) and much later by the Apostle Paul (Acts 20:9–10).

18:1 third year: The drought continues for three years and six months (Lk 4:25; Jas 5:17). **Ahab:** King of Israel. See note on 16:28.

18:2 Samaria: Capital of the Northern Kingdom of Israel. See note on 16:24.

18:3 over the household: Suggests that Obadiah is the royal steward (= prime minister) of the Northern Kingdom. See word study: *Over the Household* at 16:9.

18:4 Jezebel: Ahab's wife. See note on 16:31.

18:7 recognized him: For Elijah's distinctive appearance, see 2 Kings 1:8.

18:12 Spirit of the LORD: Known to whisk away the prophets from one location to another, giving rise to the reputation for sudden appearances and disappearances (2 Kings 2:16). • Ezekiel experienced this type of spiritual transport in the OT (Ezek 3:14–15), as did Philip the evangelist in the NT (Acts 8:39).

18:18 Baals: Here the name is plural because worship of Baal takes place at multiple sites throughout the Northern Kingdom.

and your father's house, because you have forsaken the commandments of the Lord and followed the Ba'als. ¹⁹Now therefore send and gather all Israel to me at Mount Carmel, and the four hundred and fifty prophets of Ba'al* and the four hundred prophets of Ashe'rah, who eat at Jez'ebel's table."

Elijah Triumphs over the Prophets of Baal

20 So A'hab sent to all the sons of Israel, and gathered the prophets together at Mount Carmel. ²¹And Eli'jah came near to all the people, and said, "How long will you go limping with two different opinions? If the Lord is God, follow him; but if Ba'al, then follow him." And the people did not answer him a word. ²²Then Eli'jah said to the people, "I, even I only, am left a prophet of the Lord; but Ba'al's prophets are four hundred and fifty men. ²³Let two bulls be given to us; and let them choose one bull for themselves, and cut it in pieces and lay it on the wood, but put no fire to it; and I will prepare the other bull and lay it on the wood, and put no fire to it. ²⁴And you call on the name of your god and I will call on the name of the Lord; and the God who answers by fire, he is God." And all the people answered, "It is well spoken." ²⁵Then Eli'jah said to the prophets of Ba'al, "Choose for yourselves one bull and prepare it first, for you are many; and call on the name of your god, but put no fire to it." ²⁶And they took the bull which was given them, and they prepared it, and called on the name of Ba'al from morning until noon, saying, "O Baal, answer us!" But there was no voice, and no one answered. And they limped about the altar which they had made. ²⁷And at noon Eli'jah mocked them, saying, "Cry aloud, for he is a god; either he is musing, or he has gone aside, or he is on a journey, or perhaps he is asleep and must be awakened." ²⁸And they cried aloud, and cut themselves after their custom with swords and lances, until the blood gushed out upon them. ²⁹And as midday passed, they raved on until the time of the offering of the oblation, but there was no voice; no one answered, no one heeded.

30 Then Eli'jah said to all the people, "Come near to me"; and all the people came near to him. And he repaired the altar of the Lord that had been thrown down; ³¹Eli'jah took twelve stones, according to the number of the tribes of the sons of Jacob, to whom the word of the Lord came, saying, "Israel shall be your name"; ³²and with the stones he built an altar in the name of the Lord. And he made a trench about the altar, as great as would contain two measures of seed. ³³And he put the wood in order, and cut the bull in pieces and laid it on the wood. And he said, "Fill four jars with water, and pour it on the burnt offering, and on the wood." ³⁴And he said, "Do it a second time"; and they did it a second time. And he said, "Do it a third time"; and they did it a third time. ³⁵And the water ran round about the altar, and filled the trench also with water.

36 And at the time of the offering of the oblation, Eli'jah the prophet came near and said, "O Lord, God of Abraham, Isaac, and Israel, let it be known this day that you are God in Israel, and that I am your servant, and that I have done all these things at your word. ³⁷Answer me, O Lord, answer me, that this people may know that you, O Lord, are God, and that you have turned their hearts back." ³⁸Then the fire of the Lord fell, and consumed the burnt offering, and the wood, and the stones, and the dust, and licked up the water that was in the trench. ³⁹And when all the people saw it, they fell on their faces; and they said, "The Lord, he is God; the Lord, he is God." ⁴⁰And Eli'jah said to them, "Seize

---

18:19 Mount Carmel: Rises along the Mediterranean coast in northwest Israel. **Asherah:** A Canaanite fertility goddess. **Jezebel's table:** Ahab's government gives material support to the leaders of the Baal and Asherah cults. See note on 16:31.

18:20–40 Elijah faces off against the pagan prophets of Baal. The contest is staged to determine whether Yahweh or Baal is truly God. Elijah appears to be outmatched by taking on several hundred opponents (18:22) and further disadvantaged by using an altar that is doused with water (18:33–35). Nevertheless, heaven is unmoved by the ravings of the idol prophets, while it roars down with fire at the prayer of Elijah. The standoff is successful in discrediting Baal and reawakening faith in the God of Israel (18:39) (CCC 2583). • If the words of Elijah were powerful enough to call down fire from heaven, then surely the words of Christ have power enough to change the elements of the Eucharist. They can make out of nothing things that did not exist, and so they can change things that exist into things that were not (St. Ambrose *On the Mysteries* 52).

18:21 limping: An image of Israel hobbling along with weak religious convictions. Elijah is noticeably annoyed by this and urges the people to make a decisive choice between the God of the covenant (Yahweh) and the god of the Canaanites (Baal).

18:24 answers by fire: A challenge to see which god can ignite the altar by lightning. Baal, if he is really the lord of the storm, should have no problem with this; Yahweh, for his part, has been known to incinerate sacrifices with a blast of heavenly fire (Lev 9:24; Judg 6:19–21; 2 Chron 7:1).

18:27 mocked them: Elijah uses sarcasm to poke fun at Baal and taunt his followers. **has gone aside:** A euphemism suggesting that Baal has stepped out to "relieve himself".

18:28 cut themselves: Self-laceration is a type of mourning rite. It is forbidden in Israel by the Mosaic Law (Lev 19:28).

18:29 time of the offering: Late afternoon, around 3 P.M., when the daily lamb, grain, and wine offerings are made in the sanctuary (Ex 29:38–41).

18:31 twelve stones: Elijah has a message for all 12 tribes of Israel, not just the ten northern tribes (cf. Ex 24:4). **Israel ... your name:** The words spoken to Jacob in Gen 35:10. See word study: *Israel* at Gen 32:28.

18:40 brook Kishon: Flows northwest across the Plain of Megiddo and empties into the Mediterranean just north of Mt. Carmel. **killed them:** In accord with Deuteronomy, which demands the execution of false prophets who lead Israel into idolatry (Deut 13:1–5).

---

*18:19, *prophets of Baal:* These had been brought from Phoenicia by Jezebel.

the prophets of Ba'al; let not one of them escape." And they seized them; and Elijah brought them down to the brook Ki'shon, and killed them there.

The Drought Ends

41 And Eli'jah said to A'hab, "Go up, eat and drink; for there is a sound of the rushing of rain." ⁴²So A'hab went up to eat and to drink. And Eli'jah went up to the top of Carmel; and he bowed himself down upon the earth, and put his face between his knees. ⁴³And he said to his servant, "Go up now, look toward the sea." And he went up and looked, and said, "There is nothing." And he said, "Go again seven times." ⁴⁴And at the seventh time he said, "Behold, a little cloud like a man's hand is rising out of the sea." And he said, "Go up, say to A'hab, 'Prepare your chariot and go down, lest the rain stop you.'" ⁴⁵And in a little while the heavens grew black with clouds and wind, and there was a great rain. And A'hab rode and went to Jezre'el. ⁴⁶And the hand of the LORD was on Eli'jah; and he girded up his loins and ran before A'hab to the entrance of Jezre'el.

Elijah Flees from Jezebel

19 A'hab told Jez'ebel all that Eli'jah had done, and how he had slain all the prophets with the sword. ²Then Jez'ebel sent a messenger to Eli'jah, saying, "So may the gods do to me, and more also, if I do not make your life as the life of one of them by this time tomorrow." ³Then he was afraid, and he arose and went for his life, and came to Be'er-she'ba, which belongs to Judah, and left his servant there.

4 But he himself went a day's journey into the wilderness, and came and sat down under a broom tree; and he asked that he might die, saying, "It is enough; now, O LORD, take away my life; for I am no better than my fathers." ⁵And he lay down and slept under a broom tree; and behold, an angel touched him, and said to him, "Arise and eat."

⁶And he looked, and behold, there was at his head a cake baked on hot stones and a jar of water. And he ate and drank, and lay down again. ⁷And the angel of the LORD came again a second time, and touched him, and said, "Arise and eat, else the journey will be too great for you." ⁸And he arose, and ate and drank, and walked in the strength of that food forty days and forty nights to Horeb* the mount of God.

Elijah Meets God at Mount Horeb

9 And there he came to a cave, and lodged there; and behold, the word of the LORD came to him, and he said to him, "What are you doing here, Eli'jah?" ¹⁰He said, "I have been very jealous for the LORD, the God of hosts; for the sons of Israel have forsaken your covenant, thrown down your altars, and slain your prophets with the sword; and I, even I only, am left; and they seek my life, to take it away." ¹¹And he said, "Go forth, and stand upon the mount before the LORD." And behold, the LORD passed by, and a great and strong wind tore the mountains, and broke in pieces the rocks before the LORD, but the LORD was not in the wind; and after the wind an earthquake, but the LORD was not in the earthquake; ¹²and after the earthquake a fire, but the LORD was not in the fire; and after the fire a still small voice. ¹³And when Eli'jah heard it, he wrapped his face in his mantle and went out and stood at the entrance of the cave. And behold, there came a voice to him, and said, "What are you doing here, Eli'jah?" ¹⁴He said, "I have been very jealous for the LORD, the God of hosts; for the sons of Israel have forsaken your covenant, thrown down your altars, and slain your prophets with the sword; and I, even I only, am left; and they seek my life, to take it away." ¹⁵And the LORD said to him, "Go, return on your way to the wilderness of Damascus; and when you arrive, you shall anoint Haz'ael to be

---

19:10: Rom 11:2, 3. **19:18:** Rom 11:4.

18:42 bowed himself down: Elijah humbles himself before the Lord and prays for an end to the drought. Soon a rainstorm blows in from the Mediterranean, and a downpour refreshes the land (18:45). • According to James, the prayer of Elijah is effective because the prophet is a righteous man (Jas 5:16–18). The lesson is that heaven is quick to answer the pleas of humble and holy saints (Sir 35:16–20) (CCC 2582).

18:45 Jezreel: A town over 15 miles southeast of Mt. Carmel. King Ahab maintained a second royal residence in Jezreel (21:1).

19:2 the gods do to me: A conditional self-curse. See note on Ruth 1:17.

19:3 Beer-sheba: In the deep south of Canaan, far from the realm of the Northern Kingdom. Elijah is trying to place himself beyond the reach of Jezebel's wrath.

19:4 broom tree: A type of wilderness shrub. **It is enough:** Elijah hopes aloud for death, having been pushed to this point by fear and fatigue.

19:7 angel: Sent to revive the weary prophet with food, indicating that God wants to keep him alive a while longer (CCC 332).

19:8-18 Elijah travels to Mt. Horeb (= Mt. Sinai). Several parallels indicate that Elijah is following in the steps of Moses: (1) both flee from danger to the same wilderness peak (19:8; Ex 19:1–2); (2) both spend 40 days and nights fasting (19:8; Deut 9:9); (3) both hide their faces in the presence of the Lord (19:13; Ex 3:6); (4) both find shelter in a rock crevice on the mountain (19:9; Ex 33:21–22); (5) both witness a terrifying display of storm winds, earthquakes, and fire (19:11–12; Ex 19:16–18); and (6) both hear the voice of the living God (19:12; Ex 19:19). The author of Kings, shaped by the outlook of Deuteronomy, thus portrays Elijah as a "prophet like Moses" (Deut 18:15–18) (CCC 2583).

19:15-16 A mandate for three transfers in leadership. Elijah's successor, Elisha, will bring about the first (Hazael, 2 Kings 8:7–15); one of Elisha's associates will facilitate the second (Jehu, 2 Kings 9:1–13); and Elijah himself will accomplish the third (Elisha, 19:19).

---

*19:8, *Horeb:* i.e., Mt. Sinai, where the law was given to Moses and God made a covenant with his people.

king over Syria; ¹⁶and Je'hu the son of Nimshi you shall anoint to be king over Israel; and Eli'sha the son of Sha'phat of A'bel-meho'lah you shall anoint to be prophet in your place. ¹⁷And him who escapes from the sword of Haz'ael shall Je'hu slay; and him who escapes from the sword of Jehu shall Eli'sha slay. ¹⁸Yet I will leave seven thousand in Israel, all the knees that have not bowed to Ba'al, and every mouth that has not kissed him."

Elisha Becomes Elijah's Disciple

19 So he departed from there, and found Eli'sha the son of Sha'phat, who was plowing, with twelve yoke of oxen before him, and he was with the twelfth. Eli'jah passed by him and cast his mantle upon him. ²⁰And he left the oxen, and ran after Eli'jah, and said, "Let me kiss my father and my mother, and then I will follow you." And he said to him, "Go back again; for what have I done to you?" ²¹And he returned from following him, and took

the yoke of oxen, and slew them, and boiled their flesh with the yokes of the oxen, and gave it to the people, and they ate. Then he arose and went after Eli'jah, and ministered to him.

Ahab's Wars with the Syrians

20 Ben-ha'dad the king of Syria gathered all his army together; thirty-two kings were with him, and horses and chariots; and he went up and besieged Samar'ia, and fought against it. ²And he sent messengers into the city to A'hab king of Israel, and said to him, "Thus says Ben-ha'dad: ³'Your silver and your gold are mine; your fairest wives and children also are mine.'" ⁴And the king of Israel answered, "As you say, my lord, O king, I am yours, and all that I have." ⁵The messengers came again, and said, "Thus says Ben-ha'dad: 'I sent to you, saying, "Deliver to me your silver and your gold, your wives and your children"; ⁶nevertheless I will send my servants to you tomorrow about

---

19:16 Elisha: The name translates "my God saves". **prophet in your place:** Announcing a replacement for Elijah is a divine "rebuke" for his cowardly flight to Horeb (Sir 48:7). **Abel-meholah:** South of Beth-shan in the western Jordan valley.

19:18 seven thousand: A surprise to Elijah, who thought he was the only one left in northern Israel still zealous for Yahweh (19:10). As it turns out, the Lord has preserved a remnant of the faithful several thousand strong. • Paul sees this scenario played out in his own day, when a remnant of believing Israel, accepting Jesus as the Messiah, is preserved by grace in the midst of widespread unbelief among the chosen people (Rom 11:1-7). **has not kissed him:** I.e., has not venerated a cult image of Baal (cf. Hos 13:2).

19:19 cast his mantle: Elijah performs a symbolic gesture to designate his successor in the prophetic office (cf. Num 20:25-26). Later his mantle will become Elisha's (2 Kings 2:13).

19:19-21 Elisha follows along as Elijah's apprentice-in-training until the latter's fiery departure (2 Kings 2:11-12). In bidding farewell to his parents, Elisha makes a decisive break with his past (19:20); in boiling his oxen and burning their yokes, he sacrifices the tokens of his former way of life to fulfill his prophetic mission (19:21). • Jesus alludes to the calling of Elisha, particularly his delays and family farewells,

in order to stress the greater urgency of his own call to discipleship in the kingdom of God (Lk 9:59-62).

19:21 ministered to him: Elisha becomes a personal attendant to Elijah, much as Joshua, the successor to Moses, started out as his servant (Ex 33:11; Num 11:28).

20:1 Ben-hadad: Ruler of the Aramean kingdom of Syria, whose name appears in Assyrian texts as Adad-idri. Without known provocation, he assembles a coalition army to march into Canaan and to demand tribute from the northern capital of Samaria (20:3). Twice his aggressive moves against the Northern Kingdom end in defeat (20:20, 29), although his own life is spared and a treaty between Syria and the house of Israel is eventually sealed (20:33-34). On the possible identity of Ben-hadad, see note on 15:18. **kings:** More likely chieftains than monarchs in the strict sense (as in Num 31:8).

20:4 As you say, my lord: Ahab acts the part of a vassal complying with the requests of his overlord. It is a diplomatic move to spare the city a violent destruction.

20:6 whatever pleases them: The Syrian king increases his demands. Now he wants, not only tribute, but the right to plunder Samaria without restriction. This proves too much for the Israelite leadership, and the new demand is flatly refused (20:7-9).

WORD STUDY

Voice (19:12)

qol (Heb.): means "sound" or "voice". A great variety of sounds are indicated by this term, including the gentle sound of bleating sheep (1 Sam 15:14), the melodic sound of people singing (Is 52:8), the distressing sound of mourners weeping (Is 65:19), and the deafening sounds of a trumpet blaring (Ex 19:16) or thunder booming (1 Sam 12:17). It can also refer to the voice of a man (Josh 10:14) as well as the mighty voice of God (Ps 29:3-9). The voice that Elijah encounters on Horeb is somewhat difficult to interpret. Traditionally, it is thought to be "a still small voice" that whispers to the prophet (1 Kings 19:12). On this interpretation, the modifiers "still" and "small" are related to two verbs that mean "become still" and "crush, grind small". Another possibility, based on a different interpretation of the modifiers, is that Elijah encountered a "roaring, crushing voice". Though the linguistic evidence is inconclusive, this reading would enhance the parallelism between Elijah and Moses. Recall that Moses witnessed storms, quakes, and fire (Ex 19:16-18) as a dramatic prelude to the thunderous voice of Yahweh blaring down the Ten Commandments from the mountaintop, striking fear into Israel below (Ex 19:19; Deut 4:12-13; 5:24-26).

this time, and they shall search your house and the houses of your servants, and lay hands on whatever pleases them,° and take it away.'"

7 Then the king of Israel called all the elders of the land, and said, "Mark, now, and see how this man is seeking trouble; for he sent to me for my wives and my children, and for my silver and my gold, and I did not refuse him." ⁸And all the elders and all the people said to him, "Do not heed or consent." ⁹So he said to the messengers of Ben-ha′dad, "Tell my lord the king, 'All that you first demanded of your servant I will do; but this thing I cannot do.'" And the messengers departed and brought him word again. ¹⁰Ben-ha′dad sent to him and said, "The gods do so to me, and more also, if the dust of Samar′ia shall suffice for handfuls for all the people who follow me." ¹¹And the king of Israel answered, "Tell him, 'Let not him that belts on his armor boast himself as he that puts it off.'" ¹²When Ben-ha′dad heard this message as he was drinking with the kings in the booths, he said to his men, "Take your positions." And they took their positions against the city.

A Prophet Speaks to Ahab

13 And behold, a prophet came near to A′hab king of Israel and said, "Thus says the LORD, Have you seen all this great multitude? Behold, I will give it into your hand this day; and you shall know that I am the LORD." ¹⁴And A′hab said, "By whom?" He said, "Thus says the LORD, By the servants of the governors of the districts." Then he said, "Who shall begin the battle?" He answered, "You." ¹⁵Then he mustered the servants of the governors of the districts, and they were two hundred and thirty-two; and after them he mustered all the sons of Israel, seven thousand.

The Syrians Are Defeated

16 And they went out at noon, while Ben-ha′dad was drinking himself drunk in the booths, he and the thirty-two kings who helped him. ¹⁷The servants of the governors of the districts went out first. And Ben-ha′dad sent out scouts, and they reported to him, "Men are coming out from Samar′ia." ¹⁸He said,

"If they have come out for peace, take them alive; or if they have come out for war, take them alive."

19 So these went out of the city, the servants of the governors of the districts, and the army which followed them. ²⁰And each killed his man; the Syrians fled and Israel pursued them, but Ben-ha′dad king of Syria escaped on a horse with horsemen. ²¹And the king of Israel went out, and captured^p the horses and chariots, and killed the Syrians with a great slaughter.

22 Then the prophet came near to the king of Israel, and said to him, "Come, strengthen yourself, and consider well what you have to do; for in the spring the king of Syria will come up against you."

23 And the servants of the king of Syria said to him, "Their gods are gods of the hills, and so they were stronger than we; but let us fight against them in the plain, and surely we shall be stronger than they. ²⁴And do this: remove the kings, each from his post, and put commanders in their places; ²⁵and muster an army like the army that you have lost, horse for horse, and chariot for chariot; then we will fight against them in the plain, and surely we shall be stronger than they." And he listened to their voice, and did so.

26 In the spring Ben-ha′dad mustered the Syrians, and went up to A′phek, to fight against Israel. ²⁷And the sons of Israel were mustered, and were provisioned, and went against them; the sons of Israel encamped before them like two little flocks of goats, but the Syrians filled the country. ²⁸And a man of God came near and said to the king of Israel, "Thus says the LORD, 'Because the Syrians have said, "The LORD is a god of the hills but he is not a god of the valleys," therefore I will give all this great multitude into your hand, and you shall know that I am the LORD.'" ²⁹And they encamped opposite one another seven days. Then on the seventh day the battle was joined; and the sons of Israel struck a hundred thousand Syrian foot soldiers in one day. ³⁰And the rest fled into the city of A′phek; and the wall fell upon twenty-seven thousand men that were left.

20:10 The gods do so to me: A conditional self-curse. See note on Ruth 1:17.

20:11 Let not him ... boast: A proverb that cautions soldiers against boasting before victory on the battlefield is won.

20:12 in the booths: I.e., in the war camp.

20:13 into your hand: Yahweh promises to fight for Israel and give victory over the Syrian aggressor. With the compliance of Ahab, the small army of Israel is strengthened by heaven to conquer unfavorable odds and wipe out the invaders (20:20–21).

20:14 the servants: Or "the young men". They will lead the charge against the Syrian army (20:15).

20:22 in the spring: A customary time for military expeditions (2 Sam 11:1).

20:23 gods of the hills: In the polytheistic thinking of the ancient world, local gods have only a local range of influence. The Syrians assume, therefore, that if Israel can be drawn down from the highlands, then Yahweh will be drawn away from his home turf and foreign fighters will have the advantage. Israel's crushing defeat of the Syrians on the plain will serve as a refutation of this mistaken theology (20:28–30). Also, from a tactical standpoint, the Aramean chariots (20:1) can fight most effectively on level terrain (cf. Judg 1:19).

20:26 Aphek: A walled city less than five miles east of the Sea of Galilee.

20:27 like two little flocks: A mere 7,232 fighters from Israel (20:15) are up against more than 100,000 warriors fighting for the Syrian coalition (20:29–30).

20:28 a man of God: The prophet introduced in 20:13.

20:29 on the seventh day: Reminiscent of the battle of Jericho, which commenced on the seventh day and likewise saw the walls of the city collapse (20:30; Josh 6:15–21).

°Gk Syr Vg: Heb *you*.
ᴾGk: Heb *struck*.

Ben-ha′dad also fled, and entered an inner chamber in the city. ³¹And his servants said to him, "Behold now, we have heard that the kings of the house of Israel are merciful kings; let us put sackcloth on our loins and ropes upon our heads, and go out to the king of Israel; perhaps he will spare your life." ³²So they belted sackcloth on their loins, and put ropes on their heads, and went to the king of Israel and said, "Your servant Ben-ha′dad says, 'Please, let me live.'" And he said, "Does he still live? He is my brother." ³³Now the men were watching for an omen, and they quickly took it up from him and said, "Yes, your brother Ben-ha′dad." Then he said, "Go and bring him." Then Ben-hadad came forth to him; and he caused him to come up into the chariot. ³⁴And Ben-ha′dad said to him, "The cities which my father took from your father I will restore; and you may establish bazaars for yourself in Damascus, as my father did in Samar′ia." And A′hab said, "I will let you go on these terms." So he made a covenant with him and let him go.

A Prophet Condemns Ahab

35 And a certain man of the sons of the prophets said to his fellow at the command of the Lord, "Strike me, I beg you." But the man refused to strike him. ³⁶Then he said to him, "Because you have not obeyed the voice of the Lord, behold, as soon as you have gone from me, a lion shall kill you." And as soon as he had departed from him, a lion met him and killed him. ³⁷Then he found another man, and said, "Strike me, I beg you." And the man struck him, hitting and wounding him. ³⁸So the prophet departed, and waited for the king by the way, disguising himself with a bandage over his eyes. ³⁹And as the king passed, he cried to the king and said, "Your servant went out into the midst of the battle; and behold, a soldier turned and brought a man to me, and said, 'Keep this man; if by any means he be missing, your life shall be for his life, or else you shall pay a talent of silver.' ⁴⁰And as your servant was busy here and there, he was gone." The king of Israel said to him, "So shall your judgment be; you yourself have decided it." ⁴¹Then he made haste to take the bandage away from his eyes; and the king of Israel recognized him as one of the prophets. ⁴²And he said to him, "Thus says the Lord, 'Because you have let go out of your hand the man whom I had devoted to destruction, therefore your life shall go for his life, and your people for his people.'" ⁴³And the king of Israel went to his house resentful and sullen, and came to Samar′ia.

Naboth's Vineyard

21 Now Naboth the Jezre′elite had a vineyard in Jezre′el, beside the palace of A′hab king of Samar′ia. ²And after this A′hab said to Naboth, "Give me your vineyard, that I may have it for a vegetable garden, because it is near my house; and I will give you a better vineyard for it; or, if it seems good to you, I will give you its value in money." ³But Naboth said to A′hab, "The Lord forbid that I should give you the inheritance of my fathers." ⁴And A′hab went into his house vexed and sullen because of what Naboth the Jezre′elite had said to him; for he had said, "I will not give you the inheritance of my fathers." And he lay down on his bed, and turned away his face, and would eat no food.

5 But Jez′ebel his wife came to him, and said to him, "Why is your spirit so vexed that you eat no food?" ⁶And he said to her, "Because I spoke to Naboth the Jezre′elite, and said to him, 'Give me your

---

20:31 sackcloth ... ropes: Signs of mourning and submission. In this context, they serve as visible appeals for clemency.

20:32 Your servant: Ben-hadad declares his submission to Ahab in exchange for his life, yet Ahab treats him as a king of equal rank (my brother) with whom he will make a covenant (20:34). Some see this as an astute political move on Ahab's part, since he needed an ally against the growing threat of Assyria in the east.

20:34 my father took: Seemingly a reference to the Galilean cities Ben-hadad I conquered in 15:20. covenant: Ahab forges a treaty between Israel and Syria. In return for the Syrian king's life, Israel is given commercial opportunities that could help to revive the economy of the Northern Kingdom as it struggles to recover from several years of famine (17:1; 18:1).

20:35 sons of the prophets: Junior members of a prophetic guild under the direction of a senior prophet, called a "father" (2 Kings 2:12). Strike me: The prophet wants to disguise himself as an injured soldier (20:38) before he confronts King Ahab with an incriminating parable (20:38-40).

20:36 a lion: Recalls the similar story in 13:20-25. • Morally, it is a paradox that the man who struck the prophet was spared and the man who spared the prophet was struck with punishment. For what reason? To teach that when God commands, the action must not be overly questioned but simply obeyed. Revere the One who commands, and heed his word eagerly. The man who was afraid to strike the prophet suffered punishment, and by this we are encouraged to obey every divine commandment (St. John Chrysostom, *Against Judaizing Christians* 4, 2).

20:39 a talent: Estimated at about 75 pounds.

20:42 devoted to destruction: A reference to the Deuteronomic war ban. See word study: *Devoted* at Josh 6:17.

21:1-16 The stoning of Naboth and the seizure of his vineyard. • Ahab's treachery in the "Naboth affair" is parallel to David's treachery in the "Bathsheba affair". The king covets his neighbor's property and resorts to false witness and murder to acquire it; so, too, David covets his neighbor's wife and, having committed adultery, resorts to murder to acquire the woman for himself. See note on 2 Sam 11:1-27.

21:1 Jezreel: Northwest of Mt. Gilboa in the tribal territory of Issachar (Josh 19:18). Ahab maintained a royal palace in Jezreel besides his primary residence in Samaria (16:29).

21:3 inheritance: In ancient Israel, ancestral lands belonged to tribes and families, not just to individuals. Each tribe had its territory as a gift from the Lord, and so the sale of land to buyers outside one's tribe was disallowed under normal circumstances (Num 36:7).

21:5 Jezebel: Ahab's wife (16:31). Her corruptive influence over Ahab (21:25) is evident here in a scheme to confiscate property by means of deception and murder (21:9-10).

vineyard for money; or else, if it please you, I will give you another vineyard for it'; and he answered, 'I will not give you my vineyard.'" ⁷And Jez'ebel his wife said to him, "Do you now govern Israel? Arise, and eat bread, and let your heart be cheerful; I will give you the vineyard of Naboth the Jezre'elite."

8 So she wrote letters in A'hab's name and sealed them with his seal, and she sent the letters to the elders and the nobles who dwelt with Naboth in his city. ⁹And she wrote in the letters, "Proclaim a fast, and set Naboth on high among the people; ¹⁰and set two* base fellows opposite him, and let them bring a charge against him, saying, 'You have cursed God and the king.' Then take him out, and stone him to death." ¹¹And the men of his city, the elders and the nobles who dwelt in his city, did as Jez'ebel had sent word to them. As it was written in the letters which she had sent to them, ¹²they proclaimed a fast, and set Naboth on high among the people. ¹³And the two base fellows came in and sat opposite him; and the base fellows brought a charge against Naboth, in the presence of the people, saying, "Naboth cursed God and the king." So they took him outside the city, and stoned him to death with stones. ¹⁴Then they sent to Jez'ebel, saying, "Naboth has been stoned; he is dead."

15 As soon as Jez'ebel heard that Naboth had been stoned and was dead, Jezebel said to A'hab, "Arise, take possession of the vineyard of Naboth the Jezre'elite, which he refused to give you for money; for Naboth is not alive, but dead." ¹⁶And as soon as A'hab heard that Naboth was dead, Ahab arose to go down to the vineyard of Naboth the Jezre'elite, to take possession of it.

Elijah Pronounces God's Sentence

17 Then the word of the Lᴏʀᴅ came to Eli'jah the Tishbite, saying, ¹⁸"Arise, go down to meet A'hab king of Israel, who is in Samar'ia; behold, he is in the vineyard of Naboth, where he has gone to take possession. ¹⁹And you shall say to him, 'Thus says the Lᴏʀᴅ, "Have you killed, and also taken possession?"' And you shall say to him, 'Thus says the Lᴏʀᴅ: "In the place where dogs licked up the blood of Naboth shall dogs lick your own blood."'"

20 A'hab said to Eli'jah, "Have you found me, O my enemy?" He answered, "I have found you, because you have sold yourself to do what is evil in the sight of the Lᴏʀᴅ. ²¹Behold, I will bring evil upon you; I will utterly sweep you away, and will cut off from A'hab every male, bond or free, in Israel; ²²and I will make your house like the house of Jerobo'am the son of Ne'bat, and like the house of Ba'asha the son of Ahi'jah, for the anger to which you have provoked me, and because you have made Israel to sin. ²³And of Jez'ebel the Lᴏʀᴅ also said, 'The dogs shall eat Jezebel within the bounds of Jezre'el.' ²⁴Any one belonging to A'hab who dies in the city the dogs shall eat; and any one of his who dies in the open country the birds of the air shall eat."

25 (There was none who sold himself to do what was evil in the sight of the Lᴏʀᴅ like A'hab, whom Jez'ebel his wife incited. ²⁶He did very abominably in going after idols, as the Am'orites had done, whom the Lᴏʀᴅ cast out before the sons of Israel.)

27 And when A'hab heard those words, he tore his clothes, and put sackcloth upon his flesh, and fasted and lay in sackcloth, and went about dejectedly. ²⁸And the word of the Lᴏʀᴅ came to Eli'jah the Tishbite, saying, ²⁹"Have you seen how Ahab has humbled himself before me? Because he has humbled himself before me, I will not bring the evil in his days; but in his son's days I will bring the evil upon his house."†

21:19: 2 Kings 9:26. **21:23:** 2 Kings 9:36.

21:7 Do you now govern ...?: The question is rhetorical, implying that royal power should be used to serve the selfish interests of the king. Jezebel, a princess of the Phoenician royal family, knows only the Canaanite model of kingship, where rulers wield absolute authority over their subjects and territories. By contrast, kings in Israel were forbidden to behave like tyrants but were called to be model students of the Torah (Deut 17:14-20).

21:8 his seal: Used to impress Ahab's royal insignia onto a wax or clay seal (CCC 1295).

21:10 two base fellows: False witnesses. Two persons with corroborating testimony are needed for the court to issue a death sentence (Deut 17:6). **cursed God and the king:** Both are forbidden by the Torah (Ex 22:28). Death by stoning is the penalty for cursing the name of the Lord (Lev 24:10-16).

21:13 outside the city: To avoid defiling the city with human death (Num 15:35; 19:11).

21:14 he is dead: It is implied in 2 Kings 9:26 that the sons of Naboth were also killed. All the heirs to Naboth's estate had to be wiped out in order for Ahab to claim the vineyard as royal property.

21:17 Elijah the Tishbite: See note on 17:1.

21:19 your own blood: To be lapped up by a pack of dogs after Ahab is fatally wounded in battle (22:34-38).

21:22 your house: Doom is pronounced on the royal line of Ahab. The northern dynasty of Omri, his father, like that of Jeroboam and Baasha, will eventually be cut off (14:10; 16:3).

21:23 dogs shall eat Jezebel: The gory details of her demise are given in 2 Kings 9:30-37.

21:24 dogs ... birds ... eat: A curse. See note on 14:11.

21:26 Amorites: One of the ten peoples that lived in Canaan before the Israelite takeover of the land (Gen 15:18-21).

21:27-29 Ahab repents after Elijah delivers an oracle of judgment. The king's remorse must be genuine, since the Lord shows mercy and postpones the full measure of his punitive judgment.

21:27 tore ... sackcloth ... fasted: Signs of sorrow and repentance (Gen 37:34; Joel 1:13-14).

---

*21:10: Two witnesses were required for a legal charge involving the death penalty; cf. Susanna and the elders; cf. Num 35:30; Deut 19:15; Dan 13:40; Mt 18:16.
†21:29: God has mercy on the repentant king, as before in the case of David. But he does not say here that the dynasty will be preserved.

Judah and Israel Join to Fight the Syrians

22 For three years Syria and Israel continued without war. ²But in the third year Jehosh′- aphat the king of Judah came down to the king of Israel. ³And the king of Israel said to his servants, "Do you know that Ra′moth-gil′ead belongs to us, and we keep quiet and do not take it out of the hand of the king of Syria?" ⁴And he said to Jehosh′aphat, "Will you go with me to battle at Ra′moth-gil′ead?" And Jehoshaphat said to the king of Israel, "I am as you are, my people as your people, my horses as your horses."

5 And Jehosh′aphat said to the king of Israel, "Inquire first for the word of the Lord." ⁶Then the king of Israel gathered the prophets together, about four hundred men, and said to them, "Shall I go to battle against Ra′moth-gil′ead, or shall I forbear?" And they said, "Go up; for the Lord will give it into the hand of the king." ⁷But Jehosh′- aphat said, "Is there not here another prophet of the Lord of whom we may inquire?" ⁸And the king of Israel said to Jehosh′aphat, "There is yet one man by whom we may inquire of the Lord, Micai′ah the son of Imlah; but I hate him, for he never prophesies good concerning me, but evil." And Jehosh′aphat said, "Let not the king say so." ⁹Then the king of Israel summoned an officer and said, "Bring quickly Micai′ah the son of Imlah." ¹⁰Now the king of Israel and Jehosh′aphat the king of Judah were sitting on their thrones, wearing their robes, at the threshing floor at the entrance of the gate of Samar′ia; and all the prophets were prophesying before them. ¹¹And Zedeki′ah the son of Chena′anah made for himself horns of iron, and said, "Thus says the Lord, 'With these you shall push the Syrians until they are destroyed.'" ¹²And all the prophets prophesied so, and said, "Go up to Ra′moth-gil′ead and triumph; the Lord will give it into the hand of the king."

Micaiah's Prophecy

13 And the messenger who went to summon Micai′ah said to him, "Behold, the words of the prophets with one accord are favorable to the king; let your word be like the word of one of them, and speak favorably." ¹⁴But Micai′ah said, "As the Lord lives, what the Lord says to me, that I will speak." ¹⁵And when he had come to the king, the king said to him, "Micai′ah, shall we go to Ra′moth-gil′ead to battle, or shall we forbear?" And he answered him, "Go up and triumph; the Lord will give it into the hand of the king." ¹⁶But the king said to him, "How many times shall I adjure you that you speak to me nothing but the truth in the name of the Lord?" ¹⁷And he said, "I saw all Israel scattered upon the mountains, as sheep that have no shepherd; and the Lord said, 'These have no master; let each return to his home in peace.'" ¹⁸And the king of Israel said to Jehosh′aphat, "Did I not tell you that he would not prophesy good concerning me, but evil?" ¹⁹And Micai′ah said, "Therefore hear the word of the Lord: I saw the Lord sitting on his throne, and all the host of heaven standing beside him on his right hand and on his left; ²⁰and the Lord said, 'Who will entice A′hab, that he may go up and fall at Ra′moth-gil′ead?' And one said one thing, and another said another. ²¹Then a spirit came forward and stood before the Lord, saying, 'I will entice him.' ²²And the Lord said to him, 'By

---

22:1–35: 2 Chron 18:1–34. **22:17:** Mt 9:36.

22:1–40 Israel and Judah make peace for the first time since the division of the monarchy (22:44). Nevertheless, it is not a political reunion of the two kingdoms, only a temporary military alliance to reclaim an Israelite city that had fallen under Syrian control (Ramoth-gilead, 22:4).

22:1 three years: Since the covenant was made between Israel and Syria in 20:34.

22:2 Jehoshaphat: Introduced in 15:24 as the fourth king of Judah (ca. 873 to 848 b.c.). An evaluation of his reign is given in 22:41–44.

22:3 Ramoth-gilead: A fortified city in the Transjordan, on the eastern frontier of Israel's territory. It belongs to the tribe of Gad (Josh 20:8) and was in Israelite hands during the reign of Solomon (4:13). Perhaps the Syrian conquest of Ramoth occurred when Ben-hadad I launched a series of military strikes against northern Israel (15:20). **the king of Syria:** Appears to be Ben-hadad II. See note on 15:18.

22:5 Inquire: It was customary to consult the Lord before taking military action (Judg 1:1; 20:18; 1 Sam 23:2, etc.).

22:6 four hundred men: Court prophets who serve as advisors to Ahab. Their reliability as spokesmen for God is doubtful, given the idolatrous climate that prevails in the north (16:31–32). Besides that, they have a weakness for telling the king whatever he wants to hear (implied by 22:8, 13).

22:8 Micaiah: Called in to verify the counsel of the 400 court prophets. Though imprisoned on suspicion of false prophecy (22:26–27), he is the only true prophet among them, for his prediction (22:17) is the only one that will come to pass (22:34–36). Micaiah is not to be confused with the writing prophet Micah (Micah 1:1).

22:10 threshing floor: A spacious outdoor platform used for processing grain during the harvest season. It could also function as a place of public assembly. **Samaria:** Capital of the Northern Kingdom (16:29).

22:11 horns of iron: Used to dramatize the (false) prediction that Israel will plough the Syrians out of Ramoth-gilead like a strong bull (Deut 33:17).

22:14 As the Lord lives: An oath formula.

22:15 Go up and triumph: Intended sarcastically. Ahab quickly realizes he is being mocked (22:16).

22:17 no shepherd: Ahab will be slain in battle, and the warriors of Israel will scatter in defeat (22:35–36). Kings and other leaders are often described as shepherds in the Bible (Num 27:16–17; 2 Sam 5:2; Ezek 34:23–24; Mt 25:32–34).

22:19–23 A vision of Yahweh enthroned in glory and presiding over an assembly of angels in heaven (Ps 89:5–7; Is 6:1–2). Access to the divine council is the privilege of a true prophet, who is allowed to listen in on its deliberations and decisions (Jer 23:18). Micaiah's vision reveals that Ahab's prophets are deceived in accord with God's will: the lying spirit is permitted to act so as to bring the Lord's judgment on the king by sending him to his death.

what means?' And he said, 'I will go forth, and will be a lying spirit in the mouth of all his prophets.' And he said, 'You are to entice him, and you shall succeed; go forth and do so.' ²³Now therefore behold, the LORD has put a lying spirit in the mouth of all these your prophets; the LORD has spoken evil concerning you."

24 Then Zedeki'ah the son of Chena'anah came near and struck Micai'ah on the cheek, and said, "How did the Spirit of the LORD go from me to speak to you?" ²⁵And Micai'ah said, "Behold, you shall see on that day when you go into an inner chamber to hide yourself." ²⁶And the king of Israel said, "Seize Micai'ah, and take him back to A'mon the governor of the city and to Jo'ash the king's son; ²⁷and say, 'Thus says the king, "Put this fellow in prison, and feed him with scant fare of bread and water, until I come in peace."'" ²⁸And Micai'ah said, "If you return in peace, the LORD has not spoken by me." And he said, "Hear, all you peoples!"

Defeat and Death of Ahab

29 So the king of Israel and Jehosh'aphat the king of Judah went up to Ra'moth-gil'ead. ³⁰And the king of Israel said to Jehosh'aphat, "I will disguise myself and go into battle, but you wear your robes." And the king of Israel disguised himself and went into battle. ³¹Now the king of Syria had commanded the thirty-two captains of his chariots, "Fight with neither small nor great, but only with the king of Israel." ³²And when the captains of the chariots saw Jehosh'aphat, they said, "It is surely the king of Israel." So they turned to fight against him; and Jehoshaphat cried out. ³³And when the captains of the chariots saw that it was not the king of Israel, they turned back from pursuing him. ³⁴But a certain man drew his bow by chance, and struck the king of Israel between the scale armor and the breastplate; therefore he said to the driver of his chariot, "Turn about, and carry me out of the battle, for I am wounded." ³⁵And the battle grew hot that day, and the king was propped up in his chariot facing the Syrians, until at evening

he died; and the blood of the wound flowed into the bottom of the chariot. ³⁶And about sunset a cry went through the army, "Every man to his city, and every man to his country!"

37 So the king died, and was brought to Samar'ia; and they buried the king in Samaria. ³⁸And they washed the chariot by the pool of Samar'ia, and the dogs licked up his blood, and the harlots washed themselves in it, according to the word of the LORD which he had spoken. ³⁹Now the rest of the acts of A'hab, and all that he did, and the ivory house which he built, and all the cities that he built, are they not written in the Book of the Chronicles of the Kings of Israel? ⁴⁰So A'hab slept with his fathers; and Ahazi'ah his son reigned in his stead.

Jehoshaphat Reigns over Judah

41 Jehosh'aphat the son of Asa began to reign over Judah in the fourth year of A'hab king of Israel. ⁴²Jehosh'aphat was thirty-five years old when he began to reign, and he reigned twenty-five years in Jerusalem. His mother's name was Azu'bah the daughter of Shilhi. ⁴³He walked in all the way of Asa his father; he did not turn aside from it, doing what was right in the sight of the LORD; yet the high places were not taken away, and the people still sacrificed and burned incense on the high places. ⁴⁴Jehosh'aphat also made peace with the king of Israel.

45 Now the rest of the acts of Jehosh'aphat, and his might that he showed, and how he warred, are they not written in the Book of the Chronicles of the Kings of Judah? ⁴⁶And the remnant of the male cult prostitutes who remained in the days of his father Asa, he exterminated from the land.

47 There was no king in E'dom; a deputy was king. ⁴⁸Jehosh'aphat made ships of Tar'shish to go to O'phir for gold; but they did not go, for the ships were wrecked at E'zion-ge'ber. ⁴⁹Then Ahazi'ah the son of A'hab said to Jehosh'aphat, "Let my servants go with your servants in the ships," but Jehoshaphat was not willing. ⁵⁰And Jehosh'aphat slept with his fathers, and was buried with his fathers in the city

---

22:41–43: 2 Chron 20:31–33. **22:48, 49:** 2 Chron 20:35–37.

22:27 in prison: The prophet is detained until his prediction can be tested at the battle for Ramoth-gilead (cf. Deut 18:21–22).

22:34 struck the king: Ahab is pierced in the abdomen with an arrow shot randomly or inadvertently. It only appears to be an accident, for the Lord was guiding shaft and point to the target of his judgment.

22:38 licked up his blood: Fulfills the gruesome prophecy of Elijah (21:19). **the harlots washed:** Meaning obscure.

22:39 Book of the Chronicles: See note on 14:19.

22:40 Ahaziah: The eighth king of Israel and the third of the Omride dynasty (ca. 853 to 852 B.C.). Scripture judges him harshly for embracing the evil and idolatry of his parents, Ahab and Jezebel (22:52–53). The end of his reign is related in 2 Kings 1:1–18.

22:41–50 Jehoshaphat receives mixed reviews of his long reign over Judah (ca. 873 to 848 B.C.). To his credit, he was mainly a righteous king who worked to rid the Southern Kingdom of abominations such as cultic prostitution (22:46). Even so, worship at illegitimate shrines continued unabated on his watch (22:43).

22:42 Azubah: Queen mother of the kingdom of Judah.

22:45 Book of the Chronicles: See note on 14:19.

22:46 cult prostitutes: Outlawed by Deuteronomy (Deut 23:17).

22:47 Edom: South of the Dead Sea.

22:48 ships of Tarshish: Merchant vessels. Jehoshaphat tries but fails to reestablish the lucrative trading ventures for which Solomon was so famous (9:26–28; 10:22). See note on 10:22. **Ezion-geber:** A shipping port at the northern tip of the Gulf of Aqaba (an inlet of the Red Sea).

of David his father; and Jeho'ram his son reigned in his stead.

Ahaziah Reigns over Israel

51 Ahazi'ah the son of A'hab began to reign over Israel in Samar'ia in the seventeenth year of Jehosh'aphat king of Judah, and he reigned two years over Israel. [52]He did what was evil in the sight of the LORD, and walked in the way of his father, and in the way of his mother, and in the way of Jerobo'am the son of Ne'bat, who made Israel to sin. [53]He served Ba'al and worshiped him, and provoked the LORD, the God of Israel, to anger in every way that his father had done.

22:50: 2 Chron 21:1.

22:50 Jehoram: The fifth king of Judah (ca. 848 to 841 B.C.).
22:52 his mother: Jezebel, the wife of Ahab. See note on 16:31.

22:53 Baal: The storm and fertility god of Canaanite religion (16:31–32).

Study Questions
1 Kings

Chapter 1

For understanding
1. **1:5.** Who is Adonijah? Why is he widely expected to rule as his father's successor? How does Adonijah follow in the footsteps of Absalom in his attempt to gain power? For what does the prominence of these parallels hint that Adonijah is destined?
2. **1:34.** What does anointing involve for the candidate, and who are anointed? Of what is it a sign? Aside from this official rite of installation, in what other contexts does the Bible speak about anointing?
3. **1:37.** To what kind of relationship does Benaiah's statement to David point? What is its foundation? Where else is the same language used?
4. **1:38-40.** How is Solomon's accession to the throne made known to the public? How does the event foreshadow Jesus' entry into Jerusalem on Palm Sunday?

For application
1. **1:5.** What has been your highest ambition in life? How much of your mental and spiritual resources have you devoted to it? What have you done in practice to achieve it? How successful have your efforts been?
2. **1:6-8.** What effect have your ambitions had on your family? For example, how have your desires and plans for yourself served either to unite your relatives behind you or to divide them in opposition to you?
3. **1:11-27.** Have you ever had to remind an important person in your life of a significant but unfulfilled promise made to you? How did you try to persuade this person to act on the promise?
4. **1:41-53.** Has someone else's success ever impeded or thwarted your own? How did you choose to respond? How genuine was your response?

Chapter 2

For understanding
1. **2:4.** What is Yahweh's oath to David? In what respect is the Davidic covenant conditional?
2. **2:5.** What relation is Joab to David? How does Joab on several occasions defy the wishes of the king? How do these assassinations dishonor David?
3. **2:17.** What do Adonijah's words to Bathsheba indicate about the queen mother? To what does his request (that Solomon give him Abishag) really amount? In Israel, as in the Near East, what did the passing of the harem of the king to his successor normally mean? What does Solomon detect behind Adonijah's simple request?
4. **Essay: The Queen Mother.** Who is the figure known in Hebrew as the *gebirah*, or "Great Lady"? In Israel, who held the office of queenship, and what were some reasons for that practice? What five considerations give shape and substance to our knowledge of this ancient institution, specifically in the Davidic monarchy? How does the role of the queen mother in the Old Testament lay the groundwork for Mary's role in the New Testament?
5. **2:26.** Who is Abiathar? Why, since he has remained loyal to David for many years, does Solomon strip him of priestly privileges and banish him from Jerusalem? Theologically, of what oracle are these actions a fulfillment?

For application
1. **2:1-4.** Why does David encourage Solomon to be faithful to the covenant? What result does he think Solomon will achieve by doing so? Why should you remain a committed Catholic? What result will occur if you do?
2. **2:5-9.** David wants Solomon to reward those who supported him (Barzillai) but punish those who compromised his reputation (Joab) or who cursed him (Shimei). Why do you think he commissions Solomon to do this rather than doing it himself? Why would you allow a condition to exist without intervening but have someone else deal with it for you later?
3. **2:19-20.** Read the essay "The Queen Mother". How does it influence your relation with Mary, Mother of Jesus? For example, how do you envision Mary: as a young woman, as a maternal personality, as an intercessor on your behalf, as a queen who can command obedience? How does this view affect your relationship with her?

Chapter 3

For understanding
1. **3:2.** What are the "high places", and what is Israel commanded to do with them? What actually happens to them? For what does this compromise over the strict demands of the Mosaic Law pave the way?
2. **3:4.** What is located at Gibeon at this time? What is the hyperbolic phrase "a thousand burnt offerings" meant to heighten in the reader? If this hyperbole does not mean that the details of the story are legendary, what does it mean? What are some other possible instances of hyperbole?
3. **3:9.** What does the expression "an understanding mind" mean literally? What kind of wisdom does Solomon desire?
4. **3:16-28.** What does Solomon's brilliant solution to the case of the two harlots confirm? According to St. Augustine, what do the dead child and the living child signify in relation to the Church?
5. **Word Study: Wisdom (3:28).** In reference to men, what does *ḥokmah* mean? In the moral and spiritual realm, what is wisdom? To whom does wisdom ultimately belong, and how do men come to possess it? Among those endowed with wisdom in the OT, how does Solomon demonstrate wisdom? How do Moses and Solomon compare in the ways they impart wisdom?

Study Questions

For application
1. **3:7.** Have you ever succeeded someone else in a job carrying responsibility? If so, did you feel any unease about your ability to handle it? What did you do to reassure yourself? What part did prayer play in your efforts toward self-confidence?
2. **3:9.** What kind of good and evil do you think Solomon has in mind in his prayer to God? If you are in a position of responsibility, what kinds of good and evil would be important to you?
3. **3:12–14.** Why is the word "if" in v. 14 important? Why would God impose a condition like this on a promise he makes? How do such if-conditions apply to you in the practice of your faith?
4. **3:12.** In Solomon's dream, God says, "Behold, I give you a wise and discerning mind." How will Solomon later come to know that he has such a mind? How does one acquire the sort of wisdom Solomon has in mind?

Chapter 4

For understanding
1. **4:6.** In what capacity does Ahishar seem to have served the king, and what would it make him in Solomon's kingdom? For what purpose is forced labor used?
2. **4:7–19.** How does Solomon organize his kingdom? Why do these districts not align with the tribal territories delineated in Josh 12–21? Who is prefigured, according to St. Ephrem, by the 12 district officers appointed by Solomon?
3. **4:21.** Over what does Solomon sit enthroned? Where does its geographical reach extend, and what does it represent?
4. **4:32.** In which ways does Solomon manifest his wisdom? To which biblical writings is his name attached?

For application
1. **4:1–19.** What do you know about the organization of the company for which you work, of the state and nation in which you live, or of the Church to which you belong? As a Christian, what do you think you should know about these things? What are some of the advantages of having a working knowledge of these organizations and some of the disadvantages of being ignorant about them?
2. **4:20–21.** What do you know of Catholic Church history, of the spread of Christianity, of the persecutions it has endured, of the growth and decline of Christendom, and the trials and triumphs arising from the Reformation and the Enlightenment? How can such knowledge be of service to you as you consider the state of the Church today and her prospects for the future? How might it influence your prayer?
3. **4:26.** Read the note for this verse. Why would Solomon be concerned about building up his military during peacetime? What does the Church teach about the accumulation of arms and their production and sale (see CCC 2315–17)?
4. **4:34.** To whom do people of our generation come to learn wisdom? If not to individuals or personalities, what are our sources of wisdom? How is wisdom different from scientific or technological knowledge?

Chapter 5

For understanding
1. **5:1.** Who is Hiram? What does the author indicate about Hiram in saying that he loved David?
2. **5:3.** What made David unsuitable for the task of building the Temple? What does the expression "under the soles of his feet" recall?
3. **5:6.** What makes the cedars of Lebanon ideally suited for monumental construction projects? What are the peoples of Sidon known for being? According to St. Thomas Aquinas, what do the Tabernacle of Moses and the Temple of Solomon signify, and why?
4. **5:13–16.** Whom is Solomon conscripting as laborers? What did the prophet Samuel forewarn would happen if Israel set a king over itself? What does Solomon's levy of state workers cause to build up?

For application
1. **5:5.** Solomon proposes to do something great for God. What is the greatest thing you can do for him? How would you discern whether your desire is what *he* wants you to do for him?
2. **5:10–12.** What are some of the social benefits of working with others to complete a project? What role might such work play in building up personal friendships?
3. **5:13–18.** When you are asked to participate in a diocesan fundraising campaign (say, to build or repair a church or support ongoing diocesan projects), how do you respond? What is your attitude toward the money you are asked to contribute toward the financial support of the Church?

Chapter 6

For understanding
1. **6:1–38.** Where is Solomon's Temple built? On what are its main features modeled? What are its architectural characteristics? Historically, how long does Solomon's Temple stand? Archaeologically, what remains of it, and why is the lack of artifactual confirmation not a sufficient reason to question its historical existence?
2. **6:1.** What considerations make the "four hundred and eightieth year" an important benchmark of biblical chronology? How does it give a fixed point of reference for dating the early history of Israel? How do the perceived conflicts between the biblical timeline and archaeological findings affect scholars' view of the period between the Exodus and the building of the Temple? To what does the month of Ziv correspond in our calendar?
3. **6:7.** Why are building blocks prefabricated at the quarry? According to St. Thomas Aquinas, what do the Tabernacle and the Temple signify about life?
4. **6:23.** What are the two cherubim? In the view of most scholars, what do they resemble? What is their function here?
5. **6:38.** What is the "month of Bul"? What is the time span of the Temple's construction? What is the importance of the seven time units mentioned here?

For application

1. **6:11–13.** How would you paraphrase God's promise to Solomon so that it applies to your own life? What does it mean for God to "dwell" with you? Compare this promise with Jn 15:4–11.
2. **6:14–22.** Note the size and ornamentation of the main Temple building ("the house"), and compare that with a major basilica such as St. Peter's in Rome. What spiritual values are size and ornamentation meant to symbolize? For example, what might the great height of the ceiling be intended to communicate?
3. **6:23–28.** Read the note for v. 23. What is the function of icons and images of angelic figures in Christian art? How are angels usually represented in Christian art? What do such representations communicate to you?
4. **6:31–35.** What is the natural function of a door? Spiritually speaking, what may a door signify? How may the human heart be compared to a door?

Chapter 7

For understanding

1. **7:1–12.** What does Solomon construct directly south of the Temple, and what public and private buildings does it include? In terms of elevation, what is the relation between the Temple and the royal buildings adjacent to it?
2. **7:14.** How are the craftsman Hiram's wisdom, understanding, and skill similar to those of Bezalel in Exodus 31?
3. **7:15.** What are the pillars of bronze, and what does their function appear to be? What are their names, and how might they have been derived? What is the symbolism of these uprights? Why do some scholars call them stylized trees?
4. **7:49.** What are the lampstands? What does each lampstand look like?

For application

1. **7:14.** What is it that you most admire about a skilled craft worker? What virtues must that person have in addition to "wisdom, understanding, and skill" while working? According to the note for this verse, how might such virtues be considered gifts of the Holy Spirit?
2. **7:23–44.** How is the church you attend both furnished and decorated? What are some of the liturgical implements used there? What are some of the symbolic representations shown there, and what are their meanings? What is the purpose of all these furnishings, decorations, implements, and symbols?
3. **7:48–51.** Why is it appropriate for the house of the Lord to be richly furnished, or at least to *look* well furnished? How would you answer someone who thought that it would be better to sell all these furnishings and give the money to the poor?
4. **7:49.** Read the note for this verse. How many different kinds of candles are used in your church? What is their purpose? What is the function of the sanctuary lamp near the tabernacle?

Chapter 8

For understanding

1. **8:1–66.** How does Solomon stage the events of the dedication of the Temple, and how long after its completion? What highlights does the ceremony include?
2. **8:4.** Where did the Ark of the Covenant reside before being brought into the Temple? Where is the tent of meeting at that point? What does storage of the tent inside Solomon's sanctuary indicate?
3. **8:14–26.** What two themes in Solomon's opening address celebrate the fulfillment of God's word?
4. **8:25–53.** What seven petitions does Solomon make to the Lord in his dedication prayer? In several cases, from what is Solomon requesting deliverance?
5. **8:41.** What does Solomon's prayer envision individual Gentiles doing? Theologically, what spirit does the Temple embody? What is Yahweh being asked to do here, and with what result?
6. **8:63.** What part does Solomon play, as his father, David, did? What do his priestly actions include? How is this in stark contrast to King Saul? In what is the difference rooted, and how is Melchizedek involved?

For application

1. **8:2.** According to the note for this verse, the seventh month is the holiest month in the Israelite calendar. What is the holiest time of the Christian calendar? Why do Christians celebrate feasts in a cycle called the "liturgical year"?
2. **8:9.** This verse says that there was "nothing in the ark except the two tables of stone which Moses put there at Horeb, where the Lord made a covenant with the sons of Israel." What do the tabernacles of Catholic churches usually contain? How do those contents reflect the New Covenant that Jesus made with us?
3. **8:27.** What is the response to Solomon's question: Does God dwell on earth, and if so, where? Where is the most fitting place on earth for him to dwell?
4. **8:30–53.** Note how often Solomon asks the Lord to forgive the sins of those who ask for forgiveness. How many requests for God's forgiveness and mercy do we make during a typical celebration of Mass? What is the point of this repetition? How often in your personal prayer do you pray for forgiveness and mercy?

Chapter 9

For understanding

1. **9:4–9.** Of what does the Lord remind Solomon in this second divine encounter? What will faithfulness and apostasy each bring? Theologically, in what sense is the Davidic covenant unconditional and at the same time conditional?
2. **9:11.** Where are the twenty cities that Solomon gives King Hiram of Tyre presumably located? What is unclear about this transaction? How is this gesture taken when compared to Hiram's abundant contributions to Solomon's building projects?

3. **9:15.** To what does the name Millo point? In what two ways do people identify the Millo? What are Hazor and Megiddo and Gezer? What has archaeology revealed about them?
4. **9:28.** Where are possible locations for Ophir? For what was it renowned in biblical times?

For application
1. **9:4-5.** How might the "if" statement in the Lord's renewed promise to Solomon apply to you? As a Christian, to what promises from God do you look forward? What conditions are attached to them?
2. **9:6-9.** Note that the Lord's warning of exile and disaster will fall upon the nation if Solomon or his children engage in idolatry. Why would the consequences not fall upon Solomon personally? What consequences do you personally face when you commit serious sin (e.g., sexual or substance-abuse sins)? What consequences are likely to fall upon your family when you commit them?
3. **9:13.** What point is Hiram making by addressing Solomon as "my brother" in his complaint? If you were in Hiram's position, how would you have spoken? How would 1 Cor 6:1-8 help your relationships with those who cheat, defraud, or simply shortchange you?

Chapter 10

For understanding
1. **10:1.** Where is Sheba, and what kind of empire is it? What may have been the purpose of the queen's historic visit? How is it clear in the prophecies of Isaiah that the visit serves as a paradigm of Israel's hopes for the future? How does the queen's visit figure in the teaching of Jesus?
2. **10:14—11:8.** How do these verses represent a turning point in the Solomon story from both a political and economical viewpoint? Morally, how has Solomon transgressed the three limits placed on kingship by Deuteronomy?
3. **10:14.** If each talent weighs roughly 75 pounds, what does the annual influx of 666 talents equal? What does this figure not include? How does the number 666 appear in the Book of Revelation? How does an allusion to Solomon and his gold and his wisdom seem likely?
4. **10:22.** What are the "ships of Tarshish"? Where is Tarshish?

For application
1. **10:5.** Read the note for this verse about the meaning of "no more spirit". When something "takes your breath away" (for example, a financial windfall or a "golden opportunity" for fame), are you more or less likely to want to engage with it? How willing, at that moment, are you to consider the ethical, financial, legal, or personal implications of engaging with what you admire?
2. **10:14-15.** How concerned are you about your level of income? How comfortable are you with it, how detached or how desirous of more? How close are you to St. Paul's attitude in Phil 4:12?
3. **10:16-22.** How have you decorated your home? What message do you communicate to others about yourself in the way your home is decorated? What message do you *want* to communicate?
4. **10:26-29.** Would you consider yourself a spender or a saver? a giver or a hoarder? an investor or a conserver? a show-man or a recluse? How do the things you give away or collect describe your character? What do you think is the attitude that God wants you to have toward your possessions, and how well do you reflect it?

Chapter 11

For understanding
1. **11:2.** To what prohibition does this verse refer? What is the rationale for this law? How is Solomon the foremost example of this danger?
2. **11:3.** To what do the numbers seven hundred and three hundred refer? How reliable are these numbers? What kind of marriages were these unions presumed to be? Along the path of salvation history, what does polygamy represent in relation to God's original design for marriage and to the Old Testament practice? According to St. Augustine, how did Solomon lose the wisdom he desired?
3. **11:5-7.** Who are the foreign gods venerated by Solomon?
4. **11:30.** Why does the prophet Ahijah tear his cloak into 12 pieces? Why did prophets often perform dramatic and symbolic actions? According to St. Cyprian, why can the people of Christ not be torn apart?
5. **11:36.** What does the lamp signify? On what is its signification grounded?

For application
1. **11:2.** Are there relationships to which you cling, even though you know they are not good for you? Why do you cling to them? What might your persistence in those relationships be doing to your faith?
2. **11:8.** According to CCC 1633-37, what is the Catholic Church's teaching on mixed marriages and marriages involving "disparity of cult"? Under what circumstances may a Catholic enter into such marriages? What is the danger for the Catholic partner in such marriages?
3. **11:9-13.** What do you think might have happened if Solomon had listened to the Lord's verdict and repented? What might repentance have led him to do? What does Mt 16:25-26 say to you in this context?
4. **11:36.** Read the note for this verse. According to Rev 1:20, what do the lampstands of the seven churches signify? What happens if a lampstand is removed (see Rev 2-3)? How might these images apply to the Church today?

Chapter 12

For understanding
1. **12:1-33.** What do these verses describe? What do the northern tribes of Israel do? Historically, how long will the North-ern Kingdom of Israel survive, and how long will the Southern Kingdom of Judah last?

2. **12:15.** Though the division of Solomon's kingdom is a historical disaster, with what is it in accord? How is Yahweh the helmsman of history? What does the remark by the author of Kings indicate about how God acts in these events?
3. **12:25–33.** What does Jeroboam devise, and by what are his efforts guided? What rival religious elements does he establish? Ironically, to what secular philosophy does Jeroboam bow?
4. **12:28–33.** Whose apostasy does Jeroboam reenact? What are seven parallels between both men? What is the point of the parallels?
5. **Chart: Kings of the Divided Monarchy.** What factors make the chronology of the kings of Israel and Judah difficult to reconstruct? What is clear about the two kingdoms from the data in the chart?

For application
1. **12:7.** In your experience, what makes someone a good leader? How does an attitude of service make one a good leader?
2. **12:8–15.** What kind of people should a good leader recruit as advisors? What often happens when a leader recruits advisors who tell him only what he wants to hear? What are some of the moral issues facing advisors who do that?
3. **12:16.** How justified do you think Israel was to break away from the authority of its king and establish its own kingdom? On what grounds? How would you evaluate the conduct of the Israelite rebels in the light of St. Paul's command in Rom 13:1–3?
4. **12:26–33.** What goal does Jeroboam have in mind by creating places of worship and celebratory feasts? Can you think of any examples from the history of the last hundred years or so where leaders have employed the same strategy?

Chapter 13

For understanding
1. **13:1.** What is a "man of God"? As the following account shows, what is a prophet also responsible for doing?
2. **13:6.** How is the divine authority of the prophet revealed? What does restoring the withered hand of Jeroboam anticipate?
3. **13:19.** How does the prophet fare in his test of obedience? Having delivered the word of God faithfully, in what way is he mistaken?
4. **13:34.** How many kings does the house of Jeroboam produce?

For application
1. **13:7–9.** In this story, the "man of God" utters a prophecy that is validated by two miracles. In addition to the explanation given in the note for v. 8, why else might it have been imprudent for him to accept the king's invitation and promised reward afterward? What trust would you accord the invitation of a mobster you had criticized?
2. **13:18–19.** What credence should you give a theologian who cites biblical texts and other theologians' opinions for a belief that appears to contradict what you have been taught? How should you form your conscience in such matters?
3. **13:30–32.** Even though he ensnared the "man of God" through a lie and caused his death, the prophet from Bethel honors him in burial. Why? What honor do you owe to an authority figure whose beliefs or practices you oppose?
4. **13:33.** When people continue a pattern of wrongdoing even though they know they risk divine judgment, what motivates them to persist in it? What hinders them from turning away from it?

Chapter 14

For understanding
1. **14:7–16.** According to Ahijah's oracle of judgment, what three forms will the Lord's judgment take? Why will all of this take place?
2. **14:15.** What kind of language are the words "root up" and "scatter"? What does the prophet foresee, and how far in the future is it? What are Asherim?
3. **14:19.** What are the books of the Chronicles? What did scribes record in them?
4. **14:21.** Who is Rehoboam? What facts are noted in the standardized formula used for introducing kings of Judah?
5. **14:23–24.** What activities does the degeneration of religious practice in Judah involve? What does Deuteronomy call for with respect to them?

For application
1. **14:12–13.** Have you lost a child in infancy, or do you know anyone who has? How difficult was the grieving process? Although the death of a child is grievous, why might there be cause for comfort in it?
2. **14:16.** Does God ever give up on you because of your sin? What kind of sin can God not forgive (see CCC 1864)? Even though God forgives the most heinous of sins, why does he still allow the consequences of those sins to play out?
3. **14:22.** This verse indicates a cultural shift away from right religion to its corruption. How do such changes happen over a relatively short period of time? For example, how does the culture reflect the attitudes of its leaders, and how does it in turn shape their attitudes?
4. **14:25–26.** Suppose that an enemy were to raid Vatican City and burn or take away all the treasures in the Vatican library. What do you think would be the long-term effect on the Church's life? Of what do the riches of the Church consist?

Chapter 15

For understanding
1. **15:3.** For what is the "heart of David" the standard? What is the point about David? For the author of Kings, what is it that made David the model king by which his successors are judged?
2. **15:13.** Who is Asherah? What is the brook Kidron? What does Asa's burning of the cult objects at this location anticipate?
3. **15:17.** Where is Ramah? Why does Baasha think there is an advantage to fortifying Ramah? What does the effort to block southbound traffic imply?

4. **15:18.** Who is Ben-hadad? What does his name declare him to be? What is he being bribed to do here? Judging from 1 and 2 Kings, what does the name Ben-hadad appear to be? What is clear and what is questionable about others named Ben-hadad in 1 and 2 Kings?

5. **15:26.** What does the expression "in the way of his father" mean in reference to Nadab? Just as the southern kings of Judah are measured against David's cultic fidelity, how are the northern kings of Israel judged? What is the author's chief interest in this regard?

For application

1. **15:3.** Read the note for this verse. What is the standard by which we should measure our bishops? What about ourselves?

2. **15:13.** Jesus says that he did not come to bring peace, but a sword (Mt 10:34). What does he mean? Has your commitment to his gospel ever caused division in your family? Why might some go so far as to disown their parents (or be disowned by them)?

3. **15:27-29.** Scripture speaks of how the iniquity of the fathers is visited on their children (see Ex 34:7). How do you see that happening in our culture? What are some of the reasons it happens, even though the children are innocent of their ancestors' crimes? How can such a cycle be broken?

Chapter 16

For understanding

1. **Word Study: Over the Household (16:9).** For whom does the expression "one who is over the house" serve as a title? How does it apply to Joseph in the house of Pharaoh or to the monarchies of ancient Israel? What roles do prime ministers play in the Northern Kingdom of Israel and the Southern Kingdom of Judah? How may the office possibly have developed over time, and how can an instance of this development be seen in Isaiah? What has archaeology turned up? In the NT, what role does Jesus assign Peter?

2. **16:16.** Who is Omri? What is he like? With what is his memory mainly linked? How is Omri referenced outside the Bible?

3. **16:28.** Who is Ahab? By what are memories of Ahab scarred? How does Scripture judge him? What about him is visible in the end? How is Ahab mentioned outside the Bible?

4. **16:31.** Who is Jezebel, and of what does she make herself the official sponsor? Of whom is she likewise the official enemy, and how is that evidenced? What is one of the main reasons for her downfall? Who is Ethbaal, and what does his daughter's marriage to Ahab suggest? What is Baal, and what do his devotees believe about him?

For application

1. **16:4.** What makes the prophet Jehu's prediction so horrifying to readers of Scripture? Why in most cultures are proper burials so important? How do you wish to be buried, and why?

2. **16:9.** What is Elah doing in this verse, and what does the description of his behavior suggest about his character? What are some of the warning signs that consumption of alcohol has become a problem? What kinds of problems does alcoholism cause in the alcoholic person, in families, and in society at large?

3. **16:31.** Read this verse carefully. Looking back at chap. 12, what were the sins of Jeroboam? Why does the author of Kings imply that Ahab's sins are worse? According to CCC 1868-69, how does one's personal sin make accomplices of others? How does that apply to a country such as ours?

Chapter 17

For understanding

1. **17:1—21:29.** With what do these chapters deal? With what is the narrative punctuated? Where do the high points of his ministry occur? What do many scholars believe about these prophetic traditions? Of whom is Elijah a type? How do his life and ministry anticipate that of Jesus?

2. **17:1.** What does the name Elijah mean? Where is Tishbe? How do drought and famine weigh heavily on Israel? What will the drought show about Baal?

3. **17:14.** What does Elijah promise the widow? According to St. Augustine, why did the miracle happen, and of what was it a sign?

4. **17:21.** What kind of miracle does Elijah perform? What features does it combine? Who else performs nearly identical miracles?

For application

1. **17:13-14.** According to Elijah's instruction to the widow of Zarephath about providing food for him, when was she supposed to feed herself and her child? What kind of faith did that demand of her? How does the Lord test your own faith?

2. **17:18.** Although the widow knew that her son died of an illness, why did she blame the prophet for his death? Why do people sometimes blame God for diseases or deaths in the family? What is their image of God?

3. **17:20.** Is it ever appropriate to get angry with God? If not, why do so many of the prophets and psalms express displeasure with him (e.g., Jer 15:10-18; Ps 89:38-46)? Why does anger at God not necessarily indicate a lack of faith? Ultimately, what should our attitude toward God be in the face of trouble?

Chapter 18

For understanding

1. **18:20-40.** Against whom does Elijah face off? What is the contest staged to determine? Why does Elijah appear to be outmatched and disadvantaged? In what respect is the standoff successful? How does St. Ambrose reason from this event that the words of Christ have power to change the Eucharistic elements?

2. **18:21.** What does Elijah think about Israel's religious convictions? What does he urge the people to do about them?

3. **18:24.** What is Elijah's challenge for Baal as the lord of the storm? What has been known about Yahweh?

4. **18:42.** What happens when Elijah humbles himself before the Lord and prays? According to James, why is the prayer of Elijah effective? What lesson is to be learned from this?

For application
1. **18:21.** What is a "divided heart"? Why is it important not to pray with one (see Sir 2:12, Jas 1:7–8)? What sort of prayer do you think God is most likely to answer?
2. **18:28.** Read the note for this verse. Many saints have beaten themselves with whips and chains to the point of drawing blood. What are some of the differences between their behavior and that of the priests of Baal? Why are the saints not violating Lev 19:28? What forms of self-discipline or mortification does the Church recommend for most people?
3. **18:37–39.** Jesus promises that signs and wonders will confirm the message of the gospel (Mk 16:15–18). What signs and wonders have you seen that confirm his promise? If none, for what kinds of signs and wonders are you looking?
4. **18:42.** Bodily positions are often helpful in prayer. What is the significance of prostrating oneself in prayer, of kneeling, of placing the palms of the hands together, or of praying with the arms in the form of a cross? What posture do you customarily take when you pray?

Chapter 19

For understanding
1. **19:8–18.** In his travel to Mt. Horeb, what parallels indicate that Elijah is following in the steps of Moses? How does the outlook of Deuteronomy shape the author's portrayal of Elijah?
2. **Word Study: Voice (19:12).** What kinds of sounds are indicated by the Hebrew term *qol*? To what voices can it refer? While the voice that Elijah encounters on Horeb is somewhat difficult to interpret, on what adjectives is the traditional understanding based? What is another possible interpretation? How would this latter reading enhance the parallelism between Elijah and Moses?
3. **19:18.** Why is the number seven thousand a surprise to Elijah? How does Paul see this scenario played out in his own day? What does the expression "has not kissed him" mean?
4. **19:19–21.** As an apprentice-in-training to Elijah, what is Elisha doing in bidding farewell to his parents and boiling his oxen and burning their yokes? What is Jesus' purpose in alluding to the calling of Elisha?

For application
1. **19:3.** After his miraculous victory over the priests of Baal, why should Elijah have been afraid of Jezebel and run for his life? What could cause his loss of confidence in God? If you have ever had a similar experience of great success followed by fear of failure, what was behind the latter?
2. **19:4–5.** What is the closest you have come to giving up on God or wishing no longer to live? What happened to renew your confidence in both?
3. **19:8.** Why would Elijah choose Horeb for his destination; in other words, what would the significance of Horeb have been for him? How do you seek to renew your faith when it seems to flag (e.g., through pilgrimages, retreats, conferences, books)?
4. **19:11–13.** How do you discern the voice of the Lord in your life? What characteristics convince you that it is the Lord you are hearing?
5. **19:19–21.** Read the note for these verses. Why would Elijah object to Elisha's going to "kiss my father and my mother", and why would Jesus raise a similar objection to burying one's parents? How long might such delays take? How prompt should your response to God's invitation be?

Chapter 20

For understanding
1. **20:1.** Who is the Ben-hadad referred to here? Without known provocation, what does he do, and how do his aggressive moves against the Northern Kingdom end?
2. **20:23.** In the polytheistic thinking of the ancient world, what influence do local gods have? What do the Syrians assume, and as what does their crushing defeat serve? What tactical consideration is behind getting Israel out of the highlands onto the plain?
3. **20:32.** How does Ben-hadad approach Ahab, and how does Ahab treat him? Why do some consider this an astute political move on Ahab's part?
4. **20:35.** Who are the sons of the prophets? Why does the prophet want someone to strike him?

For application
1. **20:11.** Read the note for this verse. How often do you tend to "count your chickens before they hatch"? Has a "sure thing" ever failed to materialize in your life? Why is trust in God's providence important even when good prospects seem certain?
2. **20:16.** Why do you think the writer of Kings adds the note about Ben-hadad's "drinking himself drunk" at this point in the narrative? How does drink or other substance abuse make a person overconfident?
3. **20:43.** How do you respond when someone corrects you for a lapse of judgment? If you made a much-desired arrangement, and someone warned that it was wrong or sinful, what would you tend to do? How would you respond if that "someone" were God, either directly or through his word?

Chapter 21

For understanding
1. **21:1–16.** With what do these verses deal, and how is Ahab's treachery with Naboth parallel to David's with Bathsheba?
2. **21:3.** In ancient Israel, to whom did ancestral lands belong? What did that mean for the sale of land to one outside one's tribe?

3. **21:7.** What does Jezebel's rhetorical question imply? What model of kingship does Jezebel know? How does the Israelite model of kingship contrast with it?
4. **21:14.** Why would the heirs to Naboth's estate have to be wiped out?

For application
1. **21:1-4.** What is "lust of the eyes", and what does it have to do with the tenth commandment (see 1 Jn 2:16; CCC 2514)? How does the virtue of purity help to overcome such lusts?
2. **21:11-14.** How guilty of Jezebel's sin are the elders who do as she instructs? Moral theology distinguishes between direct and indirect cooperation in evil (see CCC 1868). How do you understand the difference? What examples can you think of for each?
3. **21:20b.** According to Elijah, to what (or whom) did Ahab sell himself to do evil? When one decides to sin, how is that decision like a choice to sell oneself?

Chapter 22

For understanding
1. **22:3.** Where is Ramoth-gilead? To which tribe does it belong? When might the Syrian conquest of Ramoth have occurred? Who appears to be the king of Syria?
2. **22:8.** Though imprisoned on suspicion of false prophecy, what makes Micaiah the only true prophet among the 400 others? With whom is Micaiah not to be confused?
3. **22:19-23.** Of what does Micaiah describe a vision? Who has access to the divine council? What does Micaiah's vision reveal is happening to Ahab's prophets, and why?
4. **22:41-50.** What kinds of reviews does Jehoshaphat receive in 1 Kings? What is to his credit, and what to his blame?

For application
1. **22:7.** The note for v. 6 suggests why the reliability of the 400 prophets was doubtful, but why do you think *Jehoshaphat* doubted it? What might be some of the warning signs that nearly universal agitation in favor of a course of action should be questioned?
2. **22:13-14.** Of the four cardinal virtues, which does Micaiah demonstrate in resisting pressure to conform? What are some examples of pressures that our society places on Christians to conform to its demands? What should Christians do in response?
3. **22:19-23.** Who is the lying spirit that Micaiah envisions? How is he active in the world today?
4. **22:28.** St. Paul urges Christians not to despise prophecy but to test it. What standard of evaluation is Micaiah using? How else should prophecy be tested?

INTRODUCTION TO THE SECOND BOOK OF THE KINGS

Author and Date The author of 2 Kings is unnamed and unknown. Early rabbinic scholars identified him with the prophet Jeremiah, who lived at the end of the monarchical period, but most modern scholars are disinclined to accept this tradition. The anonymous compiler was a historian and theologian who drew upon several ancient sources in constructing his narrative. Two of his sources are identified as chronicles documenting the reigns of kings in Israel and Judah (1:18; 8:23; 10:34; 13:12; 15:6, etc.). Beyond this, he seems to have relied on written accounts concerning the prophets Elijah and Elisha, the latter of whom features prominently in 2 Kings 2–13. Some scholars also speak of an Isaianic source, based on the remarkable similarity in wording and sequence between 2 Kings 18:13–20:19 and Isaiah 36–39. Much of modern scholarship views the Books of the Kings as the product of a school of theologians called the "Deuteronomists". The complete narrative of Israel's life in the land of Canaan, stretching from Joshua to 2 Kings (minus Ruth), is attributed to this school.

Despite uncertainties of attribution, there is little doubt that the canonical form of 2 Kings can be dated around 550 B.C. Its last recorded event is the release of King Jehoiachin from prison in Babylon in 560 B.C., and the historian shows no awareness of the end of the exile in 538 B.C. For fuller discussion, see introduction to 1 Kings: *Author and Date*.

Title The Books of the Kings were originally written as a single literary work called "Kings", in Hebrew *melakim*. In the second or third century B.C., the translators of the Greek Septuagint divided the text into two books and grouped them together with the Books of Samuel under the heading "Kingdoms". Second Kings was thus known in Greek as *Basileiōn Delta*, "Fourth Kingdoms". Saint Jerome, in producing the Latin Vulgate, followed the Greek LXX tradition by dividing the work into two books but followed Hebrew tradition by supplying the title *Libri Regum*, "Books of the Kings".

Place in the Canon Second Kings stands immediately after 1 Kings because the two works originally formed a single volume devoted to the history of the Israelite monarchy. In the Jewish canon, it is the last of the "Former Prophets", a sequence of books extending from Joshua to 2 Kings (minus Ruth) that tells the story of Israel from a prophetic perspective, directly correlating its historical fortunes with its waxing and waning commitment to the Lord of the covenant. Christian tradition likewise accepts the theological outlook of 2 Kings but classifies it among the "Historical Books" of the Bible.

Structure Second Kings may be read as a story in three parts. **(1)** Chapters 1–13 follow the ministry of the prophet Elisha and contemporary events in the twin kingdoms of Israel and Judah. **(2)** Chapters 14–17 detail the decline and fall of the Northern Kingdom of Israel to Assyrian conquest in the eighth century B.C. **(3)** Chapters 18–25 recount the decline and fall of the Southern Kingdom of Judah to Babylonian conquest in the sixth century B.C.

Genre and Purpose Second Kings is a work of theological history. It exhibits an interest in chronology and basic archival information in relation to the kings of Israel and Judah. At the same time, its main objective is to show that Israel's expulsion from the Promised Land was a direct consequence of its prolonged disobedience to God and his covenant (see 17:7–23; 22:15–20). For fuller discussion, see introduction to 1 Kings: *Genre and Purpose*.

Content and Themes Second Kings brings the tragic story of the divided monarchy to its tragic end, providing a detailed account of Israel's downward slide toward national ruin and exile. Just as prosperity is a blessing that comes with obedience to the Lord's covenant (Deut 28:1–14), so adversity is a curse that comes with disobedience to the covenant (Deut 28:15–68). Unfortunately, Israel experienced more of the latter than the former for most of the monarchical period.

Careful analysis indicates that the overriding concern of 2 Kings is Deuteronomy's prescription for correct worship. Nearly everything depends on whether the twin kingdoms of Israel and Judah worship the right God (Yahweh) in the right way (according to the Mosaic covenant) and at the right place (the Jerusalem Temple). Failure to do so is idolatry, and idolatry is equivalent to spiritual adultery against Yahweh. This poses a threat to Israel's well-being far more serious than incompetent leadership or failed government policies.

Second Kings places most of the responsibility for proper worship on the shoulders of the kings of Israel and Judah. The few kings who are given a high approval rating in the book are those who make aggressive attempts to rid their kingdoms of idols and idol shrines, most notably Jehu of Israel (10:18–31), Hezekiah of Judah (18:1–6), and Josiah of Judah (23:1–25). Conversely, the kings most stridently criticized in the book are those who sponsor idol cults and plunge Israel into the darkness of pagan religion. This is most visible in Manasseh of Judah (21:1–9) and his son Amon (21:19–22).

In the end, despite intermittent reforms, the kingdoms of Israel and Judah fail the test of covenant faithfulness and are forced to reap the consequences. Disaster comes first to the Northern Kingdom with the Assyrian conquest of Israel and the fall of Samaria in 722 B.C. (17:1–23). The kingdom of Judah survives this catastrophe, but afterward the hammer of Babylon smashes down on the south, and Jerusalem and its Temple are reduced to ruins in 586 B.C. (25:1–21). Both tragedies, which devastate the homeland of Palestine and force mass numbers of the covenant people into exile, are divine punishments for sin—curses of the covenant activated for brazen rebellion against the Lord. Far from signaling Yahweh's weakness or lack of commitment to Israel, these foreign conquests show that the God of Israel is holy (intolerant of sin), powerful (determines the fate of entire kingdoms), and faithful to the covenant (enforcing its sanctions on disobedience). So, too, the exile of Israel is a sign of Yahweh's mercy: instead of annihilating his people, he chooses to humble and purify them through captivity. The hope is that Israel will "wake up" in exile and renew its commitment to love and serve the Lord from the heart (Deut 30:1–6).

Christian Perspective Several personalities and themes in 2 Kings figure prominently in a Christian reading of the Bible. For instance, the prophets Elijah and Elisha are considered prophetic anticipations of John the Baptist and Jesus, respectively. Elijah, who clad himself in haircloth and a leather belt (1:8) and was last seen on the banks of the Jordan (2:6–13), seems to reappear in John, who clothed himself in camel's hair and a leather belt (Mk 1:6) and made his prophetic debut at the Jordan (Mk 1:4–5). Parallels are also evident between Elijah's successor, Elisha, and John's successor, Jesus. Miracles performed by both include raising the dead (4:32–37; Mk 5:35–43), multiplying barely loaves (4:42–44; Jn 6:5–14), curing lepers (5:8–14; Lk 17:11–19), and giving sight to the blind (6:20; Mt 20:29–34; Jn 9:6–7). Beyond this, the Davidic kingdom that is destroyed at the conclusion of 2 Kings is the kingdom restored and reconfigured in the New Covenant. The Babylonian conquest put an end to the Israelite monarchy, but not to the Davidic line. The royal descendants of King Jehoiachin (25:27–30) disappear for a time in the fog of the exilic and postexilic periods but reappear in the Davidic genealogy of Jesus (Mt 1:1–16). As the royal and messianic heir of David, he comes to reconstitute the ancient kingdom of David by founding the universal Church (Mt 16:18–19; Lk 1:32–33) and restoring the exiled tribes of Israel to the family of God (Mt 19:28; Lk 22:28–30).

OUTLINE OF THE SECOND BOOK OF THE KINGS

1. Elisha and the Twin Kingdoms (chaps. 1–13)
  A. The Translation of Elijah (1:1—2:12)
  B. Elisha the Miracle Worker (2:13—8:15)
  C. The Kingdom of Judah: Jehoram, Ahaziah (8:16–29)
  D. The Kingdom of Israel: Jehu (9:1—10:36)
  E. The Kingdom of Judah: Joash (11:1—12:21)
  F. The Kingdom of Israel: Jehoahaz, Jehoash (13:1–25)

2. The Fall of the Northern Kingdom (chaps. 14–17)
  A. The Kingdom of Judah: Amaziah (14:1–22)
  B. The Kingdom of Israel: Jeroboam II (14:23–29)
  C. The Kingdom of Judah: Azariah (15:1–7)
  D. The Kingdom of Israel: Zechariah to Pekah (15:8–31)
  E. The Kingdom of Judah: Jotham, Ahaz (15:32—16:20)
  F. The Fall of Samaria and Exile of Israel (17:1–41)

3. The Fall of the Southern Kingdom (chaps. 18–25)
  A. Hezekiah's Reign and Reform (18:1—20:21)
  B. The Apostasy of Manasseh and Amon (21:1–26)
  C. Josiah's Reign and Reform (22:1—23:30)
  D. Jehoahaz, Jehoiakim, Jehoiachin, Zedekiah (23:31—24:20)
  E. The Fall of Jerusalem and Exile of Judah (25:1–30)

THE SECOND BOOK OF THE
KINGS

Elijah Denounces Ahaziah

1 After the death of A′hab, Moab rebelled against Israel.

2 Now Ahazi′ah fell through the lattice in his upper chamber in Samar′ia, and lay sick; so he sent messengers, telling them, "Go, inquire of Ba′al-ze′bub, the god of Ek′ron, whether I shall recover from this sickness." ³But the angel of the LORD said to Eli′jah the Tishbite, "Arise, go up to meet the messengers of the king of Samar′ia, and say to them, 'Is it because there is no God in Israel that you are going to inquire of Ba′al-ze′bub, the god of Ek′ron?' ⁴Now therefore thus says the LORD, 'You shall not come down from the bed to which you have gone, but you shall surely die.'" So Eli′jah went.

5 The messengers returned to the king, and he said to them, "Why have you returned?" ⁶And they said to him, "There came a man to meet us, and said to us, 'Go back to the king who sent you, and say to him, Thus says the LORD, Is it because there is no God in Israel that you are sending to inquire of Ba′al-ze′bub, the god of Ek′ron? Therefore you shall not come down from the bed to which you have gone, but shall surely die.'" ⁷He said to them, "What kind of man was he who came to meet you and told you these things?" ⁸They answered him, "He wore a garment of haircloth, with a belt of leather about his loins." And he said, "It is Eli′jah the Tishbite."

9 Then the king sent to him a captain of fifty men with his fifty. He went up to Eli′jah, who was sitting on the top of a hill, and said to him, "O man of God, the king says, 'Come down.'" ¹⁰But Eli′jah answered the captain of fifty, "If I am a man of God, let fire come down from heaven and consume you and your fifty." Then fire came down from heaven, and consumed him and his fifty.

11 Again the king sent to him another captain of fifty men with his fifty. And he went up[a] and said to him, "O man of God, this is the king's order, 'Come down quickly!'" ¹²But Eli′jah answered them, "If I am a man of God, let fire come down from heaven and consume you and your fifty." Then the fire of God came down from heaven and consumed him and his fifty.

13 Again the king sent the captain of a third fifty with his fifty. And the third captain of fifty went up, and came and fell on his knees before Eli′jah, and entreated him, "O man of God, I beg you, let my life, and the life of these fifty servants of yours, be precious in your sight. ¹⁴Behold, fire came down from heaven, and consumed the two former captains of fifty men with their fifties; but now let my life be precious in your sight." ¹⁵Then the angel of the LORD said to Eli′jah, "Go down with him; do not be afraid of him." So he arose and went down with him to the king, ¹⁶and said to him, "Thus says the LORD, 'Because you have sent messengers to inquire of Ba′al-ze′bub, the god of Ek′ron—is it because there is no God in Israel to inquire of his word?—therefore you shall not come down from

---

1:10–12: Lk 9:54; Rev 11:5; 20:9.

1:1 Moab rebelled: The statement is repeated with fuller context in 3:5.

1:2 Ahaziah: The eighth king of Israel (ca. 853 to 852 B.C.). Ahaziah is introduced in 1 Kings 22:51–53, but the division of 1 and 2 Kings cuts through the account of his reign. Little is known of him except that he fell from a second-story window or balcony, and his efforts to consult the Philistine idol of Baal about his recovery brought him into conflict with Elijah. **Samaria:** Capital city of the Northern Kingdom, founded by Ahaziah's grandfather Omri (1 Kings 16:23–24). **Baal-Zebub:** A Hebrew expression meaning "Lord of the Flies". It is a derogatory distortion of the name Baal-zebul, meaning "Prince Baal" (cf. Mt 10:25). Baal is the storm and fertility god of Canaanite religion whose cult was promoted in Israel by King Ahaziah's parents, Ahab and Jezebel (1 Kings 16:31–32). **Ekron:** A Philistine city over 20 miles west of Jerusalem (possibly Khirbet al-Muqanna′).

1:3 the angel of the LORD: Mediates the word of God to the prophet. See word study: *Angel of the LORD* at Gen 16:7.

Elijah: A prophet to northern Israel and a sworn enemy of Baal worship. See note on 1 Kings 17:1–21:29.

1:8 haircloth ... leather: The distinctive dress of a prophet, also described as a "hairy mantle" (Zech 13:4). It indicates that the Lord's prophets embraced an ascetical life-style. • Centuries later John the Baptist will appear as a prophet in the spirit of Elijah (Lk 1:17), clad in the rugged attire of his forebearer (Mt 3:4) and continuing his effort to restore Israel to repentance (Mt 17:10–13).

1:9 the top of a hill: Perhaps the summit of Mt. Carmel, the site of two other weather miracles by Elijah (1 Kings 18:19–45) and a place where Elisha will go as well (2:25; 4:25). **man of God:** Terminology for a prophet (1 Sam 9:6; 1 Kings 13:1).

1:10 came down: Fire roars down from heaven, presumably in the form of lightning, and incinerates the Samarian delegation. Elijah was known for spectacular feats of this sort (1 Kings 18:36–38). The incident shows not only that God protects his prophets but also that judgment falls on those who reject him in favor of other gods. • The apostles James and John have this episode in mind when they seek Jesus' permission to call down fire upon inhospitable Samaritans in Lk 9:52–54.

---

[a]Gk Compare verses 9, 13: Heb *answered*.

the bed to which you have gone, but you shall surely die.'"

Death of Ahaziah

17 So he died according to the word of the Lord which Eli'jah had spoken. Jeho'ram, his brother,ᵇ became king in his stead in the second year of Jehoram the son of Jehosh'aphat, king of Judah, because Ahazi'ah had no son. ¹⁸Now the rest of the acts of Ahazi'ah which he did, are they not written in the Book of the Chronicles of the Kings of Israel?

Elijah Is Taken Up to Heaven

2 Now when the Lord was about to take Eli'jah up to heaven by a whirlwind, Elijah and Eli'sha were on their way from Gilgal. ²And Eli'jah said to Eli'sha, "Tarry here, I beg you; for the Lord has sent me as far as Bethel." But Elisha said, "As the Lord lives, and as you yourself live, I will not leave you." So they went down to Bethel. ³And the sons of the prophets who were in Bethel came out to Eli'sha, and said to him, "Do you know that today the Lord will take away your master from over you?" And he said, "Yes, I know it; hold your peace."

4 Eli'jah said to him, "Eli'sha, tarry here, I beg you; for the Lord has sent me to Jericho." But he said, "As the Lord lives, and as you yourself live,

I will not leave you." So they came to Jericho. ⁵The sons of the prophets who were at Jericho drew near to Eli'sha, and said to him, "Do you know that today the Lord will take away your master from over you?" And he answered, "Yes, I know it; hold your peace."

6 Then Eli'jah said to him, "Tarry here, I beg you; for the Lord has sent me to the Jordan." But he said, "As the Lord lives, and as you yourself live, I will not leave you." So the two of them went on. ⁷Fifty men of the sons of the prophets also went, and stood at some distance from them, as they both were standing by the Jordan. ⁸Then Eli'jah took his coat, and rolled it up, and struck the water, and the water was parted to the one side and to the other, till the two of them could go over on dry ground.

Elisha Succeeds Elijah

9 When they had crossed, Eli'jah said to Eli'sha, "Ask what I shall do for you, before I am taken from you." And Elisha said, "I beg you, let me inherit a double share* of your spirit." ¹⁰And he said, "You have asked a hard thing; yet, if you see me as I am being taken from you, it shall be so for you; but if you do not see me, it shall not be so." ¹¹And as they still went on and talked, behold, a chariot of

---

2:11: Rev 11:12.

1:17 Jehoram: Brother of Ahaziah and the ninth king of Israel (ca. 852 to 841 B.C.). His name is sometimes shortened to "Joram" (8:16). His royal counterpart in the south, Jehoram of Judah, shares the same name (1:17; 8:16).

1:18 Book of the Chronicles: See note on 1 Kings 14:19.

2:1—8:15 Stories about the prophet Elisha, who continues the ministry of Elijah and succeeds him as headmaster of a band of prophets-in-training. He is remembered most as a miracle worker who offered his services to all—Israelites as well as Gentiles, nobles as well as peasants. Scholars surmise that the Elisha stories, which include a final miracle linked with his burial (13:20-21), were preserved initially as oral tradition among the prophetic circles of northern Israel. • Elisha is a prophet after the likeness of Moses. Miracles common to both include making a path through parted waters (2:13-14; Ex 14:21-22), cleansing foul waters to make them drinkable (2:19-22; Ex 15:22-25), and supplying water for Israel in an arid land (3:13-20; Ex 17:1-7). Elisha also prefigures the Messiah by performing miracles such as raising the dead (4:32-37; Mk 5:35-43), multiplying barley loaves (4:42-44; Jn 6:5-14), and curing lepers (5:8-14; Lk 17:11-19).

2:1 Gilgal: In the western Jordan valley near Jericho (or possibly a town of this name in the central hill country). See note on Josh 4:19.

2:3 sons of the prophets: Trainees in the prophetic ministry under the direction of a head prophet (6:1; 1 Kings 20:35). Prophetic guilds use the kinship language of "father" and "sons" for the senior prophet and his junior apprentices (1 Kings 13:11). Hence, Elisha addresses his master Elijah as "father" (2:12), and Elisha himself is addressed this way after his succession to Elijah's leadership position (6:21; 13:14).

Communities of prophets live in Gilgal (4:38), Bethel (2:3), and Jericho (2:5). Presumably Elijah, by making his final stops in these towns, is bidding farewell to his disciples before his departure (2:11).

2:4 Jericho: In the western Jordan valley, roughly six miles north of the Dead Sea. See note on Josh 2:1-24. **As the Lord lives:** An oath formula.

2:8 the water was parted: Elijah imitates the action of Moses, who divided the sea so that Israel could cross over on dry ground (Ex 14:21-22). For additional parallels between Moses and Elijah, see note on 1 Kings 19:8-18.

2:9 double share: A request to be Elijah's primary heir. The background is the inheritance law of Deuteronomy, where the first-born son was entitled to receive a "double portion" of his father's estate (Deut 21:17). Elisha is confirmed as Elijah's successor by possession of his mantle (2:13) and by a replication of his final miracle at the Jordan (compare 2:14 with 2:8) (CCC 2684). See also chart: *Elijah and Elisha* at 2 Kings 4.

2:11 chariot ... horses: Elijah's escort appears to be an angel or angels from the Lord's heavenly army (cf. 6:17; 7:6). **fire ... whirlwind:** Both raging flames and storm winds manifest God's power and presence in the world (Ex 19:18; Deut 4:24; Job 38:1; Is 29:6; Ezek 1:4; Nah 1:3). Elijah, along with the patriarch Enoch, are the only two figures of the OT whose life on earth ends with a translation into heaven (Gen 5:24; 1 Mac 2:58). • The prophet Malachi announces the future return of Elijah before the "day of the Lord" (Mal 4:5). Given Elijah's disappearance on the banks of the Jordan (2:7), it is fitting that John of Baptist, who comes "in the spirit and power of Elijah" (Lk 1:17), will make his appearance on the banks of the same river (Mk 1:4-6). See note on 1:8. • *Allegorically*, the departure of Elijah, who was taken up by angels while talking with Elisha, prefigures the Ascension of the Lord, who was drawn into heaven while speaking to his disciples. And as Elisha takes up the cloak of Elijah, calling upon God and crossing over the divided waters, so the apostles take up the sacraments of the redeemer, and,

---

*2:9, *a double share:* The eldest son inherited a double share of his father's property; cf. Deut 21:17. Elisha regarded himself as the son and so asked for Elijah's spirit as his inheritance.
ᵇGk Syr: Heb lacks *his brother.*

fire and horses of fire separated the two of them. And Eli'jah went up by a whirlwind into heaven. [12]And Eli'sha saw it and he cried, "My father, my father! the chariots of Israel and its horsemen!" And he saw him no more.

Then he took hold of his own clothes and tore them in two pieces. [13]And he took up the coat of Eli'jah that had fallen from him, and went back and stood on the bank of the Jordan. [14]Then he took the coat of Eli'jah that had fallen from him, and struck the water, saying, "Where is the LORD, the God of Elijah?" And when he had struck the water, the water was parted to the one side and to the other; and Eli'sha went over.

15 Now when the sons of the prophets who were at Jericho saw him over against them, they said,

"The spirit of Eli'jah rests on Eli'sha." And they came to meet him, and bowed to the ground before him. [16]And they said to him, "Behold now, there are with your servants fifty strong men; please, let them go, and seek your master; it may be that the Spirit of the LORD has caught him up and cast him upon some mountain or into some valley." And he said, "You shall not send." [17]But when they urged him till he was ashamed, he said, "Send." They sent therefore fifty men; and for three days they sought him but did not find him. [18]And they came back to him, while he tarried at Jericho, and he said to them, "Did I not say to you, Do not go?"

Elisha Performs Miracles

19 Now the men of the city said to Eli'sha, "Behold, the situation of this city is pleasant, as

---

having been cleansed and sanctified by them, they learn to call upon God and cross over the river of death to an undying life (St. Bede, *Homilies on the Gospels* 2, 15).

2:12 tore them: A sign of extreme grief or distress (Gen 37:34; 2 Sam 1:11–12).

2:14 the water was parted: Elisha, the successor of Elijah, makes a dry path through the Jordan, just as Joshua, the successor of Moses, made a dry path through the

Jordan (Josh 3:7–17). Reinforcing this parallel, the spirit of Elijah rests upon Elisha (2:15), just as the spirit of Moses was conferred upon Joshua (Deut 34:9).

2:16 Spirit of the LORD: Known to whisk away the prophets from place to place. See note on 1 Kings 18:12.

2:18 Did I not say . . . ?: Elisha knew the search party would never find Elijah. Permission was granted to look, however, as the failure would encourage greater faith in Elisha's word.

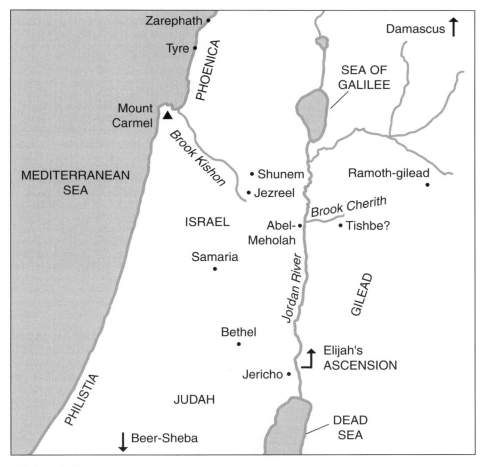

Elijah and Elisha

my lord sees; but the water is bad, and the land is unfruitful." [20]He said, "Bring me a new bowl, and put salt in it." So they brought it to him. [21]Then he went to the spring of water and threw salt in it, and said, "Thus says the LORD, I have made this water wholesome; henceforth neither death nor miscarriage shall come from it." [22]So the water has been wholesome to this day, according to the word which Eli'sha spoke.

23 He went up from there to Bethel; and while he was going up on the way, some small boys came out of the city and jeered at him, saying, "Go up, you baldhead! Go up, you baldhead!" [24]And he turned around, and when he saw them, he cursed them in the name of the LORD. And two she-bears came out of the woods and tore forty-two of the boys. [25]From there he went on to Mount Carmel, and thence he returned to Samar'ia.

Jehoram Reigns over Israel

3 In the eighteenth year of Jehosh'aphat king of Judah, Jeho'ram the son of A'hab became king over Israel in Samar'ia, and he reigned twelve years. [2]He did what was evil in the sight of the LORD, though not like his father and mother, for he put away the pillar of Ba'al which his father had made.

[3]Nevertheless he clung to the sin of Jerobo'am the son of Ne'bat, which he made Israel to sin; he did not depart from it.

War with Moab

4 *Now Me'sha king of Moab was a sheep breeder; and he had to deliver annually[c] to the king of Israel a hundred thousand lambs, and the wool of a hundred thousand rams. [5]But when A'hab died, the king of Moab rebelled against the king of Israel. [6]So King Jeho'ram marched out of Samar'ia at that time and mustered all Israel. [7]And he went and sent word to Jehosh'aphat king of Judah, "The king of Moab has rebelled against me; will you go with me to battle against Moab?" And he said, "I will go; I am as you are, my people as your people, my horses as your horses." [8]Then he said, "By which way shall we march?" Jeho'ram answered, "By the way of the wilderness of E'dom."

9 So the king of Israel went with the king of Judah and the king of E'dom. And when they had made a circuitous march of seven days, there was no water for the army or for the beasts which followed them. [10]Then the king of Israel said, "Alas! The LORD has called these three kings to give them into the hand of Moab." [11]And Jehosh'aphat said, "Is there no

---

2:21 made this water wholesome: Recalls how Moses made bitter waters drinkable by casting a purifying object into them (Ex 15:22–25). See note on 2:1–8:15. • *Allegorically*, Elisha is a type of the Savior, and the foul spring represents Adam, whose sin made the human race barren and bitter. The new vessel is the mystery of the Incarnation, in which the body of Christ is filled with the salt of divine wisdom. Sent by the Father, the incarnate Word came to restore the human race to sweetness by leading it from evil ways to the purity of charity and the fruitfulness of righteousness (St. Caesarius of Arles, *Sermons* 126, 2).

2:23 Bethel: One of two cities in the Northern Kingdom of Israel hosting the idolatrous calf cult of Jeroboam (1 Kings 12:28–30) and one of many sites where Canaanite cults flourished. Bethel is a place of apostasy and antagonism toward Yahweh during the days of the divided monarchy. See note on Judg 1:23. **small boys:** The expression can designate children as well as young men old enough for marriage and public service. Perhaps these youths are affiliated with the idol sanctuary at Bethel (2:3), who, unlike the "sons of the prophets" from Jericho (2:7, 15), refuse to acknowledge the authority of Elisha as Elijah's successor. They are mauled to death, not simply for name calling or disrespecting an elder, but for their mocking rejection of one who delivers the word of the Lord. **Go up ... Go up:** The Hebrew verb "go up" often has the connotation of traveling to engage in worship at a sanctuary, normally seated on an elevation (e.g., Judg 21:5; 1 Sam 1:3; 1 Kings 12:27; Ps 122:3–4). This suggests the boys are urging Elisha to participate in the idol cults at Bethel. The Torah deems it a capital crime to encourage fellow Israelites to serve gods other than Yahweh (Deut 13:6–11). **baldhead:** Insinuates that Elisha is unfit to assume the prophetic office of Elijah, who was covered with hair (1:8).

2:24 she-bears: Death by wild animals is sometimes a form of divine judgment (17:25; Lev 26:22; Num 21:6; 1 Kings 13:26). Moreover, death by **two** bears mirrors the two lightning miracles of Elijah that struck down the Samaritan soldiers in 1:10, 12.

2:25 Mount Carmel: Rises along the Mediterranean coast in northwest Israel.

3:1 eighteenth year: This number stands in tension with 1:17. The apparent discrepancy is best explained by the practice of co-regency: Jehoram of Judah probably ruled for several years alongside his father, Jehoshaphat of Judah, making the second year of Jehoram and the eighteenth year of Jehoshaphat one and the same year.

3:2 pillar of Baal: A cultic monument to the storm and fertility god of Canaanite religion. Jehoram's father, Ahab, was an aggressive sponsor of Baal worship in northern Israel (1 Kings 16:30–32).

3:5 Moab rebelled: Moab, east of the Dead Sea, is a vassal state of the Northern Kingdom of Israel, and refusal to pay the required tribute to an overlord (mentioned in 3:4) is tantamount to a declaration of independence. In 1868 a basalt victory monument, known as the *Mesha Inscription* (or Moabite Stone), was discovered east of the Jordan. The text, which dates back to the ninth century B.C. and mentions King Mesha by name, celebrates Moab's success in breaking free from Israelite rule, although it fails to mention Moab's humiliating defeats as described in the biblical account (3:24–26).

3:6–7 Jehoram seeks military assistance from Jehoshaphat of Judah, just as his father, Ahab, had done (1 Kings 22:1–4).

3:8 wilderness of Edom: The plan is to march around the southern end of the Dead Sea and attack Moab from the south.

3:9 Israel ... Judah ... Edom: A coalition formed to bring Moab back under Israelite control. Edom, being a vassal state of Judah, is obligated to participate in the war effort (cf. 8:20).

3:11 poured water: Indicates that Elisha was once Elijah's servant (1 Kings 19:21).

---

*3:4–27: The Moabite Stone, or Stele of Mesha, in the Louvre, found in Trans-Jordan in 1868, describes the liberation of Moab from Israel, but understandably is silent about its subjection.
[c]Tg: Heb lacks *annually*.

prophet of the LORD here, through whom we may inquire of the LORD?" Then one of the king of Israel's servants answered, "Eli'sha the son of Sha'phat is here, who poured water on the hands of Eli'jah." ¹²And Jehosh'aphat said, "The word of the LORD is with him." So the king of Israel and Jehoshaphat and the king of E'dom went down to him.

13 And Eli'sha said to the king of Israel, "What have I to do with you? Go to the prophets of your father and the prophets of your mother." But the king of Israel said to him, "No; it is the LORD who has called these three kings to give them into the hand of Moab." ¹⁴And Eli'sha said, "As the LORD of hosts lives, whom I serve, were it not that I have regard for Jehosh'aphat the king of Judah, I would neither look at you, nor see you. ¹⁵But now bring me a minstrel." And when the minstrel played, the power of the LORD came upon him. ¹⁶And he said, "Thus says the LORD, 'I will make this dry stream-bed full of pools.' ¹⁷For thus says the LORD, 'You shall not see wind or rain, but that stream-bed shall be filled with water, so that you shall drink, you, your cattle, and your beasts.' ¹⁸This is a light thing in the sight of the LORD; he will also give the Moabites into your hand, ¹⁹and you shall conquer every fortified city, and every choice city, and shall fell every good tree, and stop up all springs of water, and ruin every good piece of land with stones." ²⁰The next morning, about the time of offering the sacrifice, behold, water came from the direction of E'dom, till the country was filled with water.

21 When all the Moabites heard that the kings had come up to fight against them, all who were able to put on armor, from the youngest to the oldest, were called out, and were drawn up at the frontier. ²²And when they rose early in the morning, and the sun shone upon the water, the Moabites saw the water opposite them as red as blood. ²³And they said, "This is blood; the kings have surely fought

together, and slain one another. Now then, Moab, to the spoil!" ²⁴But when they came to the camp of Israel, the Israelites rose and attacked the Moabites, till they fled before them; and they went forward, slaughtering the Moabites as they went.ᵈ ²⁵And they overthrew the cities, and on every good piece of land every man threw a stone, until it was covered; they stopped every spring of water, and felled all the good trees; till only its stones were left in Kir-har'-eseth, and the slingers surrounded and conquered it. ²⁶When the king of Moab saw that the battle was going against him, he took with him seven hundred swordsmen to break through, opposite the king of E'dom; but they could not. ²⁷Then he took his eldest son who was to reign in his stead, and offered him for a burnt offering upon the wall. And there came great wrath upon Israel; and they withdrew from him and returned to their own land.

Elisha and the Widow's Jar of Oil

4 Now the wife of one of the sons of the prophets cried to Eli'sha, "Your servant my husband is dead; and you know that your servant feared the LORD, but the creditor has come to take my two children to be his slaves." ²And Eli'sha said to her, "What shall I do for you? Tell me; what have you in the house?" And she said, "Your maidservant has nothing in the house, except a jar of oil." ³Then he said, "Go outside, borrow vessels of all your neighbors, empty vessels and not too few. ⁴Then go in, and shut the door upon yourself and your sons, and pour into all these vessels; and when one is full, set it aside." ⁵So she went from him and shut the door upon herself and her sons; and as she poured they brought the vessels to her. ⁶When the vessels were full, she said to her son, "Bring me another vessel." And he said to her, "There is not another." Then the oil stopped flowing. ⁷She came and told the man of God, and he said, "Go, sell the oil and pay your debts, and you and your sons can live on the rest."

3:13 Go to the prophets: I.e., to the court prophets of Ahab (1 Kings 22:6) and to the pagan prophets of Jezebel (1 Kings 18:19).

3:15 the minstrel played: The sound of musical instruments helped prepare the prophet to receive a word from God (1 Sam 10:5; 1 Chron 25:1).

3:17 You shall not see wind or rain: Elisha promises a water miracle even more amazing than that of Elijah, whose prayer called forth "wind" and "great rain" (1 Kings 18:45). **filled with water:** By an act of God, the dried-up riverbed will overflow its banks to refresh the whole army along with its animals (3:9).

3:20 time of offering: When the daily sacrificial liturgy was conducted each morning in the Temple (Ex 29:38-40).

3:22 red as blood: The reddish sandstone of Edom makes the water look bloodied by war. The elements in question

constitute a wordplay in Hebrew: Edom is 'edom, red is 'adom, and blood is dam.

3:25 Kir-hareseth: The capital of Moab, about 11 miles east of the Dead Sea (Is 16:7).

3:27 offered him: Mesha sacrifices his first-born son, the crown prince, in full view of his warriors. His action is a desperate appeal to the Moabite god Chemosh for deliverance of the capital city. **wrath upon Israel:** Not divine wrath, but an outburst of human fury. The spectacle inspires Mesha's fighters to launch a ferocious counterattack that sends coalition forces running home.

4:1 sons of the prophets: See note on 2:3. **his slaves:** Poverty was often a path to slavery in the ancient Near East, where unpaid debts could force the sale of family members into bondage (Ex 21:7; Neh 5:5; Is 50:1).

4:2 jar of oil: Multiplied to fill a roomful of storage vessels (4:5-6). Selling the oil will bring sufficient income for the widow to pay off her debts and live independently with her sons (4:7). The story recalls Elijah's oil miracle for the widow of Zarephath (1 Kings 17:8-16).

ᵈGk: Heb uncertain.

Elisha and the Shunammite Couple

8 One day Eli′sha went on to Shu′nem, where a wealthy woman lived, who urged him to eat some food. So whenever he passed that way, he would turn in there to eat food. ⁹And she said to her husband, "Behold now, I perceive that this is a holy man of God, who is continually passing our way. ¹⁰Let us make a small roof chamber with walls, and put there for him a bed, a table, a chair, and a lamp, so that whenever he comes to us, he can go in there."

11 One day he came there, and he turned into the chamber and rested there. ¹²And he said to Geha′zi his servant, "Call this Shu′nammite." When he had called her, she stood before him. ¹³And he said to him, "Say now to her, See, you have taken all this trouble for us; what is to be done for you? Would you have a word spoken on your behalf to the king or to the commander of the army?" She answered, "I dwell among my own people." ¹⁴And he said, "What then is to be done for her?" Geha′zi answered, "Well, she has no son, and her husband is old." ¹⁵He said, "Call her." And when he had called her, she stood in the doorway. ¹⁶And he said, "At this season, when the time comes round, you shall embrace a son." And she said, "No, my lord, O man of God; do not lie to your maidservant." ¹⁷But the woman conceived, and she bore a son about that time the following spring, as Eli′sha had said to her.

Elisha Restores the Shunammite's Son

18 When the child had grown, he went out one day to his father among the reapers. ¹⁹And he said to his father, "Oh, my head, my head!" The father said to his servant, "Carry him to his mother." ²⁰And when he had lifted him, and brought him to his mother, the child sat on her lap till noon, and then he died. ²¹And she went up and laid him on the bed of the man of God, and shut the door upon him, and went out. ²²Then she called to her husband, and said, "Send me one of the servants and one of the donkeys, that I may quickly go to the man of God, and come back again." ²³And he said, "Why will you go to him today? It is neither new moon nor sabbath." She said, "It will be well." ²⁴Then she saddled the donkey, and she said to her servant, "Urge the beast on; do not slacken the pace for me unless I tell you." ²⁵So she set out, and came to the man of God at Mount Carmel.

When the man of God saw her coming, he said to Geha′zi his servant, "Look, yonder is the Shu′-nammite; ²⁶run at once to meet her, and say to her, Is it well with you? Is it well with your husband? Is it well with the child?" And she answered, "It is well." ²⁷And when she came to the mountain to the man of God, she caught hold of his feet. And Geha′zi came to thrust her away. But the man of God said, "Let her alone, for she is in bitter distress; and the Lord has hidden it from me, and has not told me." ²⁸Then she said, "Did I ask my lord for a son? Did I not say, Do not deceive me?" ²⁹He said to Geha′zi, "Gird up your loins, and take my staff in your hand, and go. If you meet any one, do not salute him; and if any one salutes you, do not reply; and lay my staff upon the face of the child." ³⁰Then the mother of the child said, "As the Lord lives, and as you yourself live, I will not leave you." So he arose and followed her. ³¹Geha′zi went on ahead and laid the staff upon the face of the child, but there was no sound or sign of life. Therefore he returned to meet him, and told him, "The child has not awaked."

32 When Eli′sha came into the house, he saw the child lying dead on his bed. ³³So he went in and shut the door upon the two of them, and prayed to the Lord.

4:33: Mt 6:6.

4:8 Shunem: In lower Galilee, southeast of Mt. Carmel.
4:12 Gehazi: Elisha's personal assistant (5:20). He serves the needs of Elisha, just as Elisha once ministered to Elijah (3:11; 1 Kings 19:21).
4:16 embrace a son: God will grant the woman a male heir despite the advanced age of her husband (4:14). It is a blessing for her generosity toward the prophet in serving him many meals (4:8) and offering him a furnished guestroom (4:10). Lack of a biological heir put the family name and estate in jeopardy, along with the well-being of a surviving widow (cf. Deut 25:5–10). • Elisha's words recall the promise to Abraham and Sarah, also aged and lacking a biological heir, that their hospitality to the Lord's messengers (Gen 18:1–8) would be followed by the conception and birth of Isaac (Gen 18:13–14). There are many miracles in the Bible where God blesses women with the birth of a son (Gen 25:21; 30:22–24; Judg 13:2–7; 1 Sam 1:3–20; Lk 1:5–25).
4:23 Why . . . today?: The father appears unaware that his son has died (4:20). new moon nor sabbath: Suggests that visits with prophets normally took place on holy days. A new moon festival was held on the first day of every month (Num 28:11–15), and the Sabbath fell on the last day of every week (Ex 20:8–11).

4:29 do not salute: Greetings could be long and elaborate in Semitic culture. Avoiding these drawn-out exchanges is a way of preventing delay. • Jesus gives this same instruction to 70 disciples in order to stress the urgency of their mission as preachers of the kingdom (Lk 10:4).
4:30 As the Lord lives: An oath formula. I will not leave you: The woman is not content to have Gehazi go on Elisha's behalf but insists that the prophet must intervene directly.
4:32–37 Elisha performs the second resurrection miracle in Scripture. Restoration to life is the result of intercessory prayer (4:33) and symbolic actions (4:34), both in response to the persistent faith of the child's mother (4:24–25, 27, 30). • Elijah was the first to raise the dead when he stretched himself upon a lifeless child in 1 Kings 17:17–24. The Apostle Paul will perform a similar miracle in Acts 20:9–10. • Allegorically, just as Elisha raised the child of the Shunammite woman, not when he sent his servant with a staff, but when he came in person and breathed seven times into the dead body, so God brought us back to life, not when he sent his servant Moses with the rod of the Law, but when he came in person and imparted the sevenfold grace of the Spirit to those who lie prostrate in death (St. Gregory the Great, *Moralia in Job* 9, 40).

³⁴Then he went up and lay upon the child, putting his mouth upon his mouth, his eyes upon his eyes, and his hands upon his hands; and as he stretched himself upon him, the flesh of the child became warm. ³⁵Then he got up again, and walked once back and forth in the house, and went up, and stretched himself upon him; the child sneezed seven times, and the child opened his eyes. ³⁶Then he summoned Geha'zi and said, "Call this Shu'nammite." So he called her. And when she came to him, he said, "Take up your son." ³⁷She came and fell at his feet, bowing to the ground; then she took up her son and went out.

Elisha Purifies the Pot of Pottage

38 And Eli'sha came again to Gilgal when there was a famine in the land. And as the sons of the prophets were sitting before him, he said to his ser-vant, "Put on the great pot, and boil pottage for the sons of the prophets." ³⁹One of them went out into the field to gather herbs, and found a wild vine and gathered from it his lap full of wild gourds, and came and cut them up into the pot of pottage, not knowing what they were. ⁴⁰And they poured out for the men to eat. But while they were eating of the pottage, they cried out, "O man of God, there is death in the pot!" And they could not eat it. ⁴¹He said, "Then bring meal." And he threw it into the pot, and said, "Pour out for the men, that they may eat." And there was no harm in the pot.

Elisha Feeds a Hundred Men

42 A man came from Ba'al-shal'ishah, bringing the man of God bread of the first fruits, twenty loaves of barley, and fresh ears of grain in his sack.

4:35 the child sneezed: A sign that the breath of life is returning to the boy. Recall that in Genesis the breath of human life enters through the nostrils (Gen 2:7).

4:38 Gilgal: See note on 2:1. **a famine in the land:** The backdrop for Elisha's next two food miracles in 4:38–41 and 4:42–44.

4:40 death in the pot: The wild plants mixed in the stew are inedible, perhaps poisonous.

4:42 Baal-shalishah: In the hill country of Ephraim in central Canaan. **twenty loaves of barley:** Multiplied to feed 100 men with some left over (4:44). Once again, the prophet provides an abundance of food beyond the immediate need of those he serves (as in 4:1–7). • Jesus will surpass the miracle of Elisha when he multiplies fewer loaves (five) for a larger crowd (over 5000 people) with much left over (Mt 14:15–21). The Gospel account specifies that Jesus, like Elisha, multiplied "barley loaves" (Jn 6:9).

Elijah and Elisha

Few prophets are as celebrated in the Bible as Elijah and Elisha. Unlike the prophets Isaiah, Jeremiah, Ezekiel, and others, who left behind written collections of oracles, these two are most remembered for miraculous works. The narrative of Kings attributes *eight* miracles to Elijah and *sixteen* miracles to Elisha. Perhaps this is the author's way of demonstrating that Elisha received a double portion of Elijah's spirit (2 Kings 2:9, 15).

The Miracles of Elijah
1. Causes a drought by his word (1 Kings 17:1).
2. Multiplies flour and oil for a woman and her son (1 Kings 17:8–16).
3. Brings a woman's dead son back to life (1 Kings 17:17–24).
4. Calls down fire from heaven on sacrifices (1 Kings 18:30–39).
5. Summons a rainstorm to end a famine caused by drought (1 Kings 18:41–46).
6. Calls down fire from heaven on a Samaritan delegation (2 Kings 1:9–10).
7. Calls down fire from heaven on another Samaritan delegation (2 Kings 1:11–12).
8. Parts the Jordan River with his mantle (2 Kings 2:8).

The Miracles of Elisha
1. Parts the Jordan River with his mantle (2 Kings 2:14).
2. Purifies undrinkable water with salt (2 Kings 2:19–22).
3. Summons bears to execute a curse (2 Kings 2:23–24).
4. Produces pools of drinking water in the wilderness (2 Kings 3:13–20).
5. Multiplies oil for a poor woman to sell and pay her debts (2 Kings 4:1–7).
6. Enables a woman with an elderly husband to conceive a son (2 Kings 4:8–17).
7. Brings a woman's dead son back to life (2 Kings 4:18–37).
8. Makes poisonous pottage into edible food (2 Kings 4:38–41).
9. Multiplies loaves of bread to feed a multitude (2 Kings 4:42–44).
10. Heals a foreigner, Naaman the Syrian, of leprosy (2 Kings 5:1–14).
11. Inflicts leprosy on his greedy and lying servant (2 Kings 5:19–27).
12. Causes an iron axe head to float in the Jordan (2 Kings 6:1–7).
13. Perceives and reveals the secret plans of the Syrian army (2 Kings 6:8–10).
14. Grants spiritual vision to his servant (2 Kings 6:15–17).
15. Strikes a besieging Syrian army with blindness (2 Kings 6:18).
16. Contact with his bones restores a dead man to life (2 Kings 13:20–21).

And Eli'sha said, "Give to the men, that they may eat." 43But his servant said, "How am I to set this before a hundred men?" So he repeated, "Give them to the men, that they may eat, for thus says the Lord, 'They shall eat and have some left.'" 44So he set it before them. And they ate, and had some left, according to the word of the Lord.

Naaman Is Cured of Leprosy

5 Na'aman, commander of the army of the king of Syria, was a great man with his master and in high favor, because by him the Lord had given victory to Syria. He was a mighty man of valor, but he was a leper. 2Now the Syrians on one of their raids had carried off a little maid from the land of Israel, and she waited on Na'aman's wife. 3She said to her mistress, "Would that my lord were with the prophet who is in Samar'ia! He would cure him of his leprosy." 4So Na'aman went in and told his lord, "Thus and so spoke the maiden from the land of Israel." 5And the king of Syria said, "Go now, and I will send a letter to the king of Israel."

So he went, taking with him ten talents of silver, six thousand shekels of gold, and ten festal garments. 6And he brought the letter to the king of Israel, which read, "When this letter reaches you, know that I have sent to you Na'aman my servant, that you may cure him of his leprosy." 7And when the king of Israel read the letter, he tore his clothes and said, "Am I God, to kill and to make alive, that this man sends word to me to cure a man of his leprosy? Only consider, and see how he is seeking a quarrel with me."

8 But when Eli'sha the man of God heard that the king of Israel had torn his clothes, he sent to the king, saying, "Why have you torn your clothes? Let him come now to me, that he may know that there is a prophet in Israel." 9So Na'aman came with his horses and chariots, and halted at the door of Eli'sha's house. 10And Eli'sha sent a messenger to him, saying, "Go and wash in the Jordan seven times, and your flesh shall be restored, and you shall be clean." 11But Na'aman was angry, and went away, saying, "Behold, I thought that he would surely come out to me, and stand, and call on the name of the Lord his God, and wave his hand over the place, and cure the leper. 12Are not Aba'na℮ and Pharpar, the rivers of Damascus, better than all the waters of Israel? Could I not wash in them, and be clean?" So he turned and went away in a rage. 13But his servants came near and said to him, "My father, if the prophet had commanded you to do some great thing, would you not have done it? How much rather, then, when he says to you, 'Wash, and be clean'?" 14So he went down and dipped himself seven times in the Jordan, according to the word of the man of God; and his flesh was restored like the flesh of a little child, and he was clean.

15 Then he returned to the man of God, he and all his company, and he came and stood before him; and he said, "Behold, I know that there is no God in all the earth but in Israel;* so accept now a present from your servant." 16But he said, "As the Lord lives, whom I serve, I will receive none." And he urged him to take it, but he refused. 17Then Na'aman said,

---

5:1 victory to Syria: A reminder that Yahweh is God of all the earth and that the destiny of nations beyond Israel rests in the hands of his Providence. **a leper:** Leprosy in this account is not the debilitating condition known today as Hansen's disease but a type of infection that turned the skin white (5:27; cf. Lev 13:10–11). Apparently it did not prevent Naaman from serving as a military commander (5:1).

5:2 one of their raids: For the ongoing conflict between Israel and Syria at this time, see 1 Kings 15:20; 20:1–34; 22:1–40.

5:5 ten talents: Over 700 pounds of silver.

5:7 tore his clothes: A sign of extreme distress (Josh 7:6; 2 Sam 1:11). **Am I God . . . ?:** King Jehoram misunderstands the Syrian request as a pretext for war, just as the king of Syria misunderstands Elisha's relation to Jehoram, assuming him to be a court prophet who answers directly to the king (5:6).

5:10 Go and wash: The instruction demands faith, especially since Naaman expected the prophet to greet him in person and conduct a more dramatic and ceremonious healing (5:11). • Jesus performs similar miracles when he instructs a group of ten lepers to "Go" and be cleansed (Lk 17:12–14) and when he directs the blind man to "Go" and "wash" in the pool of Siloam in order to regain his sight (Jn 9:7).

5:12 Abana and Pharpar: Rivers to the north and south of Damascus.

5:14 dipped himself: Washing in the murky waters of the Jordan underscores the fact that Yahweh—not the river itself—is cleansing the man of leprosy. The Greek LXX says that Naaman "immersed" or "baptized" himself in the waters. **seven times:** Perhaps a hint that his body would experience a new creation, just as the old creation came forth from God in seven days (Gen 1:1—2:4). Likewise, Leviticus stipulates that a person suspected of having leprosy must be quarantined for seven days to see if the infection spreads (Lev 13:1–8). • *Allegorically*, men who are covered with leprosy are cleansed by our Lord, the spiritual Elisha. Naaman washed, fulfilling the mystery of Baptism, and his flesh became like that of a child born in the washing of rebirth (Origen of Alexandria, *Homilies on Luke* 33). People are lepers before they are baptized in the mystical river, but afterward they are purified from the stains of soul and body. Naaman is a figure of future salvation, and his immersion in the Jordan makes us recognize the grace of Baptism (St. Ambrose, *Exposition of Luke* 4, 50–51).

5:15–27 The departure story highlights Naaman's generosity (5:15–16), Gehazi's greed (5:20–24), and Elisha's detachment from personal gain (5:16).

5:15 there is no God . . . but in Israel: An instance of Gentile conversion, the Syrian officer embracing the monotheistic faith of Israel. For other examples, see Josh 2:8–11 and Ruth 1:16–17.

5:16 As the Lord lives: An oath formula (1 Kings 1:29).

5:17 burden of earth: Soil from the land of Israel. Naaman wants to haul it back to Syria to make an altar of worship for Yahweh.

---

*5:15: A forthright monotheism that not even an Israelite could improve on. However, Naaman realized that Yahweh had a special relation to Israel; cf. verse 17.

℮Another reading is *Amana*.

"If not, I beg you, let there be given to your servant two mules' burden of earth; for henceforth your servant will not offer burnt offering or sacrifice to any god but the LORD. [18]In this matter may the LORD pardon your servant: when my master goes into the house of Rimmon to worship there, leaning on my arm, and I bow myself in the house of Rimmon, when I bow myself in the house of Rimmon, the LORD pardon your servant in this matter." [19]He said to him, "Go in peace."

But when Na′aman had gone from him a short distance, [20]Geha′zi, the servant of Eli′sha the man of God, said, "See, my master has spared this Na′aman the Syrian, in not accepting from his hand what he brought. As the LORD lives, I will run after him, and get something from him." [21]So Geha′zi followed Na′aman. And when Naaman saw some one running after him, he alighted from the chariot to meet him, and said, "Is all well?" [22]And he said, "All is well. My master has sent me to say, 'There have just now come to me from the hill country of E′phraim two young men of the sons of the prophets; please, give them a talent of silver and two festal garments.'" [23]And Na′aman said, "Be pleased to accept two talents." And he urged him, and tied up two talents of silver in two bags, with two festal garments, and laid them upon two of his servants; and they carried them before Geha′zi. [24]And when he came to the hill, he took them from their hand, and put them in the house; and he sent the men away, and they departed. [25]He went in, and stood before his master, and Eli′sha said to him, "Where have you been, Geha′zi?" And he said, "Your servant went nowhere." [26]But he said to him, "Did I not go with you in spirit when the man turned from his chariot to meet you? Was it a time to accept money and garments, olive orchards and vineyards, sheep and oxen, menservants and maidservants? [27]Therefore the leprosy of Na′aman shall cling to you, and to your descendants for ever." So he went out from his presence a leper, as white as snow.

The Miracle of the Axe Head

6 Now the sons of the prophets said to Eli′sha, "See, the place where we dwell under your charge is too small for us. [2]Let us go to the Jordan and each of us get there a log, and let us make a place for us to dwell there." And he answered, "Go." [3]Then one of them said, "Be pleased to go with your servants." And he answered, "I will go." [4]So he went with them. And when they came to the Jordan, they cut down trees. [5]But as one was felling a log, his axe head fell into the water; and he cried out, "Alas, my master! It was borrowed." [6]Then the man of God said, "Where did it fall?" When he showed him the place, he cut off a stick, and threw it in there, and made the iron float. [7]And he said, "Take it up." So he reached out his hand and took it.

A Syrian Attack Is Thwarted

8 Once when the king of Syria was warring against Israel, he took counsel with his servants, saying, "At such and such a place shall be my camp." [9]But the man of God sent word to the king of Israel, "Beware that you do not pass this place, for the Syrians are going down there." [10]And the king of Israel sent to the place of which the man of God told him. Thus he used to warn him, so that he saved himself there more than once or twice.

11 And the mind of the king of Syria was greatly troubled because of this incident; and he called his servants and said to them, "Will you not show me who of us is for the king of Israel?" [12]And one of his servants said, "None, my lord, O king; but Eli′sha, the prophet who is in Israel, tells the king of Israel the words that you speak in your bedchamber." [13]And he said, "Go and see where he is, that I may send and seize him." It was told him, "Behold, he is in Do′than." [14]So he sent there horses and chariots and a great army; and they came by night, and surrounded the city.

15 When the servant of the man of God rose early in the morning and went out, behold, an army with horses and chariots was round about the city. And

---

5:18 house of Rimmon: A temple in Syria dedicated to the worship of a Semitic storm god also known as Hadad (Zech 12:11). **pardon:** Naaman hopes that he can still "go through the motions" of Syrian religion as a new believer in the God of Israel. Participation in the cult of Rimmon is probably a requirement of his office as commander of the Syrian army (5:1).

5:20 get something from him: In a twist of tragic irony, the greedy and lying Gehazi will "get" the leprosy of Naaman (5:27).

6:1 sons of the prophets: Students under the direction of Elisha. See note on 2:3.

6:5 axe head: Made of iron and therefore expensive to replace. Making it float to the surface is a miracle (6:6), showing that Elisha puts his extraordinary gifts at the service of all, including the poor who are forced to borrow tools from the wealthy. • *Allegorically*, just as Elisha, by throwing wood into the Jordan, raised the axe head so that the prophets could make a building for studying the precepts of God, so Christ, by the wood of the Cross and the water that

sanctifies, raised us from the mire of our sins and made us a house of prayer and worship (St. Justin Martyr, *Dialogue with Trypho* 86). Elisha invoked the name of the Lord, and the axe head came up from the water. We, too, are pressed down and submerged before Baptism, but afterward we are raised up. The wood tossed into the water shows that the Cross of Christ raises us up from infirmity (St. Ambrose, *On the Sacraments* 2, 4).

6:8—7:20 Stories that highlight the political side of Elisha's ministry. Beyond ministering to common folk, he also has dealings with elders (6:32) and kings (6:21) and counsels them on moral questions (6:21–22) and strategies for national defense (6:9–10).

6:9 the king of Israel: Jehoram (1:17).

6:10 used to warn him: Elisha, by his prophetic knowledge, supplies military intelligence to the king of Israel about the location of Syrian ambushes. This makes the Syrian king suspicious that one of his officers is a secret informant (6:11–13).

6:13 Dothan: In the hill country of central Israel.

the servant said, "Alas, my master! What shall we do?" [16]He said, "Fear not, for those who are with us are more than those who are with them." [17]Then Eli'sha prayed, and said, "O Lᴏʀᴅ, I beg you, open his eyes that he may see." So the Lᴏʀᴅ opened the eyes of the young man, and he saw; and behold, the mountain was full of horses and chariots of fire round about Eli'sha. [18]And when the Syrians came down against him, Eli'sha prayed to the Lᴏʀᴅ, and said, "Strike this people, I pray you, with blindness." So he struck them with blindness in accordance with the prayer of Elisha. [19]And Eli'sha said to them, "This is not the way, and this is not the city; follow me, and I will bring you to the man whom you seek." And he led them to Samar'ia.

20 As soon as they entered Samar'ia, Eli'sha said, "O Lᴏʀᴅ, open the eyes of these men, that they may see." So the Lᴏʀᴅ opened their eyes, and they saw; and behold, they were in the midst of Samaria. [21]When the king of Israel saw them he said to Eli'sha, "My father, shall I slay them? Shall I slay them?" [22]He answered, "You shall not slay them. Would you slay those whom you have taken captive with your sword and with your bow? Set bread and water before them, that they may eat and drink and go to their master." [23]So he prepared for them a great feast; and when they had eaten and drunk, he sent them away, and they went to their master. And the Syrians came no more on raids into the land of Israel.

Ben-hadad's Siege of Samaria

24 Afterward Ben-ha'dad king of Syria mustered his entire army, and went up, and besieged Samar'ia. [25]And there was a great famine in Samar'ia, as they besieged it, until a donkey's head was sold for eighty shekels of silver, and the fourth part of a kab of dove's dung for five shekels of silver. [26]Now as the king of Israel was passing by upon the wall, a woman cried out to him, saying, "Help, my lord, O king!" [27]And he said, "If the Lᴏʀᴅ will not help you, how shall I help you? From the threshing floor, or from the wine press?" [28]And the king asked her, "What is your trouble?" She answered, "This woman said to me, 'Give your son, that we may eat him today, and we will eat my son tomorrow.' [29]So we boiled my son, and ate him. And on the next day I said to her, 'Give your son, that we may eat him'; but she has hidden her son." [30]When the king heard the words of the woman he tore his clothes—now he was passing by upon the wall—and the people looked, and behold, he had sackcloth beneath upon his body—[31]and he said, "May God do so to me, and more also, if the head of Eli'sha the son of Sha'phat remains on his shoulders today."

32 Eli'sha was sitting in his house, and the elders were sitting with him. Now the king had dispatched a man from his presence; but before the messenger arrived Elisha said to the elders, "Do you see how this murderer has sent to take off my head? Look, when the messenger comes, shut the door, and hold the door fast against him. Is not the sound of his master's feet behind him?" [33]And while he was still speaking with them, the king[f] came down to him and said, "This trouble is from the Lᴏʀᴅ! Why should I wait for the Lᴏʀᴅ any longer?" [1]But Eli'sha said, "Hear the word of the Lᴏʀᴅ: thus says the Lᴏʀᴅ, Tomorrow about this time a measure of fine meal shall be sold for a shekel, and two measures of barley for a shekel, at the gate of Samar'ia." [2]Then the captain on whose hand the king leaned said to the man of God, "If the Lᴏʀᴅ himself should make windows in heaven, could this thing be?" But he said, "You shall see it with your own eyes, but you shall not eat of it."

The Syrians Flee

3 Now there were four men who were lepers at the entrance to the gate; and they said to one another, "Why do we sit here till we die? [4]If we say, 'Let us enter the city,' the famine is in the city, and we shall die there; and if we sit here, we die also. So now come, let us go over to the camp of the Syrians; if they spare our lives we shall live, and if they kill

---

6:17–20 These verses illustrate the Lord's control over physical and spiritual sight as well as physical and spiritual blindness. Spiritual vision is given to the servant, while physical sight is taken from the Syrians and then restored again in response to the prayers of Elisha. See note on 1 Kings 18:42.

6:17 chariots of fire: The heavenly hosts that took Elijah from the earth (2:11) now come to rescue Elisha from the Syrian siege and will likewise deliver Samaria (7:6).

6:19 Samaria: Capital of the Northern Kingdom. See note on 1 Kings 16:24.

6:22 shall not slay: Prisoners of war are not ordinarily executed unless the military ban of Deut 20:16–18 is put into effect. In this case, Elisha calls for hospitality rather than violent hostility.

6:24 Ben-hadad: Ben-hadad I or, more likely, Ben-hadad II. See note on 1 Kings 15:18.

6:25 great famine: Siege brings a scarcity of food, and this means greatly inflated prices, even for unappealing portions. Eventually the city is forced to witness the desperation and horror of cannibalism (6:29). **donkey's head:** Not only unsavory but legally unclean (Lev 11:26). **kab:** Over a quart.

6:30 sackcloth: A penitential sign of mourning (1 Kings 21:27; Jon 3:5).

6:31 God do so to me: A conditional self-curse. See note on Ruth 1:17.

7:1 Tomorrow: Elisha announces a swift end to the food shortage in Samaria. Thanks to the divine miracle mentioned in 7:6, normal foods will be sold at normal market prices the very next day. **the gate:** Could serve as a public marketplace during peacetime.

7:2 captain: A trusted advisor to the king. **could this thing be?:** The captain openly doubts the word of the Lord. Unbelief will cost him his life, for he will see the fulfillment of Elisha's words, but he will not survive to benefit from them (7:16–20).

7:3 lepers: Separated from Israelite settlements due to their legal uncleanness (Lev 13:45–46; Num 5:1–4).

---

f See 7:2: Heb *messenger*.

us we shall but die." ⁵So they arose at twilight to go to the camp of the Syrians; but when they came to the edge of the camp of the Syrians, behold, there was no one there. ⁶For the Lord had made the army of the Syrians hear the sound of chariots, and of horses, the sound of a great army, so that they said to one another, "Behold, the king of Israel has hired against us the kings of the Hittites and the kings of Egypt to come upon us." ⁷So they fled away in the twilight and forsook their tents, their horses, and their donkeys, leaving the camp as it was, and fled for their lives. ⁸And when these lepers came to the edge of the camp, they went into a tent, and ate and drank, and they carried off silver and gold and clothing, and went and hid them; then they came back, and entered another tent, and carried off things from it, and went and hid them.

9 Then they said to one another, "We are not doing right. This day is a day of good news; if we are silent and wait until the morning light, punishment will overtake us; now therefore come, let us go and tell the king's household." ¹⁰So they came and called to the gatekeepers of the city, and told them, "We came to the camp of the Syrians, and behold, there was no one to be seen or heard there, nothing but the horses tied, and the donkeys tied, and the tents as they were." ¹¹Then the gatekeepers called out, and it was told within the king's household. ¹²And the king rose in the night, and said to his servants, "I will tell you what the Syrians have prepared against us. They know that we are hungry; therefore they have gone out of the camp to hide themselves in the open country, thinking, 'When they come out of the city, we shall take them alive and get into the city.'" ¹³And one of his servants said, "Let some men take five of the remaining horses, seeing that those who are left here will fare like the whole multitude of Israel that have already perished; let us send and see." ¹⁴So they took two mounted men, and the king sent them after the army of the Syrians, saying, "Go and see." ¹⁵So they went after them as far as the Jordan; and, behold, all the way was littered with garments and equipment which the Syrians had thrown away in their haste. And the messengers returned, and told the king.

16 Then the people went out, and plundered the camp of the Syrians. So a measure of fine meal was sold for a shekel, and two measures of barley for a shekel, according to the word of the Lord. ¹⁷Now the king had appointed the captain on whose hand he leaned to have charge of the gate; and the people trod upon him in the gate, so that he died, as the man of God had said when the king came down to him. ¹⁸For when the man of God had said to the king, "Two measures of barley shall be sold for a shekel, and a measure of fine meal for a shekel, about this time tomorrow in the gate of Samar'ia," ¹⁹the captain had answered the man of God, "If the Lord himself should make windows in heaven, could such a thing be?" And he had said, "You shall see it with your own eyes, but you shall not eat of it." ²⁰And so it happened to him, for the people trod upon him in the gate and he died.

The Shunammite Woman's Land Restored

8 Now Eli'sha had said to the woman whose son he had restored to life, "Arise, and depart with your household, and sojourn wherever you can; for the Lord has called for a famine, and it will come upon the land for seven years." ²So the woman arose, and did according to the word of the man of God; she went with her household and sojourned in the land of the Philis'tines seven years. ³And at the end of the seven years, when the woman returned from the land of the Philis'tines, she went forth to appeal to the king for her house and her land. ⁴Now the king was talking with Geha'zi the servant of the man of God, saying, "Tell me all the great things that Eli'sha has done." ⁵And while he was telling the king how Eli'sha had restored the dead to life, behold, the woman whose son he had restored to life appealed to the king for her house and her land. And Geha'zi said, "My lord, O king, here is the woman, and here is her son whom Elisha restored to life." ⁶And when the king asked the woman, she told him. So the king appointed an official for her, saying, "Restore all that was hers, together with all the produce of the fields from the day that she left the land until now."

The Death of Ben-hadad

7 Now Eli'sha came to Damascus. Ben-ha'dad the king of Syria was sick; and when it was told him, "The man of God has come here," ⁸the king said to Haz'ael, "Take a present with you and go to meet the man of God, and inquire of the Lord

---

7:6 a great army: Not a horde of mercenary troops hired from elsewhere, as the Syrians suppose, but Yahweh's heavenly hosts. The sound of an approaching cavalry and chariotry sends the enemy into a panicked flight back to their homeland. **Hittites:** Peoples of the Syro-Hittite states north of Damascus.

7:9 We are not doing right: The testimony of a guilty conscience joined to a fear of divine retribution.

7:12 hide themselves: The king fears an ambush that will lead to the violent overthrow of Samaria.

7:16–20 The fulfillment of Elisha's prophecy in 7:1–2.

7:17 he died: I.e., he was trampled to death by the starving inhabitants of Samaria as they rushed out of the city in search of food.

8:1 the woman: The Shunammite woman from 4:8–37. **seven years:** Twice as long as the drought that weighed upon Israel in the days of Elijah. See note on 1 Kings 18:1.

8:2 Philistines: Occupied the coastlands of southwest Canaan. Temporary relocation was one way to survive a regional famine in ancient times (Gen 12:10; 26:1; Ruth 1:1).

8:3 her house: The woman returns to reclaim her family estate in Shunem (4:8). It was taken over, perhaps by the state, while she and her household sojourned in Philistia. Her appeal to the king of Israel is graciously accepted (8:6).

8:4 Gehazi: Elisha's personal attendant (4:12).

8:7 Damascus: Capital of the Aramean kingdom of Syria, north of Israel. Elisha undertakes a mission, first made known

through him, saying, 'Shall I recover from this sickness?'" ⁹So Haz′ael went to meet him, and took a present with him, all kinds of goods of Damascus, forty camel loads. When he came and stood before him, he said, "Your son Ben-ha′dad king of Syria has sent me to you, saying, 'Shall I recover from this sickness?'" ¹⁰And Eli′sha said to him, "Go, say to him, 'You shall certainly recover'; but the LORD has shown me that he shall certainly die." ¹¹And he fixed his gaze and stared at him, until he was ashamed. And the man of God wept. ¹²And Haz′ael said, "Why does my lord weep?" He answered, "Because I know the evil that you will do to the sons of Israel; you will set on fire their fortresses, and you will slay their young men with the sword, and dash in pieces their little ones, and rip up their women with child." ¹³And Haz′ael said, "What is your servant, who is but a dog, that he should do this great thing?" Eli′sha answered, "The LORD has shown me that you are to be king over Syria." ¹⁴Then he departed from Eli′sha, and came to his master, who said to him, "What did Elisha say to you?" And he answered, "He told me that you would certainly recover." ¹⁵But the next day he took the coverlet and dipped it in water and spread it over his face, till he died. And Haz′ael became king in his stead.

Jehoram Reigns over Judah

16 In the fifth year of Jo′ram the son of A′hab, king of Israel,ᵍ Jeho′ram the son of Jehosh′aphat, king of Judah, began to reign. ¹⁷He was thirty-two years old when he became king, and he reigned eight years in Jerusalem. ¹⁸And he walked in the way of the kings of Israel, as the house of A′hab had done, for the daughter of Ahab was his wife. And he did what was evil in the sight of the LORD. ¹⁹Yet the LORD would not destroy Judah, for the sake of David his servant, since he promised to give a lamp to him and to his sons for ever.

20 In his days E′dom revolted from the rule of Judah, and set up a king of their own. ²¹Then Jo′ram passed over to Za′ir with all his chariots, and rose by night, and he and his chariot commanders struck the E′domites who had surrounded him; but his army fled home. ²²So E′dom revolted from the rule of Judah to this day. Then Libnah revolted at the same time. ²³Now the rest of the acts of Jo′ram, and all that he did, are they not written in the Book of the Chronicles of the Kings of Judah? ²⁴So Jo′ram slept with his fathers, and was buried with his fathers in the city of David; and Ahazi′ah his son reigned in his stead.

Ahaziah Reigns over Judah

25 In the twelfth year of Jo′ram the son of A′hab, king of Israel, Ahazi′ah the son of Jeho′ram, king of Judah, began to reign. ²⁶Ahazi′ah was twenty-two years old when he began to reign, and he reigned one year in Jerusalem. His mother's name was Athali′ah; she was a granddaughter of Omri king of Israel. ²⁷He also walked in the way of the house of A′hab, and did what was evil in the sight of the LORD, as the house of Ahab had done, for he was son-in-law to the house of Ahab.

28 He went with Jo′ram the son of A′hab to make war against Haz′ael king of Syria at Ra′moth-gil′ead, where the Syrians wounded Joram. ²⁹And King

---

8:17–24: 2 Chron 21:5–10, 20. **8:24–29:** 2 Chron 22:1–6.

---

to Elijah, that Hazael is to be anointed king of Syria (1 Kings 19:15). **Ben-hadad:** See note on 6:24.

8:10 certainly recover ... certainly die: A riddle about the fate of Ben-hadad. Sickness will not take the king's life, and in time he would have experienced a full recovery. However, death is certain because Hazael, ruthless and ambitious, will suffocate the bedridden king before his health has a chance to return (8:15).

8:12 I know the evil: Elisha foresees that Hazael will bring bitter suffering on Israel.

8:13 but a dog: Words of self-deprecation (1 Sam 24:14; 2 Sam 9:8).

8:16 Jehoram: The fifth king of Judah (ca. 848 to 841 B.C.). He is criticized for imitating the corruption of King Ahab, who promoted the idolatrous worship of Baal in the Northern Kingdom (1 Kings 16:30–33). Jehoram's political marriage with Ahab's daughter (Athaliah, 8:26) occasioned a similar apostasy down south (8:18). The shortened form of his name is "Joram" (8:21). **began to reign:** Jehoram's independent rule over Judah comes after several years of joint rule with his father, Jehoshaphat. See note on 3:1.

8:19 a lamp: A sign of the Davidic covenant. See note on 1 Kings 11:36.

8:20 Edom: South of the Dead Sea. **revolted:** Edom had been a vassal state subject to Judah since the time of David (2 Sam 8:13–14). Jehoram's attempt to reclaim lordship over the rebel Edomites is unsuccessful (8:21–22).

8:21 Zair: Possibly a reference to Zoar near the southern edge of the Dead Sea.

8:22 Libnah: A city in western Judah near the Philistine border.

8:23 Book of the Chronicles: See note on 1 Kings 14:19.

8:24 the city of David: The southeastern part of Jerusalem.

8:25 Ahaziah: The sixth king of Judah (ca. 841 B.C.). His short reign is judged an evil reign, mainly because of the influence of Athaliah, the reigning queen mother (8:26), who was the daughter of Ahab and Jezebel (8:18) and thus a princess of the idolatrous Omride dynasty holding power in the north (2 Chron 22:3).

8:28 Jehoram: A shortened form of "Jehoram" (1:17). **Ramoth-gilead:** A fortified city in the Transjordan on the eastern frontier of Israel's territory. The name is shortened to "Ramah" in 8:29. **wounded:** Joram's father Ahab was injured fighting for the same city under similar circumstances (1 Kings 22:1–4, 34). And just as Ahab was pierced with an arrow and died in his chariot, so will Joram be (9:24).

8:29 Jezreel: Northwest of Mt. Gilboa in the tribal territory of Issachar (Josh 19:18). It seems the kings of Israel ruled from Samaria but maintained a second royal residence in Jezreel (1 Kings 21:1).

ᵍGk Syr: Heb *Israel, Jehoshaphat being king of Judah.*

Jo'ram returned to be healed in Jezre'el of the wounds which the Syrians had given him at Ra'mah, when he fought against Haz'ael king of Syria. And Ahazi'ah the son of Jeho'ram king of Judah went down to see Joram the son of A'hab in Jezre'el, because he was sick.

Anointing of Jehu

9 Then Eli'sha the prophet called one of the sons of the prophets and said to him, "Gird up your loins, and take this flask of oil in your hand, and go to Ra'moth-gil'ead. ²And when you arrive, look there for Je'hu the son of Jehosh'aphat, son of Nimshi; and go in and bid him rise from among his fellows, and lead him to an inner chamber. ³Then take the flask of oil, and pour it on his head, and say, 'Thus says the Lord, I anoint you king over Israel.' Then open the door and flee; do not tarry."

4 So the young man, the prophet,ʰ went to Ra'moth-gil'ead. ⁵And when he came, behold, the commanders of the army were in council; and he said, "I have an errand to you, O commander." And Je'hu said, "To which of us all?" And he said, "To you, O commander." ⁶So he arose, and went into the house; and the young man poured the oil on his head, saying to him, "Thus says the Lord the God of Israel, I anoint you king over the people of the Lord, over Israel. ⁷And you shall strike down the house of A'hab your master, that I may avenge on Jez'ebel the blood of my servants the prophets, and the blood of all the servants of the Lord. ⁸For the whole house of A'hab shall perish; and I will cut off from Ahab every male, bond or free, in Israel. ⁹And I will make the house of A'hab like the house of Jerobo'am the son of Ne'bat, and like the house of Ba'asha the son of Ahi'jah. ¹⁰And the dogs shall eat

Jez'ebel in the territory of Jezre'el, and none shall bury her." Then he opened the door, and fled.

11 When Je'hu came out to the servants of his master, they said to him, "Is all well? Why did this mad fellow come to you?" And he said to them, "You know the fellow and his talk." ¹²And they said, "That is not true; tell us now." And he said, "Thus and so he spoke to me, saying, 'Thus says the Lord, I anoint you king over Israel.'" ¹³Then in haste every man of them took his garment, and put it under him on the bareⁱ steps, and they blew the trumpet, and proclaimed, "Je'hu is king."

Joram of Israel Killed

14 Thus Je'hu the son of Jehosh'aphat the son of Nimshi conspired against Jo'ram. (Now Joram with all Israel had been on guard at Ra'moth-gil'ead against Haz'ael king of Syria; ¹⁵but King Jo'ram had returned to be healed in Jezre'el of the wounds which the Syrians had given him, when he fought with Haz'ael king of Syria.) So Je'hu said, "If this is your mind, then let no one slip out of the city to go and tell the news in Jezreel." ¹⁶Then Je'hu mounted his chariot, and went to Jezre'el, for Jo'ram lay there. And Ahazi'ah king of Judah had come down to visit Joram.

17 Now the watchman was standing on the tower in Jezre'el, and he spied the company of Je'hu as he came, and said, "I see a company." And Jo'ram said, "Take a horseman, and send to meet them, and let him say, 'Is it peace?'" ¹⁸So a man on horseback went to meet him, and said, "Thus says the king, 'Is it peace?'" And Je'hu said, "What have you to do with peace? Turn round and ride behind me." And the watchman reported, saying, "The messenger reached them, but he is not coming back." ¹⁹Then

---

9:1—10:36: 2 Chron 22:7–9.

9:1—10:36 Chapters 9 and 10 turn the spotlight on Jehu, the tenth king of Israel (ca. 841 to 814 B.C.). He is the least criticized of all the northern kings, partly because he puts an end to the wicked dynasty of Omri (9:21–10:17), but also because he launches a religious reform aimed at eradicating Baal worship from the Northern Kingdom (10:18–28). Nevertheless, he is faulted for making no effort to suppress the calf cult in Dan and Bethel (10:29). Jehu's own dynasty, the fifth in the Northern Kingdom, will extend for four generations after him (10:30). Outside the Bible, the *Black Obelisk of Shalmaneser III* makes reference to Jehu of Israel and depicts him bowing and offering tribute to the Assyrian king Shalmaneser III.

9:1 sons of the prophets: Students under the direction of Elisha. See note on 2:3.

9:6 oil on his head: Anointing symbolizes the power and authority of God's Spirit pouring down over the recipient, equipping him for covenant ministry (1 Sam 16:13; Is 61:1). The rite was performed for prophets (1 Kings 19:16), priests (Lev 8:12), and kings in Israel (1 Kings 1:39). Emptying the flask upon Jehu fulfills the instruction given to Elijah on Mt. Horeb (1 Kings 19:16).

9:7 the house of Ahab: Jehu is tasked with terminating the line of Omride rulers in power in the Northern Kingdom of Israel. Jehoram, the son of Ahab, is the fourth member of this dynasty to hold the royal office. **the blood of my servants:** Jezebel put numerous prophets of Yahweh to death (1 Kings 18:4; 19:10) and orchestrated the murder of an innocent man, Naboth the Jezreelite (1 Kings 21:5–14).

9:8 the whole house of Ahab: The royal family will be slaughtered in 10:1–17. **every male:** Every potential heir to the throne, as specified by Elijah in 1 Kings 21:21.

9:9 Jeroboam ... Baasha: Previous kings of Israel whose dynasties came to a violent end (1 Kings 15:28–29; 16:8–10).

9:11 mad fellow: The eccentric behavior of the prophets was sometimes considered a sign of insanity (Jer 29:26; Hos 9:7).

9:13 garment ... under him: A ceremonial act indicating submission to a new king's royal authority. • In a similar way, the crowds throw their garments under Jesus on Palm Sunday, making his ride into Jerusalem a public proclamation of his kingship (Mk 11:7–10; Lk 19:35–38).

9:14 Joram: Jehoram of Israel (1:17). **Ramoth-gilead:** See note on 8:28.

9:15 Jezreel: See note on 8:29.

9:17 Is it peace?: Shorthand for "Is the battle at Ramoth-gilead going well?"

ʰGk Syr: Heb *the young man, the young man, the prophet.*
ⁱThe meaning of the Hebrew word is uncertain.

he sent out a second horseman, who came to them, and said, "Thus the king has said, 'Is it peace?'" And Je′hu answered, "What have you to do with peace? Turn round and ride behind me." ²⁰Again the watchman reported, "He reached them, but he is not coming back. And the driving is like the driving of Je′hu the son of Nimshi; for he drives furiously."

21 Jo′ram said, "Make ready." And they made ready his chariot. Then Joram king of Israel and Ahazi′ah king of Judah set out, each in his chariot, and went to meet Je′hu, and met him at the property of Naboth the Jezre′elite. ²²And when Jo′ram saw Je′hu, he said, "Is it peace, Jehu?" He answered, "What peace can there be, so long as the harlotries and the sorceries of your mother Jez′e-bel are so many?" ²³Then Jo′ram reined about and fled, saying to Ahazi′ah, "Treachery, O Ahaziah!" ²⁴And Je′hu drew his bow with his full strength, and shot Jo′ram between the shoulders, so that the arrow pierced his heart, and he sank in his chariot.* ²⁵Je′hu said to Bidkar his aide, "Take him up, and cast him on the plot of ground belonging to Naboth the Jezre′elite; for remember, when you and I rode side by side behind A′hab his father, how the Lord uttered this oracle against him: ²⁶'As surely as I saw yesterday the blood of Naboth and the blood of his sons—says the Lord—I will repay you on this plot of ground.' Now therefore take him up and cast him on the plot of ground, in accordance with the word of the Lord."

Ahaziah of Judah Killed

27 When Ahazi′ah the king of Judah saw this, he fled in the direction of Beth-hag′gan. And Je′hu

pursued him, and said, "Shoot him also"; and they shot him ʲ in the chariot at the ascent of Gur, which is by Ib′leam. And he fled to Megid′do, and died there. ²⁸His servants carried him in a chariot to Jerusalem, and buried him in his tomb with his fathers in the city of David.

29 In the eleventh year of Jo′ram the son of A′hab, Ahazi′ah began to reign over Judah.

Jezebel's Violent Death

30 When Je′hu came to Jezre′el, Jez′ebel heard of it; and she painted her eyes, and adorned her head, and looked out of the window. ³¹And as Je′hu entered the gate, she said, "Is it peace, you Zimri, murderer of your master?" ³²And he lifted up his face to the window, and said, "Who is on my side? Who?" Two or three eunuchs looked out at him. ³³He said, "Throw her down." So they threw her down; and some of her blood spattered on the wall and on the horses, and they trampled on her. ³⁴Then he went in and ate and drank; and he said, "See now to this cursed woman, and bury her; for she is a king's daughter." ³⁵But when they went to bury her, they found no more of her than the skull and the feet and the palms of her hands. ³⁶When they came back and told him, he said, "This is the word of the Lord, which he spoke by his servant Eli′jah the Tishbite, 'In the territory of Jezre′el the dogs shall eat the flesh of Jez′ebel; ³⁷and the corpse of Jez′ebel shall be as dung upon the face of the field in the territory of Jezre′el, so that no one can say, This is Jezebel.'"

Massacre of Ahab's Descendants

10 Now A′hab had seventy sons in Samar′ia. So Je′hu wrote letters, and sent them to

---

9:25: 1 Kings 21:19.   9:36: 1 Kings 21:23.

9:21 went to meet Jehu: Joram is anxious for an update on the war effort. He does not appear suspicious that a coup is in the works. **Naboth the Jezreelite:** Once the rightful owner of a vineyard in Jezreel that was treacherously seized by Ahab and Jezebel (1 Kings 21:1–16).

9:22 harlotries ... sorceries: The superstitious rituals of Canaanite religion sponsored by Jezebel (1 Kings 16:31; 18:19). Her corruption of Israel was infamous to the point that her name came to stand for any woman who dared to lead the covenant people into moral and religious apostasy (Rev 2:20).

9:26 says the Lord: A paraphrase of Elijah's judgment oracles in 1 Kings 21:19, 29. These are fulfilled when the blood of Ahab's son, Joram, soaks into the ground of Naboth's field.

9:27 Beth-haggan: South of Jezreel. **they shot him:** Jehu's men assassinate Ahaziah, king of Judah, presumably because of his blood-ties (8:26) with the royal house of Ahab, which is now doomed to destruction (9:8). **Megiddo:** West of Jezreel.

9:29 the eleventh year: Repeats the information in 8:25 with a discrepancy of one year. Since the kingdoms of Israel and Judah calculated regnal years differently, it seems likely that the compiler of Kings drew his information from both Israelite and Judean sources. See chart: *Kings of the Divided Monarchy* at 1 Kings 12.

9:31 Zimri: Jehu is sarcastically associated with Zimri, another military officer who seized the throne of Israel by violence. Jezebel implies by this that Jehu will turn out to be a failure like Zimri, whose reign lasted a mere seven days (1 Kings 16:8–20).

9:34 a king's daughter: Jezebel was a Phoenician princess, the daughter of Ethbaal, king of Tyre (1 Kings 16:31).

9:36 the dogs shall eat: Elijah's gruesome prophecy appears in 1 Kings 21:23. It implies that Jezebel's disgraceful death is a fitting payback for her disgraceful deeds in life. • *Morally*, there is a stark difference between Ahab, who fell in battle, was mourned by his servants, and was buried with honor, and Jezebel, who was thrown to the ground, trampled by horses, and torn by dogs. The reason is because Ahab, despite his many crimes, showed a measure of repentance, whereas Jezebel never turned from the path of perversity. Hence there was cause for an especially harsh judgment against her (St. Ephraem the Syrian, *On Second Kings 9*, 32).

10:1–17 Jehu fulfills Elijah's oracle that the house of Ahab is doomed to extinction (1 Kings 21:21). The founding of a new dynasty was often a bloody affair in the ancient Near East, as it often involved a massacre of the royal predecessor's entire family (1 Kings 15:29; 16:11).

10:1 seventy sons: All male descendants, sons as well as grandsons, having a potential claim on the throne of Israel (9:8; Judg 9:5–6). **Samaria:** Capital of the Northern Kingdom. See note on 1 Kings 16:24.

---

*9:24: So was the sin of Ahab visited upon his son, according to the word of the Lord; cf. 1 Kings 21:29.
ʲ Syr Vg Compare Gk: Heb lacks *and they shot him*.

Samar′ia, to the rulers of the city,ᵏ to the elders, and to the guardians of the sons of Ahab, saying, ²"Now then, as soon as this letter comes to you, seeing your master's sons are with you, and there are with you chariots and horses, fortified cities also, and weapons, ³select the best and fittest of your master's sons and set him on his father's throne, and fight for your master's house." ⁴But they were exceedingly afraid, and said, "Behold, the two kings could not stand before him; how then can we stand?" ⁵So he who was over the palace, and he who was over the city, together with the elders and the guardians, sent to Je′hu, saying, "We are your servants, and we will do all that you bid us. We will not make any one king; do whatever is good in your eyes." ⁶Then he wrote to them a second letter, saying, "If you are on my side, and if you are ready to obey me, take the heads of your master's sons, and come to me at Jezre′el tomorrow at this time." Now the king's sons, seventy persons, were with the great men of the city, who were bringing them up. ⁷And when the letter came to them, they took the king's sons, and slew them, seventy persons, and put their heads in baskets, and sent them to him at Jezre′el. ⁸When the messenger came and told him, "They have brought the heads of the king's sons," he said, "Lay them in two heaps at the entrance of the gate until the morning." ⁹Then in the morning, when he went out, he stood, and said to all the people, "You are innocent. It was I who conspired against my master, and slew him; but who struck down all these? ¹⁰Know then that there shall fall to the earth nothing of the word of the Lᴏʀᴅ, which the Lᴏʀᴅ spoke concerning the house of A′hab; for the Lᴏʀᴅ has done what he said by his servant Eli′jah." ¹¹So Je′hu slew all that remained of the house of A′hab in Jezre′el, all his great men, and his familiar friends, and his priests, until he left him none remaining.

12 Then he set out and went to Samar′ia. On the way, when he was at Beth-ek′ed of the Shepherds, ¹³Je′hu met the kinsmen of Ahazi′ah king of Judah, and he said, "Who are you?" And they answered, "We are the kinsmen of Ahazi′ah, and we came down to visit the royal princes and the sons of the queen mother." ¹⁴He said, "Take them alive." And they took them alive, and slew them at the pit of Beth-ek′ed, forty-two persons, and he spared none of them.

15 And when he departed from there, he met Jehon′adab the son of Re′chab coming to meet

---

10:3 fight: Jehu engages in psychological warfare, hoping that the threat of military action will bring Samaria into submission to his reign. The tactic proves successful (10:5).

10:4 the two kings: Joram of Israel, who perished in 9:24, and Ahaziah of Judah, who died in 9:27.

10:5 over the palace: Literally "over the house". This is either the chief administrator of the royal palace or the prime minister of the Northern Kingdom. See word study: *Over the Household* at 1 Kings 16:9. **over the city:** The mayor of Samaria.

10:8 two heaps: Piling up severed heads in public is an intimidation tactic also attributed to the Assyrian rulers Ashurbanipal and Shalmaneser III.

10:10 fall to the earth: The fate of a prophetic word that goes unfulfilled (cf. 1 Sam 3:19).

10:11 men ... friends ... priests: Jehu's violent action exceeds his prophetic mandate (9:7-9). The Lord condemned Ahab's entire family to death, but Jehu refuses to stop at this and proceeds to exterminate all known associates of the dethroned regime. In speaking to the prophet Hosea, the Lord promises to punish the house of Jehu for this savage killing spree in Jezreel (Hos 1:4).

10:12 Beth-eked: Exact location unknown but somewhere between Jezreel and Samaria in central Israel.

10:13 kinsmen of Ahaziah: Members of the Judean royal family. They become victims of Jehu's coup because Ahaziah's mother was a daughter of King Ahab and thus a princess of the Northern Kingdom (8:25-27). **the queen mother:** Literally "the great Lady". For this position in biblical Israel, see essay: *The Queen Mother* at 1 Kings 2.

10:15 Jehonadab ... of Rechab: Jehu welcomes support from the Rechabites, a conservative clan known for its zealous devotion to Yahweh. They idealized Israel's nomadic life-style during the Exodus period and denied themselves advantages associated with urban and sedentary culture (Jer 35:1-11). For Jehu, they represent political allies in his campaign of religious reform (10:18-28).

ᵏGk Vg: Heb *Jezreel.*

WORD STUDY

Heads (10:6)

ro'sh (Heb.): A noun with various meanings in the Bible. It often refers to the uppermost part of the body, such as the "head" of person (Num 6:9), animal (Gen 3:15), or statue (Dan 2:32). Sometimes it refers to the "top" of an inanimate object, like the highest part of a tower (Gen 11:4) or the summit of a mountain (2 Sam 15:32). With reference to time, it can designate the first month of the calendar and thus the "beginning" of a new year (Ex 12:2). In the realm of human authority, a head is often understood as a leader, e.g., a military commander (2 Sam 23:8), a chief priest (2 Kings 25:18), a tribal judge (Ex 18:25), or a king who rules other nations (Ps 18:43). The flexibility of this term is exploited in Jehu's letter in 2 Kings 10:6, where he commands the officials of Samaria to bring him the "heads" of the sons of Ahab. This could mean that Jehu wants an audience with the leading figures of the royal family, or it could mean that he wants them decapitated. The inherent ambiguity in the word *ro'sh* enables Jehu to get what he wants (the death of Ahab's offspring) and yet disclaim responsibility for the murders (10:9).

him; and he greeted him, and said to him, "Is your heart true to my heart as mine is to yours?" [1] And Jehonadab answered, "It is." Je'hu said,[m] "If it is, give me your hand." So he gave him his hand. And Jehu took him up with him into the chariot. [16]And he said, "Come with me, and see my zeal for the LORD." So he[n] had him ride in his chariot. [17]And when he came to Samar'ia, he slew all that remained to A'hab in Samaria, till he had wiped them out, according to the word of the LORD which he spoke to Eli'jah.

Jehu Slaughters the Worshipers of Baal

18 Then Je'hu assembled all the people, and said to them, "A'hab served Ba'al a little; but Jehu will serve him much. [19]Now therefore call to me all the prophets of Ba'al, all his worshipers and all his priests; let none be missing, for I have a great sacrifice to offer to Baal; whoever is missing shall not live." But Je'hu did it with cunning in order to destroy the worshipers of Ba'al. [20]And Je'hu ordered, "Sanctify a solemn assembly for Ba'al." So they proclaimed it. [21]And Je'hu sent throughout all Israel; and all the worshipers of Ba'al came, so that there was not a man left who did not come. And they entered the house of Baal, and the house of Baal was filled from one end to the other. [22]He said to him who was in charge of the wardrobe, "Bring out the vestments for all the worshipers of Ba'al." So he brought out the vestments for them. [23]Then Je'hu went into the house of Ba'al with Jehon'adab the son of Re'chab; and he said to the worshipers of Baal, "Search, and see that there is no servant of the LORD here among you, but only the worshipers of Baal." [24]Then he[o] went in to offer sacrifices and burnt offerings.

Now Je'hu had stationed eighty men outside, and said, "The man who allows any of those whom I give into your hands to escape shall forfeit his life." [25]So as soon as he had made an end of offering the burnt offering, Je'hu said to the guard and to the officers, "Go in and slay them; let not a man escape." So when they put them to the sword, the guard and the officers cast them out and went into the inner room[p] of the house of Ba'al [26]and they brought out the pillar that was in the house of Ba'al, and burned it. [27]And they demolished the pillar of Ba'al, and demolished the house of Baal, and made it a latrine to this day.

28 Thus Je'hu wiped out Ba'al from Israel. [29]But Je'hu did not turn aside from the sins of Jerobo'am the son of Ne'bat, which he made Israel to sin, the golden calves that were in Bethel, and in Dan. [30]And the LORD said to Je'hu, "Because you have done well in carrying out what is right in my eyes, and have done to the house of A'hab according to all that was in my heart, your sons of the fourth generation shall sit on the throne of Israel." [31]But Je'hu was not careful to walk in the law of the LORD the God of Israel with all his heart; he did not turn from the sins of Jerobo'am, which he made Israel to sin.

Death of Jehu

32 In those days the LORD began to cut off parts of Israel. Haz'ael defeated them throughout the territory of Israel: [33]from the Jordan eastward, all the land of Gilead, the Gadites, and the Reubenites, and the Manas'sites, from Aro'er, which is by the valley of the Arnon, that is, Gilead and Bashan. [34]Now the rest of the acts of Je'hu, and all that he did, and all his might, are they not written in the Book of the Chronicles of the Kings of Israel? [35]So Je'hu slept with his fathers, and they buried him in Samar'ia. And Jeho'ahaz his son reigned in his stead. [36]The time that Je'hu reigned over Israel in Samar'ia was twenty-eight years.

10:17 spoke to Elijah: The oracle appears in 1 Kings 21: 21–22.

10:18 Baal: The storm and fertility god of Canaanite religion. Ahab and Jezebel introduced Baal worship into the Northern Kingdom and financed the construction of a Baal temple in Samaria (called the "house of Baal" in 10:21 and 1 Kings 16:32).

10:19 prophets of Baal: Supported by state monies on the authority of Jezebel (1 Kings 18:19). **cunning:** The author acknowledges that Jehu uses sinful tactics (deception leading to murder) to achieve a praiseworthy outcome (the suppression of Baal worship) without endorsing his actions. According to Christian moral standards, evil may never be done with the intention that good may result from it. In other words, the ends do not justify the means (Rom 3:8; CCC 1789).

10:27 pillar of Baal: An upright stone venerated as a cultic object. Pillars are destroyed by heating them with fire and then splashing cold water on them so that the stone splits and cracks apart. **latrine:** Baal's temple is not only destroyed but permanently desecrated.

10:29 the golden calves: Idols worshiped as "other gods" (1 Kings 14:9). See note on 1 Kings 12:28.

10:30 fourth generation: The promise of a modest dynasty. Four of Jehu's descendants will rule over the Northern Kingdom of Israel in succession: Jehoahaz, Jehoash, Jeroboam II, and Zechariah. See chart: *Kings of the Divided Monarchy* at 1 Kings 12.

10:31 not ... all his heart: Jehu falls short of the Deuteronomic ideal of loving the Lord with his entire heart, soul, and strength (Deut 6:4–5). Tolerating the northern calf cult is clear evidence that Jehu's commitment to Yahweh is partial rather than complete (10:29). **the sins of Jeroboam:** See note on 1 Kings 15:26.

10:32–33 Syria conquers the Transjordan, annexing the tribal territories of Reuben, Gad, and Manasseh. The Northern Kingdom is thus downsized and confined to the tribal lands west of the Jordan (and north of Bethel).

10:34 Book of the Chronicles: See note on 1 Kings 14:19.

10:35 Jehoahaz: The account of his reign appears in 13:1–9.

---

[1]Gk: Heb *Is it right with your heart, as my heart is with your heart?*
[m]Gk: Heb lacks *Jehu said.*
[n]Gk Syr Tg: Heb *they.*
[o]Gk Compare verse 25: Heb *they.*
[p]Cn: Heb *city.*

Athaliah Reigns over Judah

11 Now when Athali′ah the mother of Ahazi′ah saw that her son was dead, she arose and destroyed all the royal family. ²But Jehosh′eba, the daughter of King Jo′ram, sister of Ahazi′ah, took Jo′ash the son of Ahaziah, and stole him away from among the king's sons who were about to be slain, and she put^q him and his nurse in a bedchamber. Thus she^r hid him from Athali′ah, so that he was not slain; ³and he remained with her six years, hid in the house of the LORD, while Athali′ah reigned over the land.

Jehoiada Anoints the Child Joash

4 But in the seventh year Jehoi′ada sent and brought the captains of the Cari′tes and of the guards, and had them come to him in the house of the LORD; and he made a covenant with them and put them under oath in the house of the LORD, and he showed them the king's son. ⁵And he commanded them, "This is the thing that you shall do: one third of you, those who come off duty on the sabbath and guard the king's house ⁶(another third being at the gate Sur and a third at the gate behind the guards), shall guard the palace; ⁷and the two divisions of you, which come on duty in force on the sabbath and guard the house of the LORD,^s ⁸shall surround the king, each with his weapons in his hand; and whoever approaches the ranks is to be slain. Be with the king when he goes out and when he comes in."

9 The captains did according to all that Jehoi′ada the priest commanded, and each brought his men who were to go off duty on the sabbath, with those who were to come on duty on the sabbath, and came to Jehoiada the priest. ¹⁰And the priest delivered to the captains the spears and shields that had been King David's, which were in the house of the LORD; ¹¹and the guards stood, every man with his weapons in his hand, from the south side of the house to the north side of the house, around the altar and the house.^t ¹²Then he brought out the king's son, and put the crown upon him, and gave him the covenant; and they proclaimed him king, and anointed him; and they clapped their hands, and said, "Long live the king!"

Death of Athaliah

13 When Athali′ah heard the noise of the guard and of the people, she went into the house of the LORD to the people; ¹⁴and when she looked, there was the king standing by the pillar, according to the custom, and the captains and the trumpeters beside the king, and all the people of the land rejoicing and blowing trumpets. And Athali′ah tore her clothes, and cried, "Treason! Treason!" ¹⁵Then Jehoi′ada the priest commanded the captains who were set over the army, "Bring her out between the ranks; and slay with the sword any one who follows her." For the priest said, "Let her not be slain in the house of the LORD." ¹⁶So they laid hands on her; and she went through the horses' entrance to the king's house, and there she was slain.

17 And Jehoi′ada made a covenant between the LORD and the king and people, that they should

---

11:1–20: 2 Chron 22:10—23:21.

11:1–21 The rise and fall of Athaliah, a usurper queen who seized control of the kingdom of Judah for six years (ca. 841 to 835 B.C.). Her rule was illegitimate from the start: being the daughter of Ahab and Jezebel from the north, she was not a biological member of the royal family of David (8:18); rather, she was the granddaughter of King Omri of Israel (8:29). Athaliah tried to exterminate the Davidic line (11:1) and apparently followed the example of her parents by introducing Baal worship into her domain (compare 11:18 with 1 Kings 16:30–33).
11:1 dead: Ahaziah was fatally wounded by Jehu's archers (9:27).
11:2 Jehosheba: The wife of Jehoiada, introduced in 11:4, and thus the aunt of the young Joash (2 Chron 22:11). **Joash:** The sole survivor of David's royal line, thanks to the shrewd actions of Davidic loyalists who stashed him away in the Temple (11:3) until the time for his coronation (11:12). Joash comes to the throne as a seven-year-old boy and reigns forty years in Jerusalem (ca. 835 to 796 B.C.). The long form of his name is "Jehoash" (11:21).
11:3 while Athaliah reigned: The absence of a regnal formula, used elsewhere to provide chronological and biographical information about the kings of Israel and Judah, suggests the author of Kings did not view her rule as lawful.

11:4 Jehoiada: The priest in Jerusalem who choreographs both the enthronement of young Joash (11:4–12) and the dethronement of Queen Athaliah (11:13–16). He is the uncle of the boy-king and will serve as his religious instructor (12:2). **Carites:** A mercenary guard unit, perhaps linked to the "Cherethites" hired by David (2 Sam 8:18). They provide security for the royal palace and Temple of Jerusalem. The changing of the guard occurs on the Sabbath (11:5, 7).
11:6 the gate Sur: Called the "Gate of the Foundation" in 2 Chron 23:5.
11:10 spears and shields: Weapons confiscated as plunder from David's victories on the battlefield (2 Sam 8:3–11).
11:12 the crown: The royal headpiece is a sign of the covenant God made with David (Ps 89:39). See essay: *The Davidic Covenant* at 2 Sam 7. **the covenant:** A copy of Deuteronomy, which the kings of Israel were to acquire from the Levitical priests (see Deut 17:18–20). **anointed:** With oil from a flask. See note on 9:6. **Long live the king!:** For similar royal acclamations, see 9:13 and 1 Kings 1:39.
11:14 the pillar: One of the two bronze pillars, Jachin and Boaz, that stand at the entrance to the Temple (1 Kings 7:15–22). **the custom:** Also mentioned in connection with Josiah's renewal of the covenant (23:3). **the people of the land:** Appears to be a class of wealthy and influential citizens within the general population of Judah. Its loyalty to the dynastic house of David is seen on several occasions (see also 14:21; 21:24; 23:30).
11:17 a covenant: The people renew their commitment to the Deuteronomic covenant, which lays important obligations

---

^q With 2 Chron 22:11: Heb lacks *and she put*.
^r Gk Syr Vg Compare 2 Chron 22:11: Heb *they*.
^s Heb *the* LORD *to the king*.
^t Heb *the house to the king*.

be the Lord's people; and also between the king and the people. [18]Then all the people of the land went to the house of Ba'al, and tore it down; his altars and his images they broke in pieces, and they slew Mattan the priest of Baal before the altars. And the priest posted watchmen over the house of the Lord. [19]And he took the captains, the Cari'tes, the guards, and all the people of the land; and they brought the king down from the house of the Lord, marching through the gate of the guards to the king's house. And he took his seat on the throne of the kings. [20]So all the people of the land rejoiced; and the city was quiet after Athali'ah had been slain with the sword at the king's house.

Reign of Jehoash and the Repair of the Temple

[21][u]Jeho'ash was seven years old when he began to reign.

12 In the seventh year of Je'hu Jeho'ash began to reign, and he reigned forty years in Jerusalem. His mother's name was Zib'iah of Be'ershe'ba. [2]And Jeho'ash did what was right in the eyes of the Lord all his days, because Jehoi'ada the priest instructed him. [3]Nevertheless the high places were not taken away; the people continued to sacrifice and burn incense on the high places.

[4]Jeho'ash said to the priests, "All the money of the holy things which is brought into the house of the Lord, the money for which each man is assessed— the money from the assessment of persons—and the money which a man's heart prompts him to bring into the house of the Lord, [5]let the priests take, each from his acquaintance; and let them repair the house wherever any need of repairs is discovered." [6]But by the twenty-third year of King Jeho'ash the priests had made no repairs on the house. [7]Therefore King Jeho'ash summoned Jehoi'ada the priest and the other priests and said to them, "Why are you not repairing the house? Now therefore take no more money from your acquaintances, but hand it over for the repair of the house." [8]So the priests agreed that they should take no more money from the people, and that they should not repair the house.

[9]Then Jehoi'ada the priest took a chest, and bored a hole in the lid of it, and set it beside the altar on the right side as one entered the house of the Lord; and the priests who guarded the threshold put in it all the money that was brought into the house of the Lord. [10]And whenever they saw that there was much money in the chest, the king's secretary and the high priest came up and they counted and tied up in bags the money that was found in the house of the Lord. [11]Then they would give the money that was weighed out into the hands of the workmen who had the oversight of the house of the Lord; and they paid it out to the carpenters and the builders who worked upon the house of the Lord, [12]and to the masons and the stonecutters, as well as to buy timber and quarried stone for making repairs on the house of the Lord, and for any outlay upon the repairs of the house. [13]But there were not made for the house of the Lord basins of silver, snuffers, bowls, trumpets, or any vessels of gold, or of silver, from the money that was brought into the house of the Lord, [14]for that was given to the workmen who were repairing the house of the Lord with it. [15]And they did not ask an accounting from the men into whose hand they delivered the money to pay out to the workmen, for they dealt honestly. [16]The money from the guilt offerings and the money from the sin offerings was not brought into the house of the Lord; it belonged to the priests.

Hazael of Syria Threatens Jerusalem

[17]At that time Haz'ael king of Syria went up and fought against Gath, and took it. But when Hazael set his face to go up against Jerusalem, [18]Jeho'ash king of Judah took all the votive gifts that Jehosh'aphat

---

11:21—12:14: 2 Chron 24:1–14.   **12:17-21:** 2 Chron 24:23–26.

---

on the king (Deut 17:14–20) and declares Israel to be the holy People of God (Deut 7:6–11).

11:18 house of Baal: A temple dedicated to worship of the Canaanite storm and fertility god. Athaliah, who hails from a family of avid Baal worshipers (Ahab and Jezebel, 1 Kings 16:30–32), must have sponsored the building of this shrine during her six years in power (11:3). **slew ... the priest:** On the authority of Deut 13:1–11, which demands the execution of anyone who leads the covenant people into idolatry.

12:1 Jehoash: A longer form of the name "Joash" (12:19). See note on 11:2.

12:2 instructed him: The Levitical priests are the official teachers of Mosaic religion (Lev 10:11; Deut 33:10).

12:3 high places: Pagan shrines that should have been destroyed (Deut 12:2). See word study: *High Places* at 23:5.

12:4-16 Structural maintenance is needed on the Solomonic Temple, which was built more than a century before Jehoash came to power. Temple revenues are set aside to pay for the project, including money from paid vows (Lev 27:1–8) and the census tax (Ex 30:11–16). The task is first entrusted to the priesthood (12:4–8), but later the responsibility is given to construction supervisors and tradesmen who are so honest that Jehoash allows them to work without a strict accounting of expenditures (12:9–16).

12:9 a chest: A collection box for private donations. **priests who guarded:** Three priests stand guard as sentries to prevent unlawful encroachment into the sanctuary (25:18). They also receive the donations for deposit in the chest (22:4).

12:16 guilt offerings: See Lev 5:14—6:7. **sin offerings:** See Lev 4:1—5:13.

12:17 Gath: Either the Philistine city of Gath southwest of Jerusalem (1 Sam 6:17) or the Israelite city of Gittaim northwest of Jerusalem (2 Sam 4:3).

12:18 votive gifts: Monies and precious metals dedicated to the sanctuary by a vow. Here donations to the treasury by previous kings are given to the Syrians in exchange for calling off a planned assault on Jerusalem. Gifts of silver and gold were often the "price" of peace in the days of the kings (18:13–16; 1 Kings 15:18–19).

---

[u]Ch 12:1 in Heb.

and Jeho'ram and Ahazi'ah, his fathers, the kings of Judah, had dedicated, and his own votive gifts, and all the gold that was found in the treasuries of the house of the LORD and of the king's house, and sent these to Haz'ael king of Syria. Then Hazael went away from Jerusalem.

Death of Joash

19 Now the rest of the acts of Jo'ash, and all that he did, are they not written in the Book of the Chronicles of the Kings of Judah? ²⁰His servants arose and made a conspiracy, and slew Jo'ash in the house of Millo, on the way that goes down to Silla. ²¹It was Jo'zacar the son of Shim'eath and Jeho'zabad the son of Shomer, his servants, who struck him down, so that he died. And they buried him with his fathers in the city of David, and Amazi'ah his son reigned in his stead.

Jehoahaz Reigns over Israel

13 In the twenty-third year of Jo'ash the son of Ahazi'ah, king of Judah, Jeho'ahaz the son of Je'hu began to reign over Israel in Samar'ia, and he reigned seventeen years. ²He did what was evil in the sight of the LORD, and followed the sins of Jerobo'am the son of Ne'bat, which he made Israel to sin; he did not depart from them. ³And the anger of the LORD was kindled against Israel, and he gave them continually into the hand of Haz'ael king of Syria and into the hand of Ben-ha'dad the son of Hazael. ⁴Then Jeho'ahaz besought the LORD, and the LORD listened to him; for he saw the oppression of Israel, how the king of Syria oppressed them. ⁵(Therefore the LORD gave Israel a savior, so that they escaped from the hand of the Syrians; and the sons of Israel dwelt in their homes as formerly. ⁶Nevertheless they did not depart from the sins of the house of Jerobo'am, which he made Israel to

sin, but walked^v in them; and the Ashe'rah also remained in Samar'ia.) ⁷For there was not left to Jeho'ahaz an army of more than fifty horsemen and ten chariots and ten thousand footmen; for the king of Syria had destroyed them and made them like the dust at threshing. ⁸Now the rest of the acts of Jeho'ahaz and all that he did, and his might, are they not written in the Book of the Chronicles of the Kings of Israel? ⁹So Jeho'ahaz slept with his fathers, and they buried him in Samar'ia; and Jo'ash his son reigned in his stead.

Jehoash Reigns over Israel

10 In the thirty-seventh year of Jo'ash king of Judah Jeho'ash the son of Jeho'ahaz began to reign over Israel in Samar'ia, and he reigned sixteen years. ¹¹He also did what was evil in the sight of the LORD; he did not depart from all the sins of Jerobo'am the son of Ne'bat, which he made Israel to sin, but he walked in them. ¹²Now the rest of the acts of Jo'ash, and all that he did, and the might with which he fought against Amazi'ah king of Judah, are they not written in the Book of the Chronicles of the Kings of Israel? ¹³So Jo'ash slept with his fathers, and Jerobo'am sat upon his throne; and Joash was buried in Samar'ia with the kings of Israel.

Death of Elisha

14 Now when Eli'sha had fallen sick with the illness of which he was to die, Jo'ash king of Israel went down to him, and wept before him, crying, "My father, my father! The chariots of Israel and its horsemen!" ¹⁵And Eli'sha said to him, "Take a bow and arrows"; so he took a bow and arrows. ¹⁶Then he said to the king of Israel, "Draw the bow"; and he drew it. And Eli'sha laid his hands upon the king's hands. ¹⁷And he said, "Open the window eastward"; and he opened it. Then Eli'sha said, "Shoot"; and he

---

12:19 Book of the Chronicles: See note on 1 Kings 14:19.

12:20 conspiracy: No motive for this is given in 2 Kings. The reason for the assassination is spelled out in 2 Chron 24:17-27. **the house of Millo:** Perhaps part of a terraced structure in southeast Jerusalem. See note on 1 Kings 9:15. **Silla:** Otherwise unknown.

12:21 Amaziah: The account of his reign appears in 14:1-20.

13:1 Jehoahaz: The 11th king of Israel (ca. 814 to 798 B.C.). The narrator faults him for maintaining the state religion of Jeroboam (described in 1 Kings 12:25-33) and claims that foreign oppression is Yahweh's discipline upon Israel for this wrongdoing (17:5-7). Conflicts with Syria reduced his cavalry and chariot corps to the size of a large police squad (13:7). **Samaria:** Capital of the Northern Kingdom. See note on 1 Kings 16:24.

13:2 the sins of Jeroboam: See note on 1 Kings 15:26.

13:3 anger of the LORD: A theological explanation for Israel's troubles. **Hazael:** Became king of Syria in 8:15. **Ben-hadad:** Most likely Ben-hadad III. See note on 1 Kings 15:18.

13:5 a savior: A deliverer who will free Israel from foreign oppression. The narrator has in mind Jehoahaz's grandson, Jeroboam II, who will recover lands belonging to Israel from Syrian control (14:25-27).

13:6 Asherah: A sacred tree or pole dedicated to Asherah, a fertility goddess of Canaanite religion. Ahab was responsible for erecting this cultic object in Samaria (1 Kings 16:32-33).

13:7 ten thousand footmen: A sizeable infantry despite heavy losses in other divisions of the army. For large numbers in the Bible, see note on Num 1:46.

13:8 Book of the Chronicles: See note on 1 Kings 14:19.

13:10 Jehoash: The 12th king of Israel (ca. 798 to 782 B.C.). His kingship is criticized as a time of evil (13:11), although he managed to reclaim several Israelite cities that had fallen into Syrian hands (13:25). The shorter form of his name is "Joash" (13:12, 13, 14).

13:11 the sins of Jeroboam: See note on 1 Kings 15:26.

13:12 fought against Amaziah: Documented in 14:8-14.

13:13 Jeroboam: Jeroboam II, whose reign is summarized in 14:23-29.

13:14-21 The conclusion of the Elisha cycle. See note on 2:1—8:15.

13:14 My father ... chariots ... horsemen!: Exclamations that Elisha himself uttered at Elijah's departure at the end of his life (2:12).

13:17 arrow of victory: Prophetic actions such as this one announce God's plans for the future. Helping the king shoot the bow out the east window is a sign that Yahweh will help him achieve victory over the Syrians, who had conquered the

---

^v Gk Syr Tg Vg: Heb *he walked*.

shot. And he said, "The Lord's arrow of victory, the arrow of victory over Syria! For you shall fight the Syrians in A'phek until you have made an end of them." ¹⁸And he said, "Take the arrows"; and he took them. And he said to the king of Israel, "Strike the ground with them"; and he struck three times, and stopped. ¹⁹Then the man of God was angry with him, and said, "You should have struck five or six times; then you would have struck down Syria until you had made an end of it, but now you will strike down Syria only three times."

20 So Eli'sha died, and they buried him. Now bands of Moabites used to invade the land in the spring of the year. ²¹And as a man was being buried, behold, a marauding band was seen and the man was cast into the grave of Eli'sha; and as soon as the man touched the bones of Elisha, he revived, and stood on his feet.

Israel Recaptures Its Cities from Syria

22 Now Haz'ael king of Syria oppressed Israel all the days of Jeho'ahaz. ²³But the Lord was gracious to them and had compassion on them, and he turned toward them, because of his covenant with Abraham, Isaac, and Jacob, and would not destroy them; nor has he cast them from his presence until now.

24 When Haz'ael king of Syria died, Ben-ha'dad his son became king in his stead. ²⁵Then Jeho'ash the son of Jeho'ahaz took again from Ben-ha'dad the son of Haz'ael the cities which he had taken from Jehoahaz his father in war. Three times Jo'ash defeated him and recovered the cities of Israel.

Amaziah Reigns over Judah

14 In the second year of Jo'ash the son of Jo'ahaz, king of Israel, Amazi'ah the son of Joash, king of Judah, began to reign. ²He was twenty-five years old when he began to reign, and he reigned twenty-nine years in Jerusalem. His mother's name was Je'ho-ad'din of Jerusalem. ³And he did what was right in the eyes of the Lord, yet not like David his father; he did in all things as Jo'ash his father had done. ⁴But the high places were not removed; the people still sacrificed and burned incense on the high places. ⁵And as soon as the royal power was firmly in his hand he killed his servants who had slain the king his father. ⁶But he did not put to death the children of the murderers; according to what is written in the book of the law of Moses, where the Lord commanded, "The fathers shall not be put to death for the children, or the children be put to death for the fathers; but every man shall die for his own sin."

7 He killed ten thousand E'domites in the Valley of Salt and took Se'la by storm, and called it Jok'the-el, which is its name to this day.

8 Then Amazi'ah sent messengers to Jeho'ash the son of Jeho'ahaz, son of Je'hu, king of Israel, saying, "Come, let us look one another in the face."

14:2–6: 2 Chron 25:1–4.   **14:7:** 2 Chron 25:11.   **14:8–14:** 2 Chron 25:17–24.

Israelite territories east of the Jordan (10:32–33). **Aphek:** East of the Sea of Galilee and the site of Israel's triumph over the Syrians once before (1 Kings 20:26–30).

13:19 only three times: The king fails to grasp the prophetic import of the sign. His lack of enthusiasm points to a lack of faith, and this will result in a partial victory over Syria rather than a complete and decisive one. For a similar instance where God called for a sign that was incorrectly performed, see Num 20:2–13.

13:20 in the spring: The usual time for military expeditions. See note on 2 Sam 11:1.

13:21 bones of Elisha: Even in death the prophet imparts life to others. For Elisha's earlier resurrection miracle, see 4:32–35. • Catholic teaching on the efficacy of holy relics is illustrated by this episode, where healing power is transmitted through contact with the buried remains of Elisha. This shows that the bodies and belongings of the saints can occasion great miracles (see also Mt 14:36; Acts 19:11–12). • Regarding those who live with God, even their relics are not without honor. The prophet Elisha, after falling into the sleep of death, raises a dead man to life, for that man's body touches Elisha's bones and he revives. Such would not have happened unless the body of Elisha was holy (*Apostolic Constitutions* 6, 30).

13:23 covenant with Abraham: The basis of Israel's election as the Lord's chosen people (Deut 7:6–8). God's pledge to the patriarchs also functions as an insurance policy against Israel's annihilation (Ex 32:9–14). It is because of this covenant that Yahweh shows mercy and patience, allowing his people time to repent (Rom 2:4; 2 Pet 3:9).

13:25 the cities: Unidentified but probably west of the Jordan.

14:1 Amaziah: The eighth king of Judah (ca. 796 to 767 B.C.). He is praised for doing many things "right" (14:3); at the same time, he is criticized for tolerating unlawful worship in the Southern Kingdom (14:4) and for letting his pride bring disgrace upon Jerusalem (14:8–14). Chronological factors suggest that Amaziah must have reigned jointly with his son, Azariah, during his final years (14:21). See chart: *Kings of the Divided Monarchy* at 1 Kings 12.

14:3 not like David: See note on 1 Kings 15:3.

14:4 high places: Pagan shrines that should have been destroyed (Deut 12:2). See word study: *High Places* at 23:5.

14:5 killed his servants: His father's assassins are named in 12:21.

14:6 the law of Moses: The quotation that follows comes from Deut 24:16.

14:7 Edomites: Descendants of Esau, brother of the patriarch Jacob (Gen 36:1–43). They broke away from Judah in 8:20 after years of political vassalage imposed by David (2 Sam 8:13–14). Amaziah is attempting to bring the Edomites once again under Judean control (2 Chron 25:11–12). **Valley of Salt:** South of the Dead Sea. **Sela:** Exact location uncertain.

14:8 in the face: Amaziah is brimming with overconfidence because of his recent triumph over Edom. Foolishly, he challenges the kingdom of Israel to face off in battle against the kingdom of Judah. The king is about to learn that pride comes before a fall (Prov 16:18).

⁹And Jeho′ash king of Israel sent word to Amazi′ah king of Judah, "A thistle in Lebanon sent to a cedar in Lebanon, saying, 'Give your daughter to my son for a wife'; and a wild beast of Lebanon passed by and trampled down the thistle. ¹⁰You have indeed struck down E′dom, and your heart has lifted you up. Be content with your glory, and stay at home; for why should you provoke trouble so that you fall, you and Judah with you?"

11 But Amazi′ah would not listen. So Jeho′ash king of Israel went up, and he and Amaziah king of Judah faced one another in battle at Beth-she′mesh, which belongs to Judah. ¹²And Judah was defeated by Israel, and every man fled to his home. ¹³And Jeho′ash king of Israel captured Amazi′ah king of Judah, the son of Jehoash, son of Ahazi′ah, at Beth-she′mesh, and came to Jerusalem, and broke down the wall of Jerusalem for four hundred cubits, from the E′phraim Gate to the Corner Gate. ¹⁴And he seized all the gold and silver, and all the vessels that were found in the house of the Lord and in the treasuries of the king's house, also hostages, and he returned to Samar′ia.

15 Now the rest of the acts of Jeho′ash which he did, and his might, and how he fought with Amazi′ah king of Judah, are they not written in the Book of the Chronicles of the Kings of Israel? ¹⁶And Jeho′ash slept with his fathers, and was buried in Samar′ia with the kings of Israel; and Jerobo′am his son reigned in his stead.

17 Amazi′ah the son of Jo′ash, king of Judah, lived fifteen years after the death of Jeho′ash son of Jeho′ahaz, king of Israel. ¹⁸Now the rest of the deeds of Amazi′ah, are they not written in the Book of the Chronicles of the Kings of Judah? ¹⁹And they made a conspiracy against him in Jerusalem, and he fled to La′chish. But they sent after him to Lachish, and slew him there. ²⁰And they brought him upon horses; and he was buried in Jerusalem with his fathers in the city of David. ²¹And all the people of Judah took Azari′ah,* who was sixteen years old, and made him king instead of his father Amazi′ah. ²²He built E′lath and restored it to Judah, after the king slept with his fathers.

Jeroboam II Reigns over Israel

23 In the fifteenth year of Amazi′ah the son of Jo′ash, king of Judah, Jerobo′am the son of Joash, king of Israel, began to reign in Samar′ia, and he reigned forty-one years. ²⁴And he did what was evil in the sight of the Lord; he did not depart from all the sins of Jerobo′am the son of Ne′bat, which he made Israel to sin. ²⁵He restored the border of Israel from the entrance of Ha′math as far as the Sea of the Ar′abah, according to the word of the Lord, the God of Israel, which he spoke by his servant Jonah the son of Amit′tai, the prophet, who was from Gath-he′pher. ²⁶For the Lord saw that the affliction of Israel was very bitter, for there was none left, bond or free, and there was none to help Israel. ²⁷But the Lord had not said that he would blot out the name of Israel from under heaven, so he saved them by the hand of Jerobo′am the son of Jo′ash.

28 Now the rest of the acts of Jerobo′am, and all that he did, and his might, how he fought, and how he recovered for Israel Damascus and Ha′math, which had belonged to Judah, are they not written in the Book of the Chronicles of the

---

14:17–20: 2 Chron 25:25–28. **14:21, 22:** 2 Chron 26:1, 2.

14:9 sent word: The message is a parable. Judah is the small and annoying **thistle**; Israel is the tall and mighty **cedar**; and Jehoash is the trampling **beast**.

14:11 Beth-shemesh: Over 15 miles west of Jerusalem.

14:13–14 An anticipation of things to come, when Babylonian conquerors will capture the king of Judah, tear down the walls of Jerusalem, plunder the Temple of precious metals and sacred vessels, and take captives into exile (see 25:1–15).

14:13 broke down the wall: Roughly 600 feet of Jerusalem's north wall is dismantled. The breach is made between the Ephraim Gate, which faces north, and the Corner Gate, which opens at the angle where the north wall meets the west wall.

14:15 Book of the Chronicles: See note on 1 Kings 14:19.

14:16 Jeroboam: The account of his reign appears in 14:23–29.

14:18 Book of the Chronicles: See note on 1 Kings 14:19.

14:19 conspiracy: His father was likewise the victim of a conspiracy in 12:20–21. **Lachish:** About 30 miles southwest of Jerusalem (Tell ed-Duweir).

14:21 the people of Judah: See note on 11:14. **Azariah:** The account of his reign appears in 15:1–7.

14:22 Elath: A shipping port in lower Edom, at the northern tip of the Gulf of Aqaba (called "Eloth" in 1 Kings 9:26). It must have switched hands from Judah to Edom when the latter declared its independence from the former (8:20–22).

14:23 Jeroboam: Jeroboam II, the 13th king of Israel (ca. 793 to 753 B.C.). To his credit, he reclaims lands seized by the Syrians, expanding Israel's northern and eastern borders to their full Solomonic dimensions (compare 14:25 with 1 Kings 8:65). Jeroboam's success in throwing back the enemies of Israel and recovering ancestral territory makes him a political "savior" of sorts (13:5; 14:27). Nevertheless, the narrator declares his reign "evil" because he continues to tolerate the idolatrous state religion devised by Jeroboam I (1 Kings 12:25–33).

14:24 the sins of Jeroboam: See note on 1 Kings 15:26.

14:25 entrance of Hamath: Identified with modern Lebweh, north of Damascus. It marks the northern border of the Promised Land (Num 34:8). **Sea of the Arabah:** Another name for the Dead Sea (Josh 3:16). **Jonah:** The prophet whose misadventures are told in the biblical Book of Jonah (Jon 1:1). The oracle attributed to him here is not otherwise known. **Gath-hepher:** In the territory of Zebulun in lower Galilee (Josh 19:13).

14:27 blot out the name: A covenant curse (Deut 29:20).

14:28 Book of the Chronicles: See note on 1 Kings 14:19.

---

*14:21, *Azariah:* Otherwise known as Uzziah; cf. 15:13; 2 Chron 26:1–23.

Kings of Israel? ²⁹And Jerobo'am slept with his fathers, the kings of Israel, and Zechari'ah his son reigned in his stead.

Azariah Reigns over Judah

15 In the twenty-seventh year of Jerobo'am king of Israel Azari'ah the son of Amazi'ah, king of Judah, began to reign. ²He was sixteen years old when he began to reign, and he reigned fifty-two years in Jerusalem. His mother's name was Jecoli'ah of Jerusalem. ³And he did what was right in the eyes of the Lᴏʀᴅ, according to all that his father Amazi'ah had done. ⁴Nevertheless the high places were not taken away; the people still sacrificed and burned incense on the high places. ⁵And the Lᴏʀᴅ struck the king, so that he was a leper to the day of his death, and he dwelt in a separate house. And Jo'tham the king's son was over the household, governing the people of the land. ⁶Now the rest of the acts of Azari'ah, and all that he did, are they not written in the Book of the Chronicles of the Kings of Judah? ⁷And Azari'ah slept with his fathers, and they buried him with his fathers in the city of David, and Jo'tham his son reigned in his stead.

Zechariah Reigns over Israel

8 In the thirty-eighth year of Azari'ah king of Judah Zechari'ah the son of Jerobo'am reigned over Israel in Samar'ia six months. ⁹And he did what was evil in the sight of the Lᴏʀᴅ, as his fathers had done. He did not depart from the sins of Jerobo'am the son of Ne'bat, which he made Israel to sin. ¹⁰Shallum the

son of Ja'besh conspired against him, and struck him down at Ib'leam,ʷ and killed him, and reigned in his stead. ¹¹Now the rest of the deeds of Zechari'ah, behold, they are written in the Book of the Chronicles of the Kings of Israel. ¹²(This was the promise of the Lᴏʀᴅ which he gave to Je'hu, "Your sons shall sit upon the throne of Israel to the fourth generation." And so it came to pass.)

Shallum Reigns over Israel

13 Shallum the son of Ja'besh began to reign in the thirty-ninth year of Uzzi'ah king of Judah, and he reigned one month in Samar'ia. ¹⁴Then Men'ahem the son of Gadi came up from Tirzah and came to Samar'ia, and he struck down Shallum the son of Ja'besh in Samaria and slew him, and reigned in his stead. ¹⁵Now the rest of the deeds of Shallum, and the conspiracy which he made, behold, they are written in the Book of the Chronicles of the Kings of Israel. ¹⁶At that time Men'ahem sacked Tap'pu-ahˣ and all who were in it and its territory from Tirzah on; because they did not open it to him, therefore he sacked it, and he ripped up all the women in it who were with child.

Menahem Reigns over Israel

17 In the thirty-ninth year of Azari'ah king of Judah Men'ahem the son of Gadi began to reign over Israel, and he reigned ten years in Samar'ia. ¹⁸And he did what was evil in the sight of the Lᴏʀᴅ; he did not depart all his days from all the sins of Jerobo'am the son of Ne'bat, which he made Israel to sin. ¹⁹Pul the king of Assyria came against the

---

15:2, 3: 2 Chron 26:3, 4.   **15:5–7:** 2 Chron 26:20–23.

14:29 Zechariah: The account of his reign appears in 15:8–12.

15:1 Azariah: The ninth king of Judah (ca. 792 to 740 ʙ.ᴄ.), also known as "Uzziah" (15:13, 30, 32; Is 1:1; Hos 1:1; Amos 1:1, etc.). He is an admirable king overall (15:3); however, the narrator criticizes him for allowing illegal worship to continue unchecked in the Southern Kingdom (15:4). The parallel account in Chronicles indicates that Azariah/Uzziah promoted agricultural development (2 Chron 26:10) and took steps to strengthen Judah's military (2 Chron 26:11–15). Likewise, the king's leprosy, which is left unexplained in Kings, is traced to its source in Chronicles: the Lord struck him with leprosy as punishment for attempting to conduct worship like an Aaronic priest (2 Chron 26:16–21). Chronologically, the first years of Azariah's reign overlap with the final years of Amaziah's reign.

15:4 high places: Pagan shrines that should have been destroyed (Deut 12:2). See word study: *High Places* at 23:5.

15:5 a leper: A person afflicted with a skin infection. See note on 5:1. **a separate house:** Lepers live in isolation from others due to their legal uncleanness (Num 5:1–4). **over the household:** Jotham, the royal steward or prime minister of Judah, serves as the acting ruler of the Southern Kingdom during his father's declining years of illness. See word study: *Over the Household* at 1 Kings 16:9.

15:6 Book of the Chronicles: See note on 1 Kings 14:19.

15:7 Jotham: The account of his reign appears in 15:32–38.

15:8–31 Turmoil takes hold of the Northern Kingdom in the eighth century ʙ.ᴄ. The rising threat of Assyria in the east, combined with political instability within, make for a time of power struggles and escalating violence. Four of the last five kings of Israel assassinate their predecessors in attempts to establish new dynasties. The prophet Hosea condemns these final kings of the north for acting without divine approval (Hos 8:4).

15:8 Zechariah: The 14th king of Israel (ca. 753 ʙ.ᴄ.) and the last of Jehu's dynasty (15:12). He is not to be confused with the prophet Zechariah (Zech 1:1). See note on 10:30.

15:9 the sins of Jeroboam: See note on 1 Kings 15:26.

15:11 Book of the Chronicles: See note on 1 Kings 14:19.

15:12 the promise of the Lᴏʀᴅ: Announced to Jehu in 10:30.

15:13 Shallum: The 15th king of Israel (ca. 752 ʙ.ᴄ.) and the would-be founder of its sixth dynasty.

15:16 Tappuah: On the tribal border between Ephraim and Manasseh (Josh 17:8). **Tirzah:** Former capital of the Northern Kingdom (see note on 1 Kings 14:17). **ripped up:** This level of savage brutality is normally associated with foreign armies such as the Syrians (8:12) and the Assyrians (Hos 13:16).

15:17 Menahem: The 16th king of Israel (ca. 752 to 742 ʙ.ᴄ.) and the founder of its seventh dynasty (15:22). Mention is made of "Menahem of Samaria" outside the Bible in the eighth-century *Annals of Tiglath-Pileser III*, which includes a roster of kings who paid tribute to the Assyrians (as in 15:19). Israel is made a vassal of the Assyrian empire about 740 ʙ.ᴄ.

15:18 the sins of Jeroboam: See note on 1 Kings 15:26.

15:19 Pul: Another name for Tiglath-pileser III, king of Assyria from 745 to 727 ʙ.ᴄ.

ʷGk Compare 9:27: Heb *before the people.*
ˣCompare Gk: Heb *Tiphsah.*

land; and Men′ahem gave Pul* a thousand talents of silver, that he might help him to confirm his hold of the royal power. ²⁰Men′ahem exacted the money from Israel, that is, from all the wealthy men, fifty shekels of silver from every man, to give to the king of Assyria. So the king of Assyria turned back, and did not stay there in the land. ²¹Now the rest of the deeds of Men′ahem, and all that he did, are they not written in the Book of the Chronicles of the Kings of Israel? ²²And Men′ahem slept with his fathers, and Pekahi′ah his son reigned in his stead.

Pekahiah Reigns over Israel

23 In the fiftieth year of Azari′ah king of Judah Pekahi′ah the son of Men′ahem began to reign over Israel in Samar′ia, and he reigned two years. ²⁴And he did what was evil in the sight of the Lord; he did not turn away from the sins of Jerobo′am the son of Ne′bat, which he made Israel to sin. ²⁵And Pe′kah the son of Remali′ah, his captain, conspired against him with fifty men of the Gileadites, and slew him in Samar′ia, in the citadel of the king's house;ʸ he slew him, and reigned in his stead. ²⁶Now the rest of the deeds of Pekahi′ah, and all that he did, behold, they are written in the Book of the Chronicles of the Kings of Israel.

Pekah Reigns over Israel

27 In the fifty-second year of Azari′ah king of Judah Pe′kah the son of Remali′ah began to reign over Israel in Samar′ia, and he reigned twenty years. ²⁸And he did what was evil in the sight of the Lord; he did not depart from the sins of Jerobo′am the son of Ne′bat, which he made Israel to sin.

29 In the days of Pe′kah king of Israel Tig′lath-pile′ser king of Assyria came and captured I′jon, A′bel-beth-ma′acah, Jano′ah, Ke′desh, Ha′zor, Gilead, and Galilee, all the land of Naph′tali; and he carried the people captive to Assyria. ³⁰Then Hoshe′a the son of E′lah made a conspiracy against Pe′kah the son of Remali′ah, and struck him down, and slew him, and reigned in his stead, in the twentieth year of Jo′tham the son of Uzzi′ah. ³¹Now the rest of the acts of Pe′kah, and all that he did, behold, they are written in the Book of the Chronicles of the Kings of Israel.

Jotham Reigns over Judah

32 In the second year of Pe′-kah the son of Remali′ah, king of Israel, Jo′tham the son of Uzzi′ah, king of Judah, began to reign. ³³He was twenty-five years old when he began to reign, and he reigned sixteen years in Jerusalem. His mother's name was Jeru′sha the daughter of Za′dok. ³⁴And he did what was right in the eyes of the Lord, according to all that his father Uzzi′ah had done. ³⁵Nevertheless the high places were not removed; the people still sacrificed and burned incense on the high places. He built the upper gate of the house of the Lord. ³⁶Now the rest of the acts of Jotham, and all that he did, are they not written in the Book of the Chronicles of the Kings of Judah? ³⁷In those days the Lord began to send Re′zin the king of Syria and Pe′kah the son of Remali′ah against Judah. ³⁸Jo′tham slept with his fathers, and was buried with his fathers in the city of David his father; and A′haz his son reigned in his stead.

15:33–35: 2 Chron 27:1–3. **15:38:** 2 Chron 27:9.

15:20 fifty shekels: An estimated 60,000 wealthy citizens would be needed to make an annual tribute of "a thousand talents of silver" (15:19).

15:21 Book of the Chronicles: See note on 1 Kings 14:19.

15:23 Pekahiah: The 17th king of Israel (ca. 742 to 740 B.C.) and the sole heir of King Menahem (15:22).

15:24 the sins of Jeroboam: See note on 1 Kings 15:26.

15:25 Gileadites: Men from the region of Gilead directly east of the Jordan.

15:26 Book of the Chronicles: See note on 1 Kings 14:19.

15:27 Pekah: The 18th king of Israel (ca. 752 to 732 B.C.) and the would-be founder of its eighth dynasty. Unlike his predecessors, Menahem and Pekahiah, who made Israel a vassal state of Assyria, Pekah forms a coalition with Damascus with the aim of blocking the westward expansion of Assyria into Syria-Palestine (cf. Is 7:1–9). His defiant stance against the Mesopotamian superpower will eventually backfire, and the wrath of Assyria will fall hard both upon Syria (16:9) and upon the Northern Kingdom of Israel (15:29).

15:28 the sins of Jeroboam: See note on 1 Kings 15:26.

15:29 Tiglath-pileser: Tiglath-pileser III, also called "Pul" (15:19). **Ijon ... Galilee:** Cites and territories of northern Israel sacked by the Assyrians. Tiglath-pileser III launched a series of campaigns between 734 and 732 B.C. and managed to annex the western coastlands, the region of Galilee (Is 9:1), and the entire Transjordan strip (1 Chron 5:26). With these lands made part of the Assyrian empire, the Northern Kingdom is reduced in size to the capital of Samaria and the hill country of central Canaan that surrounds it. **captive to Assyria:** The Assyrians execute a policy of "selective deportation" at this time, meaning that all Israelites of influence, wealth, and education are hauled off into exile, while a remnant of peasantry is left behind in the land (cf. 2 Chron 30:6). Archaeology confirms this picture of a significant population decrease in eighth-century Galilee.

15:30 Hoshea: The account of his reign appears in 17:1–6.

15:31 the Book of the Chronicles: See note on 1 Kings 14:19.

15:32 Jotham: The tenth king of Judah (ca. 750 to 731 B.C.).

15:35 high places: Pagan shrines that should have been destroyed (Deut 12:2). See word study: *High Places* at 23:5. **the upper gate:** Also called the Benjamin Gate because it faced north in the direction of Benjaminite territory (Jer 20:2; Ezek 9:2).

15:36 the Book of the Chronicles: See note on 1 Kings 14:19.

15:37 Rezin: The last ruler of the Aramean kingdom of Syria. He will perish with his capital when Assyrian forces conquer Damascus in 732 B.C. (16:9). **Pekah:** King of Israel. See note on 15:27. **against Judah:** The Israel-Syria coalition tries to intimidate Judah into joining the blockade against Assyrian expansion into the region (16:5; Is 7:1–9). Scholars often refer to this situation from Judah's perspective as the "Syro-Ephraimite Crisis" (ca. 735 B.C.).

---

*15:19, *Pul*: i.e., Tiglath-pileser III; cf. verse 29.
ʸHeb adds *Argob and Arieh,* which probably belong to the list of places in verse 29.

Ahaz Reigns over Judah

16 In the seventeenth year of Pe′kah the son of Remali′ah, A′haz the son of Jo′-tham, king of Judah, began to reign. ²Ahaz was twenty years old when he began to reign, and he reigned sixteen years in Jerusalem. And he did not do what was right in the eyes of the Lord his God, as his father David had done, ³but he walked in the way of the kings of Israel. He even burned his son as an offering,ᶻ according to the abominable practices of the nations whom the Lord drove out before the people of Israel.* ⁴And he sacrificed and burned incense on the high places, and on the hills, and under every green tree.

5 Then Re′zin king of Syria and Pe′kah the son of Remali′ah, king of Israel, came up to wage war on Jerusalem, and they besieged A′haz but could not conquer him. ⁶At that timeᵃ the king of E′domᵇ recovered E′lath for Edom,ᵇ and drove the men of Judah from Elath; and the E′domites came to Elath, where they dwell to this day. ⁷So A′haz sent messengers to Tig′lath-pile′ser king of Assyria, saying, "I am your servant and your son. Come up, and rescue me from the hand of the king of Syria and from the hand of the king of Israel, who are attacking me." ⁸A′haz also took the silver and gold that was found in the house of the Lord and in the treasures of the king's house, and sent a present to the king of Assyria. ⁹And the king of Assyria listened to him; the king of Assyria marched up against Damascus, and took it, carrying its people captive to Kir, and he killed Re′zin.

10 When King A′haz went to Damascus to meet Tig′lath-pile′ser king of Assyria, he saw the altar that was at Damascus. And King Ahaz sent to Uri′ah the priest a model of the altar, and its pattern, exact in all its details. ¹¹And Uri′ah the priest built the altar; in accordance with all that King A′haz had sent from Damascus, so Uriah the priest made it, before King Ahaz arrived from Damascus. ¹²And when the king came from Damascus, the king viewed the altar. Then the king drew near to the altar, and went up on it, ¹³and burned his burnt offering and his cereal offering, and poured his drink offering, and threw the blood of his peace offerings upon the altar. ¹⁴And the bronze altar which was before the Lord he removed from the front of the house, from the place between his altar and the house of the Lord, and put it on the north side of his altar. ¹⁵And King A′haz commanded Uri′ah the priest, saying, "Upon the great altar burn the morning burnt offering, and the evening cereal offering, and the king's burnt offering, and his cereal offering, with the burnt offering of all the people of the land, and their cereal offering, and their drink offering; and throw upon it all the blood of the burnt offering, and all the blood of the sacrifice; but the bronze altar shall be for me to inquire by." ¹⁶Uri′ah the priest did all this, as King A′haz commanded.

17 And King A′haz cut off the frames of the stands, and removed the laver from them, and he took down the sea from off the bronze oxen that

---

16:2–4: 2 Chron 28:1–4.

16:1 Ahaz: The 11th king of Judah (ca. 735 to 715 B.C.). He is severely criticized for the crime of child sacrifice (16:3) and for participating in illegal worship at shrines outside of Jerusalem (16:4). Ahaz is likewise faulted for his foreign policy, by which he relinquished Judah's sovereignty and made it a vassal of Assyria (16:5–9), and for his liturgical innovations, having transferred the sacrificial rites of Mosaic worship to a non-Mosaic altar (16:10–16).
16:2 David: See note on 1 Kings 15:3.
16:3 burned his son: Ahaz participated in the Canaanite cult of Molech, which is sternly condemned in the Torah (Lev 20:1–5; Deut 18:10–12). The king is not the only one in Israel who sinks to the horrible depths of child sacrifice (21:6; 23:10; Jer 7:31).
16:4 high places: Pagan shrines that should have been destroyed (Deut 12:2). See word study: *High Places* at 23:5.
16:5 war on Jerusalem: Also mentioned in Is 7:1. The Israel-Syria alliance wants to oust Ahaz from power and set up a new king in his place, the "son of Tabeel" (Is 7:6). The plan, which never comes to pass, is to force Judah into joining their coalition against the rising power of Assyria.
16:6 Elath: The northern port of the Gulf of Aqaba. Edom jumps at the chance to reclaim it while Judah is pinned down in Jerusalem. See note on 14:22.

16:7 Tiglath-pileser: Tiglath-pileser III, also called "Pul" (15:19). **your servant and your son:** Diplomatic language indicating that Ahaz declares Judah's subservience to Assyria in exchange for military protection against aggression from Israel-Syria. Judah thus becomes a vassal state that pays annual tribute to the Assyrian king (16:8). The prophet Isaiah advised Ahaz against this alliance, insisting that Israel and Syria were already doomed (Is 7–8).
16:8 a present: A bribe, as in Deut 16:19 and Prov 17:23.
16:9 Damascus: Conquered by the Assyrians in 732 B.C. **Kir:** Exact location uncertain but clearly in Mesopotamia (Amos 1:5).
16:10 the altar: Probably the altar in the house of Rimmon, a temple in Syria dedicated to the Near Eastern storm god Hadad (5:18). Ahaz commissions an exact replica to stand in the Jerusalem Temple, where he himself will perform the dedication sacrifices for the altar (16:12–13), just as kings before him had done (Solomon, 1 Kings 8:63; Jeroboam, 1 Kings 12:32). The Damascus-style altar is called "the great altar" in 16:15. **Uriah the priest:** Also mentioned by name in Is 8:2.
16:14 the bronze altar: The main altar of sacrifice in the Solomonic Temple (2 Chron 4:1). It is now demoted to a place where the king can consult the Lord's will (16:15).
16:17 the stands: The ten wheeled frames that supported large water basins and were decorated with bronze panels (1 Kings 7:27–39). **the bronze oxen:** The cast pedestal that supported the molten sea or laver (1 Kings 7:23-26). Ahaz is stripping the Temple of metals to be used as a tribute payment to the Assyrians (cf. 16:8).

---

*16:3: Human sacrifice to Moloch was practiced in Phoenicia.
ᶻOr *made his son to pass through the fire*.
ᵃHeb *At that time Rezin*.
ᵇHeb *Aram (Syria)*.

were under it, and put it upon a pediment of stone. ¹⁸And the covered way for the sabbath which had been built inside the palace, and the outer entrance for the king he removed from[c] the house of the LORD, because of the king of Assyria. ¹⁹Now the rest of the acts of A'haz which he did, are they not written in the Book of the Chronicles of the Kings of Judah? ²⁰And A'haz slept with his fathers, and was buried with his fathers in the city of David; and Hezeki'ah his son reigned in his stead.

16:20: 2 Chron 28:27.

16:18 covered way: Perhaps a metal roof or awning.

16:19 the Book of the Chronicles: See note on 1 Kings 14:19.

16:20 Hezekiah: The account of his reign appears in chaps. 18–20.

[c]Cn: Heb *turned to.*

Near Eastern Kings and the Israelite Monarchy

The history of Israel often intersects with the broader history of the ancient Near East. The Bible documents many of these encounters with reference to the foreign king in power at the time. It is significant from a historical standpoint that the witness of Scripture coheres closely with the testimony of extrabiblical texts, monuments, artifacts, etc., as to the chronology and dates of these ancient monarchs. Being responsible historians, the biblical writers make mention of Near Eastern kings at the right time and in the right order. Below is a list of the kings that Scripture mentions for their involvement with the kings of Israel and Judah. Some of the dates are well established down to the first and last year of the king's reign, while others can be dated only within a century or less.

Kings of EGYPT

Shishak (Shohenq I)	945–924	1 Kings 11:40; 14:25; 2 Chron 12:2
So (Osorkon IV)	730–716	2 Kings 17:4
Tirhakah (Taharqa)	690–664	2 Kings 19:9; Is 37:9
Neco (Necho II)	610–595	2 Kings 23:29, 33–35; 2 Chron 36:4
Hophra	589–570	Jer 44:30

Kings of ASSYRIA

Tiglath-pileser (III, Pul)	745–727	2 Kings 15:19, 29; 16:7; 1 Chron 5:6
Shalmaneser (V)	727–722	2 Kings 17:3; 18:9; Tob 1:2
Sargon (II)	722–705	Is 20:1 (also 2 Kings 17:24–26)
Sennacherib	705–681	2 Kings 18:13; 19:16, 20, 36; Is 36:1
Esarhaddon	681–669	2 Kings 19:37; Ezra 4:2; Is 37:38

Kings of BABYLON

Merodach-Baladan (II)	721–710, 703	2 Kings 20:12; Is 39:1
Nebuchadnezzar (II)	605–562	2 Kings 24:1; 25:1; 1 Chron 6:15
Evil-Merodach	562–560	2 Kings 25:27; Jer 52:31

Kings of SYRIA-DAMASCUS

Ben-hadah (I)	9th cent.	1 Kings 15:18
Hazael	9th cent.	1 Kings 19:15; 2 Kings 8:28; Amos 1:4
Ben-hadad (II or III)	8th cent.	2 Kings 13:3, 24–25
Rezin (Rakhianu)	8th cent.	2 Kings 15:37; 16:5; Ezra 2:48; Is 7:1

Kings of PHOENICIA

Hiram of Tyre (Huram)	10th cent.	2 Sam 5:11; 1 Kings 5:1; 2 Chron 2:3
Ethbaal of Sidon (Ittobaal I)	9th cent.	1 Kings 16:31

Kings of MOAB

Mesha	9th cent.	2 Kings 3:4

Hoshea Reigns over Israel

17 In the twelfth year of A'haz king of Judah Hoshe'a the son of E'lah began to reign in Samar'ia over Israel, and he reigned nine years. ²And he did what was evil in the sight of the LORD, yet not as the kings of Israel who were before him. ³Against him came up Shalmane'ser king of Assyria; and Hoshe'a became his vassal, and paid him tribute. ⁴But the king of Assyria found treachery in Hoshe'a; for he had sent messengers to So, king of Egypt, and offered no tribute to the king of Assyria, as he had done year by year; therefore the king of Assyria shut him up, and bound him in prison. ⁵Then the king of Assyria invaded all the land and came to Samar'ia, and for three years he besieged it. ⁶In the ninth year of Hoshe'a the king of Assyria captured Samar'ia, and he carried the Israelites away to Assyria, and placed them in Ha'lah, and on the Ha'bor, the river of Gozan, and in the cities of the Medes.

Sins of Israel Lead to Deportation

7 And this was so, because the sons of Israel had sinned against the LORD their God, who had brought them up out of the land of Egypt from under the hand of Pharaoh king of Egypt, and had feared other gods ⁸and walked in the customs of the nations whom the LORD drove out before the sons of Israel, and in the customs which the kings of Israel had introduced.ᵈ ⁹And the sons of Israel did secretly against the LORD their God things that were not right. They built for themselves high places at all their towns, from watchtower to fortified city; ¹⁰they set up for themselves pillars and Ashe'rim on every high hill and under every green tree; ¹¹and there they burned incense on all the high places, as the nations did whom the LORD carried away before them. And they did wicked things, provoking the LORD to anger, ¹²and they served idols, of which the LORD had said to them, "You shall not do this." ¹³Yet the LORD warned Israel and Judah by every prophet and every seer, saying, "Turn from your evil ways and keep my commandments and my statutes, in accordance with all the law which I commanded your fathers, and which I sent to you by my servants the prophets." ¹⁴But they would not listen, but were stubborn, as their fathers had been, who did not believe in the LORD their God. ¹⁵They despised his statutes, and his covenant that he made with their fathers, and the warnings which he gave them. They went after false idols, and became false, and they followed the nations that were round about them, concerning whom the LORD had commanded them that they should not do like them. ¹⁶And

---

17:1–41 The fall of the Northern Kingdom of Israel. The Kings account combines historical information with theological interpretation. (1) *Historically*, the kingdom of Israel collapsed when the Assyrians conquered Samaria in 722 B.C. Following this catastrophe, central Israel became a province of the Assyrian Empire (called Samarina), thousands of survivors were exiled to Mesopotamia and Media, and conquered peoples from Babylonia and Arabia were forcibly resettled in the Israelite homeland, assimilating with the stragglers left behind and becoming known as the "Samaritans" (17:29). The deportations of 15:29 and 17:6 (also 1 Chron 5:26) scattered the northern tribes of Israel among foreign nations, from which they would never return, giving rise to the notion of "the lost tribes of Israel". (2) *Theologically*, the demise of the Northern Kingdom of Israel is a divine judgment on the sins of the people (17:7). Despite the warnings of the prophets, the history of the Northern Kingdom was a sorry tale of unfaithfulness to the Lord, especially of a chronic failure to rid the land of idolatrous sanctuaries and practices (17:7–16). (3) *Eschatologically*, the northern tribes of Israel all but disappear from the stage of history but not from the saving purposes of God. Several prophets envision a restoration of the lost tribes to covenant sonship and a family reunion of all 12 tribes of Israel in messianic times (Is 49:6; Jer 50:17–20; Ezek 37:15–28; Hos 1:10–11; Obad 20). On this future hope, see note on 1 Kings 11:39 and essay: *The Salvation of All Israel* at Rom 11.
17:1 Hoshea: The 19th and last king of Israel (ca. 732 to 722 B.C.). Initially, Hoshea served as a vassal king of Assyria (17:3), but when he discontinued his annual payments of tribute, the Assyrians came with violent reprisals for his rebellion (17:4–5).
17:3 Shalmaneser: Shalmaneser V, the son and successor of Tiglath-pileser III as king of Assyria (727 to 722 B.C.). He is responsible for the siege and capture of Samaria (18:9–10), although Assyrian annals indicate that his successor, Sargon II

(722 to 705 B.C.), claimed credit for the conquest, probably to enhance his political image. At any rate, Sargon II was mainly responsible for Samaria's depopulation (17:6) and repopulation with foreigners (17:24). Additional waves of non-Israelite settlers were brought to Samaria by later kings of Assyria such as Esarhaddon (Ezra 4:2) and Ashurbanipal (Ezra 4:9–10, where he is called Osnappar).
17:4 So, king of Egypt: An abbreviation for Osorkon IV of the 22nd dynasty (730 to 715 B.C.). In the mind of the prophet Hosea, appealing to Egypt for protection against Assyria was downright "silly" (Hos 7:11).
17:6 captured ... carried: Summarizes a series of events between 722 B.C., when the city fell to Shalmaneser V, and 720 B.C., when deportations began in earnest under Sargon II. It is possible, however, that Shalmaneser sent an initial wave of captives into exile (see Tob 1:1–2). **away to Assyria:** Assyrian annals indicate that more than 27,000 captives were taken from Samaria and its surrounding district. For the ancient policy of "selective deportation", see note on 15:29. **Halah:** The region of Halahhu, northeast of Nineveh on the Tigris. **the Habor:** A tributary of the upper Euphrates, east of Haran. **Gozan:** A city on the upper Habor. **cities of the Medes:** East of Assyria, near the modern Iran-Iraq border.
17:7–23 Theological commentary on Israel's national destruction as viewed through the prism of Deuteronomy.
17:9 high places: Modeled on the shrines used in Canaanite worship. See word study: *High Places* at 23:5.
17:10 pillars and Asherim: Idolatrous cult objects. Pillars are large stones turned upright as monuments to the Canaanite storm and fertility god Baal. Asherim are trees or wooden poles dedicated to the Canaanite fertility goddess Asherah. Both are banned from Israelite worship (Deut 16:21–22).
17:13 every prophet: Those who preached repentance to the Northern Kingdom include Elijah, Hosea, and Amos.
17:16 two calves: Venerated as "other gods" (1 Kings 14:9) in the idolatrous state religion of Jeroboam I (1 Kings 12:25–29). Israel was forbidden to manufacture graven images or to worship gods other than Yahweh (Deut 5:7–9). **host of heaven:**

ᵈHeb obscure.

they forsook all the commandments of the Lord their God, and made for themselves molten images of two calves; and they made an Ashe'rah, and worshiped all the host of heaven, and served Ba'al. [17]And they burned their sons and their daughters as offerings,[e] and used divination and sorcery, and sold themselves to do evil in the sight of the Lord, provoking him to anger. [18]Therefore the Lord was very angry with Israel, and removed them out of his sight; none was left but the tribe of Judah only.*

19 Judah also did not keep the commandments of the Lord their God, but walked in the customs which Israel had introduced. [20]And the Lord rejected all the descendants of Israel, and afflicted them, and gave them into the hand of spoilers, until he had cast them out of his sight.

21 When he had torn Israel from the house of David they made Jerobo'am the son of Ne'bat king. And Jeroboam drove Israel from following the Lord and made them commit great sin. [22]The sons of Israel walked in all the sins which Jerobo'am did; they did not depart from them, [23]until the Lord removed Israel out of his sight, as he had spoken by all his servants the prophets. So Israel was exiled from their own land to Assyria until this day.

Assyria Resettles Samaria

24 †And the king of Assyria brought people from Babylon, Cu'thah, Avva, Ha'math, and Sepharva'im, and placed them in the cities of Samar'ia instead of the sons of Israel; and they took possession of Samaria, and dwelt in its cities. [25]And at the beginning of their dwelling there, they did not fear the Lord; therefore the Lord sent lions among

them, which killed some of them. [26]So the king of Assyria was told, "The nations which you have carried away and placed in the cities of Samar'ia do not know the law of the god of the land; therefore he has sent lions among them, and behold, they are killing them, because they do not know the law of the god of the land." [27]Then the king of Assyria commanded, "Send there one of the priests whom you carried away from there; and let him[f] go and dwell there, and teach them the law of the god of the land." [28]So one of the priests whom they had carried away from Samar'ia came and dwelt in Bethel, and taught them how they should fear the Lord.

29 But every nation still made gods of its own, and put them in the shrines of the high places which the Samar'itans had made, every nation in the cities in which they dwelt; [30]the men of Babylon made Suc'coth-be'noth, the men of Cuth made Ner'gal, the men of Ha'math made Ashi'ma, [31]and the Avvites made Nibhaz and Tartak; and the Sephar'vites burned their children in the fire to Adram'melech and Anam'melech, the gods of Sepharva'im. [32]They also feared the Lord, and appointed from among themselves all sorts of people as priests of the high places, who sacrificed for them in the shrines of the high places. [33]So they feared the Lord but also served their own gods, after the manner of the nations from among whom they had been carried away. [34]To this day they do according to the former manner.

They do not fear the Lord, and they do not follow the statutes or the ordinances or the law or the commandment which the Lord commanded the children of Jacob, whom he named Israel. [35]The Lord made

---

The sun, moon, and stars, which were revered as deities in the ancient Near East. Israel was forbidden to engage in any kind of solar or astral worship (Deut 4:19). **Baal:** The storm and fertility god of Canaanite religion.

17:17 burned their sons: Child sacrifice is an element of Molech worship that is sternly condemned in the Torah (Lev 20:1–5; Deut 18:10). **divination and sorcery:** All forms of superstition and fortune-telling are forbidden in Israel (Deut 18:10–14).

17:18 Judah only: The kingdom of Judah survives the collapse of the kingdom of Israel. As a result, the 12-tribe family of Israel is reduced to the southern tribe of Judah, along with the small tribe of Benjamin and members of the tribe of Levi living among them (also some refugees from Ephraim and Manasseh, 2 Chron 15:9).

17:21 torn Israel: The division of the united kingdom was God's judgment on the idolatry of Solomon's declining years (1 Kings 11:9–13).

17:24 Babylon ... Sepharvaim: Five foreign peoples representing a mix of Babylonians and Syrians. Assyrian records add that Arabian tribes were also forcibly resettled in Samaria around 715 B.C. The purpose of deporting and importing captives was to crush the spirit of nationalism in conquered

territories, lest residual patriotism gain strength over time and grow into future rebellion. Note that Samaria is depopulated and then repopulated with displaced immigrants, whereas Galilee and the Transjordan, which fell to the Assyrians a decade earlier, were only depopulated (15:29; 1 Chron 5:26).

17:25 the Lord sent lions: For similar divine judgments, see 1 Kings 13:24; 20:36.

17:26 god of the land: In ancient Near Eastern mythology, each deity has a defined sphere of influence, and those in his domain are accountable for serving him properly.

17:28 Bethel: One of the cultic centers of northern Israel (1 Kings 12:28–30). See note on Judg 1:23.

17:29–34 Samaritan religion is a syncretistic religion from the start, a blending of Mosaic faith with idol cults imported from foreign lands. Hereafter the mixed population serves the Lord alongside several other deities. **Succoth-benoth** is not otherwise known, although some connect the first name with the Babylonian god Saturn ("Sakkuth" in Amos 5:26) and the second name with the Babylonian goddess Ishtar, sometimes called Banitu. **Nergal** is a god of the underworld. **Ashima** may be a Semitic goddess such as Astarte or Asherah or possibly Eshmun, a Phoenician god of healing. **Nibhaz** and **Tartak** have not been identified with certainty, although some detect a reference to the Elamite deities Ibnahaza and Dirtaq. **Adrammelech** and **Anammelech** are likewise unknown. A popular suggestion links them with the Mesopotamian storm and sky gods Hadad and Anu.

17:32 all sorts ... priests: An illegitimate priesthood, calling to mind Jeroboam's appointees in 1 Kings 12:31.

---

*17:7–18: A full explanation of how Israel had sinned and was punished accordingly.

†17:24–41: Origin of the Samaritans, written by an orthodox Jew.

[e]Or *made their sons and their daughters pass through the fire.*

[f]Syr Vg: Heb *them.*

a covenant with them, and commanded them, "You shall not fear other gods or bow yourselves to them or serve them or sacrifice to them; ³⁶but you shall fear the LORD, who brought you out of the land of Egypt with great power and with an outstretched arm; you shall bow yourselves to him, and to him you shall sacrifice. ³⁷And the statutes and the ordinances and the law and the commandment which he wrote for you, you shall always be careful to do. You shall not fear other gods, ³⁸and you shall not forget the covenant that I have made with you. You shall not fear other gods, ³⁹but you shall fear the LORD your God, and he will deliver you out of the hand of all your enemies." ⁴⁰However they would not listen, but they did according to their former manner.

41 So these nations feared the LORD, and also served their graven images; their children likewise, and their children's children—as their fathers did, so they do to this day.

Hezekiah Reigns over Judah

18 In the third year of Hoshe'a son of E'lah, king of Israel, Hezeki'ah the son of A'haz, king of Judah, began to reign. ²He was twenty-five years old when he began to reign, and he reigned twenty-nine years in Jerusalem. His mother's name was Abi the daughter of Zechari'ah. ³And he did what was right in the eyes of the LORD, according to all that David his father had done. ⁴He removed the high places, and broke the pillars, and cut down the Ashe'rah. And he broke in pieces the bronze serpent that Moses

had made, for until those days the sons of Israel had burned incense to it; it was called Nehush'tan. ⁵He trusted in the LORD the God of Israel; so that there was none like him among all the kings of Judah after him, nor among those who were before him. ⁶For he held fast to the LORD; he did not depart from following him, but kept the commandments which the LORD commanded Moses. ⁷And the LORD was with him; wherever he went forth, he prospered. He rebelled against the king of Assyria, and would not serve him. ⁸He struck the Philis'tines as far as Gaza and its territory, from watchtower to fortified city.

9 In the fourth year of King Hezeki'ah, which was the seventh year of Hoshe'a son of E'lah, king of Israel, Shalmane'ser king of Assyria came up against Samar'ia and besieged it ¹⁰and at the end of three years he took it. In the sixth year of Hezeki'ah, which was the ninth year of Hoshe'a king of Israel, Samar'ia was taken. ¹¹The king of Assyria carried the Israelites away to Assyria, and put them in Ha'lah, and on the Ha'bor, the river of Gozan, and in the cities of the Medes, ¹²because they did not obey the voice of the LORD their God but transgressed his covenant, even all that Moses the servant of the LORD commanded; they neither listened nor obeyed.

Sennacherib Invades Judah

13 In the fourteenth year of King Hezeki'ah Sennach'erib king of Assyria came up against all the fortified cities of Judah and took them. ¹⁴And Hezeki'ah king of Judah sent to the king of Assyria at La'chish, saying, "I have done wrong; withdraw

---

18:1-3: 2 Chron 29:1, 2. **18:13—19:35:** 2 Chron 32:1–21; Is 36:1—37:38.

18:1—25:30 The final chapters of Kings trace the decline and fall of the Southern Kingdom of Judah. Although Judah outlives Israel by more than a century and sees extensive reforms under Hezekiah (18:4) and Josiah (23:4–20), it also begins sliding downward toward national ruin and exile. On the regional stage of Near Eastern politics, the balance of power shifts from the Assyrians to the Babylonians in the final decades of the divided monarchy.

18:1 Hezekiah: The 12th king of Judah (ca. 729 to 686 B.C.). The narrator applauds him for trustful obedience to the Lord (18:5-6) during a time of religious and political chaos. High points of his kingship include purging Judah of idolatry (18:4) and taking a courageous stand against Assyrian aggression (18:7). It appears that Hezekiah was co-regent for many years alongside his father, Ahaz, before the start of his independent reign in 715 B.C.

18:3 David: See note on 1 Kings 15:3.

18:4 He removed: Hezekiah undertakes the most extensive cultic reform in the Southern Kingdom prior to King Josiah's efforts in 23:4–20. His actions may have been prompted by the recent devastation of the idolatrous Northern Kingdom in 722 B.C. (17:6). **high places:** Unlawful sanctuaries. See word study: *High Places* at 23:5. **pillars ... Asherah:** Canaanite cult objects. See note on 17:10. **the bronze serpent:** Manufactured by Moses after Israel suffered a deadly serpent attack (Num 21:4-9). Over time, popular piety degenerated into idolatry, and what began as a relic of healing became an object of deviant worship. **Nehushtan:** The name is a play on the Hebrew terms *naḥash*, meaning "serpent", and *naḥoshet*, meaning "bronze".

18:5 trusted: Reliance on the Lord is the secret to Hezekiah's success. **none like him:** This level of praise is restricted to two of David's royal successors, Hezekiah and Josiah (23:25).

18:7 He rebelled: Hezekiah asserted Judah's independence from the lordship of Assyria by discontinuing the required payment of tribute. It was Hezekiah's father, Ahaz, who made Judah a vassal state of the Assyrian empire (16:7-9).

18:8 Philistines: Occupied the coastal plain in southwest Canaan. Hezekiah attacked cities such as Ekron, whose rulers were loyal to Assyria.

18:9-12 A summary of the events in 17:1-23.

18:13—20:19 The account of Hezekiah's activities in these chapters parallels the account in Is 36–39.

18:13 Sennacherib: Successor to Sargon II as king of Assyria (705 to 681 B.C.). His forces invaded Judah in 701 B.C. with the intent of punishing Hezekiah for his treasonous attempt to throw off the yoke of Assyrian rule. The surviving *Annals of Sennacherib* describe how the king ravaged the Judean countryside, captured more than 46 towns and fortifications, deported more than 200,000 exiles, and cooped up Hezekiah within his capital "like a bird in a cage". Amid the duress of these circumstances, the prophet Isaiah counseled Hezekiah to trust in the Lord for deliverance and to stand firm against the boastful Assyrians, with the result that Jerusalem was spared by a miracle of God (see 19:1-36).

18:14 Lachish: More than 25 miles southwest of Jerusalem (Tell el-Duweir). Sennacherib's conquest of the city is depicted on a palace wall discovered at Nineveh. Lachish served as the command center for Sennacherib's campaign in Palestine. **thirty talents of gold:** The same figure appears in the list of spoils recounted in the *Annals of Sennacherib*.

from me; whatever you impose on me I will bear." And the king of Assyria required of Hezekiah king of Judah three hundred talents of silver and thirty talents of gold. [15]And Hezeki'ah gave him all the silver that was found in the house of the LORD, and in the treasuries of the king's house. [16]At that time Hezeki'ah stripped the gold from the doors of the temple of the LORD, and from the doorposts which Hezekiah king of Judah had overlaid and gave it to the king of Assyria. [17]And the king of Assyria sent the Tartan, the Rab'saris, and the Rab'shakeh with a great army from La'chish to King Hezeki'ah at Jerusalem. And they went up and came to Jerusalem. When they arrived, they came and stood by the conduit of the upper pool, which is on the highway to the Fuller's Field. [18]And when they called for the king, there came out to them Eli'akim the son of Hilki'ah, who was over the household, and Shebnah the secretary, and Jo'ah the son of A'saph, the recorder.

19 And the Rab'shakeh said to them, "Say to Hezeki'ah, 'Thus says the great king, the king of Assyria: On what do you rest this confidence of yours? [20]Do you think that mere words are strategy and power for war? On whom do you now rely, that you have rebelled against me? [21]Behold, you are relying now on Egypt, that broken reed of a staff, which will pierce the hand of any man who leans on it. Such is Pharaoh king of Egypt to all who rely on him. [22]But if you say to me, "We rely on the LORD our God," is it not he whose high places and altars Hezeki'ah has removed, saying to Judah and to Jerusalem, "You shall worship before this altar in Jerusalem"? [23]Come now, make a wager with my master the king of Assyria: I will give you two thousand horses, if you are able on your part to set riders upon them. [24]How then can you repulse a single captain among the least of my master's servants, when you rely on Egypt for chariots and for horsemen? [25]Moreover, is it without the LORD that I have come up against this place to destroy it? The LORD said to me, Go up against this land, and destroy it.'"

26 Then Eli'akim the son of Hilki'ah, and Shebnah, and Jo'ah, said to the Rab'shakeh, "Please, speak to your servants in the Arama'ic language, for we understand it; do not speak to us in the language of Judah within the hearing of the people who are on the wall." [27]But the Rab'shakeh said to them, "Has my master sent me to speak these words to your master and to you, and not to the men sitting on the wall, who are doomed with you to eat their own dung and to drink their own urine?"

28 Then the Rab'shakeh stood and called out in a loud voice in the language of Judah: "Hear the word of the great king, the king of Assyria! [29]Thus says the king: 'Do not let Hezeki'ah deceive you, for he will not be able to deliver you out of my hand. [30]Do not let Hezeki'ah make you to rely on the LORD by saying, The LORD will surely deliver us, and this city will not be given into the hand of the king of Assyria.' [31]Do not listen to Hezeki'ah; for thus says the king of Assyria: 'Make your peace with me and come out to me; then every one of you will eat of his own vine, and every one of his own fig tree, and every one of you will drink the water of his own cistern; [32]until I come and take you away to a land like your own land, a land of grain and wine, a land of bread and vineyards, a land of olive trees and honey, that you may live, and not die. And do not listen to Hezeki'ah when he misleads you by saying, The LORD will deliver us. [33]Has any of the gods of the nations ever delivered his land out of the hand of the king of Assyria? [34]Where are the gods of Ha'math and Arpad? Where are the gods of Sepharva'im, He'na, and Ivvah? Have they delivered Samar'ia out of my hand? [35]Who among all the gods of the countries have delivered their countries out of my hand, that the LORD should deliver Jerusalem out of my hand?'"

36 But the people were silent and answered him not a word, for the king's command was, "Do not

---

18:17 **Tartan ... Rabsaris ... Rabshakeh:** Titles for three senior officials under the Assyrian king. They form a royal embassy sent to Jerusalem to demand Hezekiah's submission. **the conduit:** Part of ancient Jerusalem's water supply system (Is 7:3). Its location is uncertain but likely outside the northwestern wall of the city.

18:18 **Eliakim ... Shebnah ... Joah:** Members of the Judean court. Eliakim, the royal steward, is mentioned elsewhere in Is 22:20. For the nature of his position, see word study: *Over the Household* at 1 Kings 16:9.

18:19–35 Sennacherib's messengers engage in psychological warfare. Intimidation tactics include mocking Judah's alliance with Egypt (18:21), ridiculing Hezekiah's reliance on the Lord (18:22, 30), and boasting that no god or nation has yet withstood the advance of the Assyrian army (18:33–35). The hope is that Jerusalem will surrender without a fight and go peacefully into exile (18:31–32).

18:19 **the great king:** The customary title for Assyrian monarchs at this time.

18:21 **relying now on Egypt:** Hezekiah had taken steps to gain Egyptian military support against Assyria, a move the prophet Isaiah denounced (Is 30:1–5; 31:1–3).

18:26 **Aramaic:** The language of diplomacy in the western Assyrian empire. The request to hold negotiations in Aramaic is a request to halt negotiations in Judean Hebrew, lest the arrogant threats of Sennacherib cause panic in the city.

18:31 **vine ... fig tree:** Images of a peaceful life undisturbed by war (1 Kings 4:25; Mic 4:4).

18:32 **olive trees and honey:** The delegation claims that the lands of Assyrian exile have all the blessings of the Promised Land (Deut 8:7–9). • *Morally,* Sennacherib is a type of the devil, as seen in the boastful speech of the envoy, who falsely promises God's people a fertile and abundant land, trying to persuade them to forsake the land given by God for a new dwelling promised by the Assyrians. In a similar way, the devil's messengers strive to seduce the simple soul (St. Ephraem the Syrian, *On Second Kings* 18, 19).

answer him." [37]Then Eli'akim the son of Hilki'ah, who was over the household, and Shebna the secretary, and Jo'ah the son of A'saph, the recorder, came to Hezeki'ah with their clothes torn, and told him the words of the Rab'shakeh.

Hezekiah Consults Isaiah

19 When King Hezeki'ah heard it, he tore his clothes, and covered himself with sackcloth, and went into the house of the LORD. [2]And he sent Eli'akim, who was over the household, and Shebna the secretary, and the senior priests, covered with sackcloth, to the prophet Isai'ah the son of A'moz. [3]They said to him, "Thus says Hezeki'ah, This day is a day of distress, of rebuke, and of disgrace; children have come to the birth, and there is no strength to bring them forth. [4]It may be that the LORD your God heard all the words of the Rab'shakeh, whom his master the king of Assyria has sent to mock the living God, and will rebuke the words which the LORD your God has heard; therefore lift up your prayer for the remnant that is left." [5]When the servants of King Hezeki'ah came to Isai'ah, [6]Isai'ah said to them, "Say to your master, 'Thus says the LORD: Do not be afraid because of the words that you have heard, with which the servants of the king of Assyria have reviled me. [7]Behold, I will put a spirit in him, so that he shall hear a rumor and return to his own land; and I will cause him to fall by the sword in his own land.'"

Sennacherib's Mockery

8 The Rab'shakeh returned, and found the king of Assyria fighting against Libnah; for he heard that the king had left La'chish. [9]And when the king heard concerning Tirha'kah king of Ethiopia, "Behold, he has set out to fight against you," he sent messengers again to Hezeki'ah, saying, [10]"Thus shall you speak to Hezeki'ah king of Judah: 'Do not let your God on whom you rely deceive you by promising that Jerusalem will not be given into the hand of the king of Assyria. [11]Behold, you have heard what the kings of Assyria have done to all lands, destroying them utterly. And shall you be delivered? [12]Have the gods of the nations delivered them, the nations which my fathers destroyed, Gozan, Haran, Rezeph, and the people of Eden who were in Tel-as'sar? [13]Where is the king of Ha'math, the king of Arpad, the king of the city of Sepharva'im, the king of He'na, or the king of Ivvah?'"

Hezekiah's Prayer

14 Hezeki'ah received the letter from the hand of the messengers, and read it; and Hezekiah went up to the house of the LORD, and spread it before the LORD. [15]And Hezeki'ah prayed before the LORD, and said: "O LORD the God of Israel, who are enthroned above the cherubim, you are the God, you alone, of all the kingdoms of the earth; you have made heaven and earth. [16]Incline your ear, O LORD, and hear; open your eyes, O LORD, and see; and hear the words of Sennach'erib, which he has sent to mock the living God. [17]Of a truth, O LORD, the kings of Assyria have laid waste the nations and their lands, [18]and have cast their gods into the fire; for they were no gods, but the work of men's hands, wood and stone; therefore they were destroyed. [19]So now, O LORD our God, save us, I beg you, from his hand, that all the kingdoms of the earth may know that you, O LORD, are God alone."

20 Then Isai'ah the son of A'moz sent to Hezeki'ah, saying, "Thus says the LORD, the God of Israel: Your prayer to me about Sennach'erib king

---

18:37 their clothes torn: A sign of extreme distress (6:30; 1 Kings 21:27).

19:1-36 The Assyrian threat to Jerusalem continues. It is not impossible that Sennacherib conducted two campaigns against the city, one of exacting tribute (18:14-16) and another demanding surrender (18:31-32). More likely, however, Jerusalem faced a single ordeal in 701 B.C., and this chapter brings the confrontation to its dramatic climax.

19:1 sackcloth: A rough, hair-spun fabric worn in times of desperation, when prayer and repentance are matters of urgency (6:30; Joel 1:13).

19:2 Eliakim ... Shebna: Hezekiah's delegates. See note on 18:18. **the prophet Isaiah:** The same figure whose thunderous oracles are preserved in the biblical Book of Isaiah (Is 1:1). Several hallmarks of Isaiah's distinctive language and style appear in this chapter, e.g., the assurance that Judah need not be "afraid" of the Assyrians (19:6; Is 10:24); the reference to Assyria's "arrogance" (19:28; Is 10:12); the reference to Jerusalem as the "daughter of Zion" (19:21; Is 1:8; 10:32); the reference to Yahweh as the "Holy One of Israel" (19:22; Is 1:4; 5:19); the promise of a "remnant" (19:4, 30-31; Is 1:9; 4:2-3; 28:5); the announcement of a "sign" that confirms the fulfillment of a divine oracle (19:29; Is 7:14; 8:18). Sending delegates to Isaiah testifies to the faith of Hezekiah, who wisely turns to prophets rather than politicians in times of national crisis.

19:4 your prayer: Israel's prophets are known for being powerful intercessors (Gen 20:7; Jer 15:1).

19:7 return: A prophecy that Sennacherib will disengage and order his troops back home to Assyria. Jerusalem has nothing to fear (19:6), for Yahweh himself will defend the city and spare it the death and devastation of war (19:32-34). **fall by the sword:** Sennacherib will be assassinated by his own sons in 681 B.C. (19:36-37).

19:8 Libnah: Southwest of Jerusalem, not far from Lachish on the Judah-Philistia border.

19:9 Tirhakah: One of several Egyptian pharaohs who ruled Ethiopia, which at this time encompassed part of southern Egypt. His reign as king did not begin until 690 B.C., which means that he was a still a military commander when Egypt prepared this strike against Assyrian forces in Palestine.

19:12-13 Sennacherib boasts that neither "gods" nor "kings" have withstood the advance of the Assyrian war machine.

19:15 the cherubim: The angelic figures whose wings form Yahweh's throne on top of the Ark of the Covenant. See note on Ex 25:18. **you alone:** Hezekiah affirms the monotheistic belief of Israel (Deut 4:35, 39; 6:4).

19:18 work of men's hands: A standard critique of pagan idols. Biblical writers declared them lifeless statues that have no real power to influence the world of the living (Deut 4:28; Ps 115:3-8; Is 44:9-20; Jer 10:1-5).

of Assyria I have heard. ²¹This is the word that the LORD has spoken concerning him:
"She despises you, she scorns you—
the virgin daughter of Zion;
she wags her head behind you—
the daughter of Jerusalem.

²²"Whom have you mocked and reviled?
Against whom have you raised your voice
and haughtily lifted your eyes?
Against the Holy One of Israel!
²³By your messengers you have mocked the LORD,
and you have said, 'With my many chariots
I have gone up the heights of the mountains,
to the far recesses of Lebanon;
I felled its tallest cedars,
its choicest cypresses;
I entered its farthest retreat,
its densest forest.
²⁴I dug wells
and drank foreign waters,
and I dried up with the sole of my foot
all the streams of Egypt.'

²⁵"Have you not heard
that I determined it long ago?
I planned from days of old what now I bring to pass,
that you should turn fortified cities
into heaps of ruins,
²⁶while their inhabitants, shorn of strength,
are dismayed and confounded,
and have become like plants of the field,
and like tender grass,
like grass on the housetops;
blighted before it is grown?

²⁷"But I know your sitting down
and your going out and coming in,
and your raging against me.

²⁸Because you have raged against me
and your arrogance has come into my ears,
I will put my hook in your nose
and my bit in your mouth,
and I will turn you back on the way
by which you came.

29 "And this shall be the sign for you: this year you shall eat what grows of itself, and in the second year what springs of the same; then in the third year sow, and reap, and plant vineyards, and eat their fruit. ³⁰And the surviving remnant of the house of Judah shall again take root downward, and bear fruit upward; ³¹for out of Jerusalem shall go forth a remnant, and out of Mount Zion a band of survivors. The zeal of the LORD will do this.

32 "Therefore thus says the LORD concerning the king of Assyria, He shall not come into this city or shoot an arrow there, or come before it with a shield or cast up a siege mound against it. ³³By the way that he came, by the same he shall return, and he shall not come into this city, says the LORD. ³⁴For I will defend this city to save it, for my own sake and for the sake of my servant David."

Sennacherib's Defeat and Death

35 And that night the angel of the LORD went forth, and slew a hundred and eighty-five thousand in the camp of the Assyrians;* and when men arose early in the morning, behold, these were all dead bodies. ³⁶Then Sennach'erib king of Assyria departed, and went home, and dwelt at Nin'eveh. ³⁷And as he was worshiping in the house of Nisroch his god, Adram'melech and Share'zer, his sons, slew him with the sword, and escaped into the land of Ar'arat. And Esarhad'don his son reigned in his stead.

Hezekiah's Illness

20 In those days Hezeki'ah became sick and was at the point of death. And Isai'ah the prophet the son of A'moz came to him, and said to him, "Thus says the LORD, 'Set your house in order;

20:1–21: 2 Chron 32:24–33; Is 38:1—39:8.

19:21–34 Yahweh's reply to Hezekiah delivered by Isaiah. The message is twofold: 19:21–28 give words of judgment against the arrogant Assyrians, and 19:29–34 offer words of comfort for a frightened Jerusalem.
19:21 daughter of Zion: A poetic description of Jerusalem (Is 1:8; Lam 2:13).
19:29 the sign: The people of Judah will harvest food for two years without planting crops, despite the fact that Assyrian forces ravaged much of the land. The miracle of the harvest illustrates how the surviving remnant of God's people will again flourish (19:30).
19:34 for the sake of ... David: By defending the city and throne of Jerusalem, the Lord is defending his covenant of kingship with David. See note on 1 Kings 11:36.
19:35 the angel of the LORD: Inflicts mass casualties in the Assyrian camp (Sir 48:21). No details are given about how

the enemy soldiers died, but perhaps the angel unleashed a plague (as in 2 Sam 24:15–16 and Ps 78:49–50). See word study: *Angel of the LORD* at Gen 16:7. **a hundred and eighty five thousand:** For a discussion of large numbers in the Bible, see note on Num 1:46.
19:36 Nineveh: The capital city of Assyria on the upper Tigris River.
19:37 Nisroch: A deity otherwise unknown. **slew him:** The assassination of Sennacherib took place in 681 B.C., as foretold by Isaiah in 701 B.C. (19:7). **Ararat:** North of Assyria in modern Armenia. **Esarhaddon:** Successor to Sennacherib as king of Assyria (681 to 669 B.C.).
20:1–21 The narrative sequence of 2 Kings 18–20 is historically dischronologized. That is, the events of chap. 20 take place *before* the events of chaps. 18–19. Among the observations supporting this: (1) Jerusalem's deliverance is promised as a future event in 20:6, but the event was already narrated in 19:35–36; (2) the Merodach-baladan who appears in 20:12 was deposed as king of Babylon by 703 B.C., and yet the

---

*19:35: It is usually supposed that the Assyrians were struck by a virulent disease.

for you shall die, you shall not recover.'" ²Then Hezeki′ah turned his face to the wall, and prayed to the LORD, saying, ³"Remember now, O LORD, I beg you, how I have walked before you in faithfulness and with a whole heart, and have done what is good in your sight." And Hezeki′ah wept bitterly. ⁴And before Isai′ah had gone out of the middle court, the word of the LORD came to him: ⁵"Turn back, and say to Hezeki′ah the prince of my people, Thus says the LORD, the God of David your father: I have heard your prayer, I have seen your tears; behold, I will heal you; on the third day you shall go up to the house of the LORD. ⁶And I will add fifteen years to your life. I will deliver you and this city out of the hand of the king of Assyria, and I will defend this city for my own sake and for my servant David's sake." ⁷And Isai′ah said, "Bring a cake of figs. And let them take and lay it on the boil, that he may recover."

8 And Hezeki′ah said to Isai′ah, "What shall be the sign that the LORD will heal me, and that I shall go up to the house of the LORD on the third day?" ⁹And Isai′ah said, "This is the sign to you from the LORD, that the LORD will do the thing that he has promised: shall the shadow go forward ten steps, or go back ten steps?" ¹⁰And Hezeki′ah answered, "It is an easy thing for the shadow to lengthen ten steps; rather let the shadow go back ten steps." ¹¹And Isai′ah the prophet cried to the LORD; and he brought the shadow back ten steps, by which the sun ᵍ had declined on the dial of A′haz.

Envoys from Babylon

12 At that time Mer′odach-bal′adan the son of Bal′adan, king of Babylon, sent envoys with letters and a present to Hezeki′ah; for he heard that Hezekiah had been sick. ¹³And Hezeki′ah welcomed them, and he showed them all his treasure house, the silver, the gold, the spices, the precious oil, his armory, all that was found in his storehouses; there was nothing in his house or in all his realm that Hezekiah did not show them. ¹⁴Then Isai′ah the prophet came to King Hezeki′ah, and said to him, "What did these men say? And from where did they come to you?" And Hezekiah said, "They have come from a far country, from Babylon." ¹⁵He said, "What have they seen in your house?" And Hezeki′ah answered, "They have seen all that is in my house; there is nothing in my storehouses that I did not show them."

16 Then Isai′ah said to Hezeki′ah, "Hear the word of the LORD: ¹⁷Behold, the days are coming, when all that is in your house, and that which your fathers have stored up till this day, shall be carried to Babylon; nothing shall be left, says the LORD. ¹⁸And some of your own sons, who are born to you, shall be taken away; and they shall be eunuchs in the palace of the king of Babylon." ¹⁹Then said Hezeki′ah to Isai′ah, "The word of the LORD which you have spoken is good." For he thought, "Why not, if there will be peace and security in my days?"

Death of Hezekiah

20 The rest of the deeds of Hezeki′ah, and all his might, and how he made the pool and the conduit and brought water into the city, are they not written in the Book of the Chronicles of the Kings of Judah? ²¹And Hezeki′ah slept with his fathers; and Manas′seh his son reigned in his stead.

---

events of the last two chapters took place in 701 B.C.; (3) the treasuries of Hezekiah are full in 20:13 but appear to have been liquidated for a tribute offering back in 18:15–16.

20:3 Remember now, O LORD: The king prays for a recovery from his terminal illness by appealing to his loyal service. He has shown himself faithful to God's commandments, even ridding the Southern Kingdom of idolatry (18:1–8). **wept bitterly:** Tears of penitent sorrow (2 Cor 7:10). • Hezekiah's repentance reverses the sentence that God passed on him. He turns toward the wall, and his mind rises up to heaven from his bed of pain, for there is no wall thick enough to thwart reverent prayer. Once forbidden to hope, the king is given fifteen more years to live, the sun reversing its course as a witness to the fact (St. Cyril of Jerusalem, *Catechesis* 2, 15).

20:5 on the third day: Anticipates a divine restoration to life (Hos 6:1–2; Mt 16:21).

20:6 fifteen years: Hezekiah died in ca. 686 B.C., fifteen years after Yahweh's deliverance of Jerusalem in 701 B.C. **David's sake:** This promise is reaffirmed on the eve of deliverance in 19:34.

20:7 cake of figs: Dried figs were believed to have healing properties. **boil:** An infection or blistering of the skin that some have diagnosed as Pemphigus.

20:8 sign: Announcing signs is a characteristic feature of Isaiah's ministry (19:9; Is 7:14).

20:11 back ten steps: A miracle of sunlight and shadow. It takes place on a time-keeping device, presumably a rooftop sundial that utilized one or more flights of stairs to mark the hours of the day by the sun's shadow. Hezekiah witnesses the shadow mysteriously retreat backward in a "counterclockwise" fashion. For another miracle in the Bible linked with the sun, see note on Josh 10:13.

20:12 Merodach-baladan: Merodach-baladan II, king of Babylon from 721 to 710 B.C. He reestablished his kingship briefly in 704 B.C. until the Assyrians ousted him from power in 703 B.C. Many believe his envoys came to Jerusalem with more than a "get well" message for Hezekiah. Merodach is probably interested in forging a political alliance with Hezekiah in opposition to Assyria. Hezekiah, for his part, leads the Babylonian dignitaries on a tour of his national treasures as a way of showing that Judah is a wealthy and worthy ally (20:13).

20:16–18 Isaiah foretells the Babylonian conquest of Jerusalem more than a century before its fulfillment in 25:8–17. He warns that a partnership with Babylon will backfire when the empire drags Hezekiah's riches and relatives into exile. More than once Isaiah advised faith in Yahweh over foreign policies that put the covenant people at risk by giving them a false sense of security (e.g., Is 7–8; 30–31).

20:19 Why not: An unflattering detail, exposing Hezekiah's resignation as self-interested.

20:20 the conduit: An underground tunnel over 1,700 feet long that channeled water to a reservoir within the walls of Jerusalem (2 Chron 32:30; Sir 48:17). Hezekiah commissioned

---

ᵍSyr See Is 38:8 and Tg: Heb lacks *the sun*.

Manasseh Reigns over Judah

21 Manas'seh was twelve years old when he began to reign, and he reigned fifty-five years in Jerusalem. His mother's name was Heph'zibah. ²And he did what was evil in the sight of the LORD, according to the abominable practices of the nations whom the LORD drove out before the people of Israel. ³For he rebuilt the high places which Hezeki'ah his father had destroyed; and he erected altars for Ba'al, and made an Ashe'rah, as A'hab king of Israel had done, and worshiped all the host of heaven, and served them. ⁴And he built altars in the house of the LORD, of which the LORD had said, "In Jerusalem will I put my name." ⁵And he built altars for all the host of heaven in the two courts of the house of the LORD. ⁶And he burned his son as an offering, and practiced soothsaying and augury, and dealt with mediums and with wizards. He did much evil in the sight of the LORD, provoking him to anger. ⁷And the graven image of Ashe'rah that he had made he set in the house of which the LORD said to David and to Solomon his son, "In this house, and in Jerusalem, which I have chosen out of all the tribes of Israel, I will put my name for ever; ⁸and I will not cause the feet of Israel to wander any more out of the land which I gave to their fathers, if only they will be careful to do according to all that I have commanded them, and according to all the law that my servant Moses commanded them." ⁹But they did not listen, and Manas'seh seduced them to do more evil than the nations had done whom the LORD destroyed before the sons of Israel.

10 And the LORD said by his servants the prophets, ¹¹"Because Manas'seh king of Judah has committed these abominations, and has done things more wicked than all that the Am'orites did, who were before him, and has made Judah also to sin with his idols; ¹²therefore thus says the LORD, the God of Israel, Behold, I am bringing upon Jerusalem and Judah such evil that the ears of every one who hears of it will tingle. ¹³And I will stretch over Jerusalem the measuring line of Samar'ia, and the plummet of the house of A'hab; and I will wipe Jerusalem as one wipes a dish, wiping it and turning it upside down. ¹⁴And I will cast off the remnant of my heritage, and give them into the hand of their enemies, and they shall become a prey and a spoil to all their enemies, ¹⁵because they have done what is evil in my sight and have provoked me to anger, since the day their fathers came out of Egypt, even to this day."

16 Moreover Manas'seh shed very much innocent blood, till he had filled Jerusalem from one end to another, besides the sin which he made Judah to sin so that they did what was evil in the sight of the LORD.

17 Now the rest of the acts of Manas'seh, and all that he did, and the sin that he committed, are they not written in the Book of the Chronicles of

---

21:1–9: 2 Chron 33:1–9.

---

this update to the city's water-supply system as a precaution against the threat of siege warfare. Archaeology has discovered a wall plaque inscribed in ancient Hebrew, the *Siloam Tunnel Inscription*, which commemorates this engineering feat. The water channel remains intact today. **Book of the Chronicles:** See note on 1 Kings 14:19.

21:1 Manasseh: The 13th king of Judah (ca. 696 to 642 B.C.). Manasseh is judged the worst Davidic king ever to wear the crown. For the Kings historian, he is the "Ahab" of the Southern Kingdom (21:3; cf. 1 Kings 16:29–33). Under Manasseh's leadership, Judah sinks into a time of unprecedented apostasy. Idolatry is not simply tolerated but aggressively promoted. Injustice abounds as the streets of Jerusalem are stained red with the blood of violence. A prism of the Assyrian king Esarhaddon mentions "Manasseh, king of Judah" by name among a list of vassals forced to contribute labor and building materials for his royal palace in Nineveh. **twelve years old:** Manasseh ruled alongside his father, Hezekiah, for about ten years. This verse marks the beginning of his co-regency, not of his independent rule. **fifty-five years:** The longest reign of any Davidic king in the OT.

21:3–7 Manasseh reverses the cultic reforms of Hezekiah (18:4). He reconstructs the illicit shrines called **high places**; he reintroduces the worship of the Canaanite storm and fertility god **Baal**; he manufactures an image of **Asherah**, a fertility goddess of Canaanite religion, and desecrates the Temple by placing the idol within it; he reinstitutes the solar and astral cults that venerate **the host of heaven**; he burns his **son** in a ceremony of child sacrifice; and he participates in occult rituals, such as **soothsaying** and **augury**. Virtually all of these actions are transgressions of the Deuteronomic covenant (Deut 4:19; 7:5; 12:1–3; 18:10–14). See word study: *High Places* at 23:5.

21:4 In Jerusalem ... my name: The promise of a central sanctuary in Israel, which Moses described as a dwelling place for Yahweh's name (Deut 12:10–11), is fulfilled in the construction of Solomon's Temple (1 Kings 8:29).

21:8 out of the land: Exile from the land of Israel was always preventable. It only became necessary when Israel refused to keep its covenant with the Lord (Deut 28:63–64).

21:9 more evil than the nations: Under Manasseh, the Judahites became worse than the Canaanites who formerly occupied the Promised Land (called "the Amorites" in 21:11).

21:10–15 The enormity of Manasseh's crimes guarantees the demise of Judah. From this point on, the Southern Kingdom is sentenced to doom. Not even the heroic reforms of Josiah in chap. 23 can undo the damage done by Manasseh or shield Jerusalem from the covenant curses to be unleashed (23:26; 24:3–4).

21:13 measuring line ... plummet: Tools normally used in construction (Job 38:4–5) but here symbolizing tools of destruction (Is 34:11; Lam 2:8). In effect, Jerusalem will be "sized up" for judgment.

21:14 the remnant: The people of Judah and Jerusalem who remain in the land (19:30–31) will eventually be taken into exile (25:11).

21:16 innocent blood: Jewish tradition holds that Isaiah was sawn in two during Manasseh's campaign of state-sponsored violence (*Martyrdom and Ascension of Isaiah* 5, 1–16; cf. Heb 11:37).

21:17 Book of the Chronicles: See note on 1 Kings 14:19.

the Kings of Judah? [18]And Manas'seh slept with his fathers, and was buried in the garden of his house, in the garden of Uzza; and A'mon his son reigned in his stead.

Amon Reigns over Judah

[19] A'mon was twenty-two years old when he began to reign, and he reigned two years in Jerusalem. His mother's name was Meshul'lemeth the daughter of Haruz of Jotbah. [20]And he did what was evil in the sight of the LORD, as Manas'seh his father had done. [21]He walked in all the way in which his father walked, and served the idols that his father served, and worshiped them; [22]he forsook the LORD, the God of his fathers, and did not walk in the way of the LORD. [23]And the servants of A'mon conspired against him, and killed the king in his house. [24]But the people of the land slew all those who had conspired against King A'mon, and the people of the land made Josi'ah his son king in his stead. [25]Now the rest of the acts of A'mon which he did, are they not written in the Book of the Chronicles of the Kings of Judah? [26]And he was buried in his tomb in the garden of Uzza; and Josi'ah his son reigned in his stead.

Josiah Reigns over Judah

22 Josi'ah was eight years old when he began to reign, and he reigned thirty-one years in Jerusalem. His mother's name was Jedi'dah the daughter of Adai'ah of Bozkath. [2]And he did what was right in the eyes of the LORD, and walked in all the way of David his father, and he did not turn aside to the right hand or to the left.

Hilkiah Finds the Book of the Law

3 In the eighteenth year of King Josi'ah, the king sent Sha'phan the son of Azali'ah, son of Meshul'lam, the secretary, to the house of the LORD, saying, [4]"Go up to Hilki'ah the high priest, that he may reckon the amount of the money which has been brought into the house of the LORD, which the keepers of the threshold have collected from the people; [5]and let it be given into the hand of the workmen who have the oversight of the house of the LORD; and let them give it to the workmen who are at the house of the LORD, repairing the house, [6]that is, to the carpenters, and to the builders, and to the masons, as well as for buying timber and quarried stone to repair the house. [7]But no accounting shall be asked from them for the money which is delivered into their hand, for they deal honestly."

8 And Hilki'ah the high priest said to Sha'phan the secretary, "I have found the book of the law* in the house of the LORD." And Hilkiah gave the book to Shaphan, and he read it. [9]And Sha'phan the secretary came to the king, and reported to the king, "Your servants have emptied out the money that was found in the house, and have delivered it into the hand of the workmen who have the oversight of the house of the LORD." [10]Then Sha'phan the secretary told the king, "Hilki'ah the priest has given me a book." And Shaphan read it before the king.

21:18: 2 Chron 33:20. **21:19–24:** 2 Chron 33:21–25. **22:1, 2:** 2 Chron 34:1, 2. **22:3–7:** 2 Chron 34:8–12.

21:18 the garden of Uzza: Location uncertain. Manasseh, an unworthy successor of David, is not dignified with a burial in the royal tombs of the city of David (1 Kings 2:10; 11:43; 14:31; 15:8, etc.).

21:19 Amon: The 14th king of Judah (ca. 642 to 640 B.C.). He continues the religious policies of his father and is assassinated in a palace coup (21:23). Political issues, especially disagreements over Judah's relation to Assyria, may have been a factor in his murder.

21:24 the people of the land: See note on 11:14.

21:25 Book of the Chronicles: See note on 1 Kings 14:19.

21:26 the garden of Uzza: His father's burial place. See note on 21:18.

22:1 Josiah: The 15th king of Judah (ca. 640 to 609 B.C.). Josiah is hailed the greatest king in Israel's history next to David himself (22:2; 23:25), mainly because he orchestrates the most comprehensive religious reform ever conducted in the Southern Kingdom (23:4–24). In the admiring words of the Book of Sirach, the king "set his heart upon the Lord; in the days of wicked men he strengthened godliness" (Sir 49:3). The Kings historian offers no criticism of Josiah at all.

22:2 David: See note on 1 Kings 15:3. **did not turn aside:** A Deuteronomic idiom for exemplary obedience to the covenant (Deut 5:32; 28:13–14).

22:3 the eighteenth year: 622 B.C. **Shaphan:** A royal scribe in charge of the king's official correspondence. His sons were supporters of the prophet Jeremiah (Jer 26:24; 29:3; 36:10–12).

22:4 Hilkiah: A member of the high priestly line of Zadok (1 Chron 6:8–15; Ezra 7:1–2). He is not Hilkiah the father of Jeremiah (Jer 1:1) but the grandfather of Seraiah, the high priest who is later exiled and executed by the Babylonians (25:18–21). **the money:** The donations collected to finance repairs on the Temple (see 12:4–16). **keepers of the threshold:** Three priests who stand guard as sentries to prevent unlawful encroachment on the sanctuary (12:9; 25:18).

22:8 the book of the law: An ancient copy of Deuteronomy, which goes by this name (Deut 29:21; 30:10; 31:24–26). Evidently the scroll disappeared for more than a generation during the dark days of Manasseh and Amon (21:1–26). Either it was misplaced, forgotten, or hidden away for safekeeping. Scholars frequently claim, with insufficient warrant, that all or part of the Book of Deuteronomy was *written* in Josiah's time and that its debut was made to look like the *discovery* of a genuine Mosaic document. Apart from the total silence of 2 Kings regarding the composition of the book, the hypothesis is problematic for several reasons: (1) Deuteronomy is referenced by kings before this time (14:6); (2) the covenant document seems to have played a role in the coronation of kings before this time (11:12); and (3) the Book of Deuteronomy has the earmarks of a work that originates in the second millennium B.C. (e.g., multiple formal parallels with Hittite vassal treaties from the Late Bronze Age). For details, see introduction to Deuteronomy.

22:9 emptied out the money: I.e., from the donation chest described in 12:9.

---

*22:8, *book of the law:* Probably Deuteronomy. In Deut 12–26 may be seen details of Josiah's reform, especially as regards the centralization of worship. The book must have been hidden or lost during the reign of the wicked Manasseh.

Josiah Hears the Law and Is Penitent

11 And when the king heard the words of the book of the law, he tore his clothes. ¹²And the king commanded Hilki′ah the priest, and Ahi′kam the son of Sha′phan, and Achbor the son of Micai′ah, and Shaphan the secretary, and Asai′ah the king's servant, saying, ¹³"Go, inquire of the LORD for me, and for the people, and for all Judah, concerning the words of this book that has been found; for great is the wrath of the LORD that is kindled against us, because our fathers have not obeyed the words of this book, to do according to all that is written concerning us."

14 So Hilki′ah the priest, and Ahi′kam, and Achbor, and Sha′phan, and Asai′ah went to Huldah the prophetess, the wife of Shallum the son of Tikvah, son of Harhas, keeper of the wardrobe (now she dwelt in Jerusalem in the Second Quarter); and they talked with her. ¹⁵And she said to them, "Thus says the LORD, the God of Israel: 'Tell the man who sent you to me, ¹⁶Thus says the LORD, Behold, I will bring evil upon this place and upon its inhabitants, all the words of the book which the king of Judah has read. ¹⁷Because they have forsaken me and have burned incense to other gods, that they might provoke me to anger with all the work of their hands, therefore my wrath will be kindled against

this place, and it will not be quenched. ¹⁸But as to the king of Judah, who sent you to inquire of the LORD, thus shall you say to him, Thus says the LORD, the God of Israel: Regarding the words which you have heard, ¹⁹because your heart was penitent, and you humbled yourself before the LORD, when you heard how I spoke against this place, and against its inhabitants, that they should become a desolation and a curse, and you have torn your clothes and wept before me, I also have heard you, says the LORD. ²⁰Therefore, behold, I will gather you to your fathers, and you shall be gathered to your grave in peace, and your eyes shall not see all the evil which I will bring upon this place.'" And they brought back word to the king.

Josiah's Reforms

23 Then the king sent, and all the elders of Judah and Jerusalem were gathered to him. ²And the king went up to the house of the LORD, and with him all the men of Judah and all the inhabitants of Jerusalem, and the priests and the prophets, all the people, both small and great; and he read in their hearing all the words of the book of the covenant which had been found in the house of the LORD. ³And the king stood by the pillar and made a covenant before the LORD, to walk after the LORD and to keep his commandments and his

---

22:11 tore his clothes: A sign of extreme distress (6:30; 19:1).

22:12 Hilkiah: See note on 22:4. **Ahikam:** The government official who intervened to save the life of the prophet Jeremiah (Jer 26:24). His son Gedaliah will become the governor of Judah after the Babylonian conquest in 586 B.C. (25:22). **Achbor:** His sons will be courtiers under Jehoiakim (Jer 26:22; 36:12). **Shaphan:** See note on 22:3. **Asaiah:** Not otherwise known.

22:14 Huldah: One of several women in Scripture endowed with the charism of prophecy, including Miriam (Ex 15:20), Deborah (Judg 4:4), Isaiah's wife (Is 8:3), Anna (Lk 2:36), and the daughters of Philip the evangelist (Acts 21:8–9). Josiah, like other righteous kings before him, is wise to consult the Lord's prophets when the fate of the nation hangs in the balance (19:1–7; 1 Kings 22:5–6). **Second Quarter:** Thought to be an expansion of ancient Jerusalem onto the western hill (Zeph 1:10).

22:15–20 Huldah's oracle combines the "bad news" that Jerusalem is ripe for destruction (22:16) with the "good news" that Josiah will not live to see these awful days (22:20).

22:17 my wrath: Manifest in history as a divine "curse" (22:19). The kingdom of Judah will endure the terrifying curses of the Deuteronomic covenant (Deut 28:15–68).

22:19 your heart was penitent: Elicits an outpouring of God's compassion (Deut 30:1–3).

22:20 to your fathers: Suggests burial in a family tomb (23:30). **to your grave in peace:** The promise of a tranquil death is never realized because of Josiah's decision to interfere in a foreign conflict (23:29–30).

23:2 the book of the covenant: The covenant text of Deuteronomy, called "the book of the law" in 22:8. It was supposed to have been read aloud in the hearing of Israel every seven years (Deut 31:10–13).

23:3 the pillar: One of the two bronze pillars, Jachin and Boaz, that stand at the entrance to the Temple (1 Kings 7:15–22). **made a covenant:** Josiah leads the nation in a covenant renewal ceremony. Both king and people would have sworn

WORD STUDY

High Places (23:5)

bamah (Heb.): often rendered "height" or "high place". Sometimes the crest of a mountain or hill is meant (Amos 4:13; Mic 3:12). Other times it denotes the top of a cloud (Is 14:14) or the swell of a wave (Job 9:8). In the majority of cases, the term refers to cultic structures or shrines traditionally called "high places". These are places where sacrifices are made (1 Kings 3:2) and incense is offered (2 Kings 17:11). In some instances, Yahweh is worshiped at high places (1 Chron 16:39; 21:29; 2 Chron 33:17). However, they are usually places of idolatry (Lev 26:30). Pagan gods such as Chemosh, Molech, and Baal are venerated there (1 Kings 11:7; Jer 19:5), sometimes by child sacrifice (Jer 7:31). Stone pillars and wooden Asherah poles stand erect in the high places (1 Kings 14:23), and the priests who officiate are oftentimes illegitimate (1 Kings 13:33; 2 Kings 17:32; 23:5). For these reasons, the high places angered the Lord (Ps 78:58). Otherwise admirable kings of Judah are criticized for not removing them from the land (2 Kings 12:3; 14:4; 15:4). Only two had the courage to shut them down, Hezekiah (2 Kings 18:4) and Josiah (2 Kings 23:8, 13–15, 19). Demolition of the high places is required by Deuteronomy in order to protect Israel from idolatry (Deut 12:2). The worship of Yahweh by sacrifice and incense was to take place exclusively at the central sanctuary in Jerusalem (Deut 12:5–11).

covenants and his statutes, with all his heart and all his soul, to perform the words of this covenant that were written in this book; and all the people joined in the covenant.

4 And the king commanded Hilki′ah, the high priest, and the priests of the second order, and the keepers of the threshold, to bring out of the temple of the LORD all the vessels made for Ba′al, for Ashe′rah, and for all the host of heaven; he burned them outside Jerusalem in the fields of the Kidron, and carried their ashes to Bethel. ⁵And he deposed the idolatrous priests whom the kings of Judah had ordained to burn incense in the high places at the cities of Judah and round about Jerusalem; those also who burned incense to Ba′al, to the sun, and the moon, and the constellations, and all the host of the heavens. ⁶And he brought out the Ashe′rah from the house of the LORD, outside Jerusalem, to the brook Kidron, and burned it at the brook Kidron, and beat it to dust and cast the dust of it upon the graves of the common people. ⁷And he broke down the houses of the male cult prostitutes which were in the house of the LORD,

where the women wove hangings for the Ashe′rah. ⁸And he brought all the priests out of the cities of Judah, and defiled the high places where the priests had burned incense, from Ge′ba to Be′er-she′ba; and he broke down the high places of the gates that were at the entrance of the gate of Joshua the governor of the city, which were on one's left at the gate of the city. ⁹However, the priests of the high places did not come up to the altar of the LORD in Jerusalem, but they ate unleavened bread among their brethren. ¹⁰And he defiled To′pheth, which is in the valley of the sons of Hin′nom, that no one might burn his son or his daughter as an offering to Mo′lech. ¹¹And he removed the horses that the kings of Judah had dedicated to the sun, at the entrance to the house of the LORD, by the chamber of Na′than-me′lech the chamberlain, which was in the precincts;ʰ and he burned the chariots of the sun with fire. ¹²And the altars on the roof of the upper chamber of A′haz, which the kings of Judah had made, and the altars which Manas′seh had made in the two courts of the house of the LORD, he pulled down and broke in pieces,ⁱ

23:4–20: 2 Chron 34:3–7.

---

oaths of loyalty to Yahweh, committing themselves to observe all the commandments of the Deuteronomic law code. Pledges of a renewed commitment to Yahweh often entailed a renunciation of idols (11:17–18; Josh 24:19–28).

23:4–25 Josiah's reform. His efforts aim at purging Judah's religious practices of all pagan elements and at centralizing worship in Jerusalem. His campaign extends throughout the Southern Kingdom and even beyond it into the former Northern Kingdom, an opportunity made possible by the political decline of Assyria at this time. • Josiah's crusade is a rigorous enforcement of Deuteronomy, which forbids worship at high places (23:8, 13, 15; Deut 12:2), worship of foreign gods (23:4, 10, 13; Deut 5:7; 6:14), worship of the sun, moon, and stars (23:5, 11; Deut 4:19), the manufacture of graven images (23:6; Deut 4:16; 7:5), the practice of cultic prostitution (23:7; Deut 23:17), the burning of children as human sacrifices (23:10; Deut 12:31; 18:10), the use of pagan altars (23:12, 16; Deut 7:5; 12:3), the erection of stone pillars and wooden Asherah poles (23:14–15; Deut 7:5; 16:21–22), and the toleration of occult mediums and wizards (23:24; Deut 18:10–12). • How do kings serve the Lord except by outlawing and restraining all actions that go against the Lord's commandments? A ruler serves God one way as a man, another way as a king. He serves him as man by a life of faith; he serves him as king by enacting laws that command what is good and forbid the opposite. Hezekiah did this by destroying the idol shrines and high places disallowed by God's commandments, and Josiah served him in similar fashion. So it is that kings serve the Lord as kings when they do what kings are uniquely able to do (St. Augustine, *Letters* 185, 19).

23:4 Baal ... Asherah: The chief fertility god and goddess of Canaanite religion. **the host of heaven:** The sun, moon, and stars, revered as gods in Mesopotamian religion. **the Kidron:** The deep ravine directly east of Jerusalem. **ashes to Bethel:** Anticipates the king's actions in 23:15–16.

23:5 idolatrous priests: Priests who serve gods other than Yahweh (Hos 10:5; Zeph 1:4).

23:6 the Asherah: A statue of the Canaanite fertility goddess installed in the Temple by Manasseh (21:7). Chiseled monuments are destroyed by heating them with fire and then splashing water on them so that the stone splits and cracks apart. **cast the dust:** Recalls the zealous action of Moses, who pulverized the golden calf and flung the powdered remains of the idol into a mountain stream on Sinai (Ex 32:20; Deut 9:21).

23:7 male cult prostitutes: Forbidden to have any part in Israel's religious service to Yahweh (Deut 23:17). **hangings:** Perhaps clothing to adorn the Asherah image, as was often done with idols in the Near East (Jer 10:9).

23:8 the priests: Removed from local shrines and summoned to the Temple in Jerusalem. It is likely they had become corrupted by the prevailing idolatry. **from Geba to Beersheba:** I.e., from the northern to the southern limits of Josiah's kingdom. **the gates:** It is possible the Hebrew should be read as "the satyrs", referring to goat idols, as in Lev 17:7 and 2 Chron 11:15. On the other hand, there is some archaeological evidence from the time of the biblical kings indicating the presence of cultic shrines at city gates in places such as Lachish, Dan, Geshur, and Tirzah. **gate of Joshua:** Location unknown.

23:10 Topheth: Infamous as a cultic site where rituals of child sacrifice are conducted. It is located in the valley southwest of Jerusalem (Jer 7:31). **Molech:** A foreign god worshiped by human sacrifice (Lev 20:1–5; 1 Kings 11:7; Jer 32:35). **valley of the sons of Hinnom.** In Hebrew, *ge hinnom*. The atrocity of child sacrifice associated with the cult of Molech and, later, the burning of garbage in this valley gives rise in the New Testament to the description of *Gehenna*, the Greek transliteration for the Hebrew *ge hinnom*, as the symbol of hell (Mt 5:22). See word study *Hell* in Mk 9:43.

23:11 horses ... chariots of the sun: In Near Eastern mythology, the sun god Shamash rode in a chariot pulled by horses. Solar worship had taken root in Judah (Ezek 8:16).

23:12 the altars: Installed by Manasseh in 21:5.

ʰ The meaning of the Hebrew word is uncertain.
ⁱ Heb *pieces from there.*

and cast the dust of them into the brook Kidron. ¹³And the king defiled the high places that were east of Jerusalem, to the south of the mount of corruption, which Solomon the king of Israel had built for Ash′toreth the abomination of the Sido′nians, and for Che′mosh the abomination of Moab, and for Milcom the abomination of the Am′monites. ¹⁴And he broke in pieces the pillars, and cut down the Ashe′rim, and filled their places with the bones of men.

15 Moreover the altar at Bethel, the high place erected by Jerobo′am the son of Ne′bat, who made Israel to sin, that altar with the high place he pulled down and he broke in pieces its stones,ʲ crushing them to dust; also he burned the Ashe′rah. ¹⁶And as Josi′ah turned, he saw the tombs there on the mount; and he sent and took the bones out of the tombs, and burned them upon the altar, and defiled it, according to the word of the Lᴏʀᴅ which the man of God proclaimed, who had predicted these things. ¹⁷Then he said, "What is yonder monument that I see?" And the men of the city told him, "It is the tomb of the man of God who came from Judah and predicted these things which you have done against the altar at Bethel." ¹⁸And he said, "Let him be; let no man move his bones." So they let his bones alone, with the bones of the prophet who came out of Samar′ia. ¹⁹And all the shrines also of the high places that were in the cities of Samar′ia, which kings of Israel had made, provoking the Lᴏʀᴅ to anger, Josi′ah removed; he did to them according to all that he had done at Bethel. ²⁰And he slew all the priests of the high places who were there, upon the altars, and burned the bones of men upon them. Then he returned to Jerusalem.

The Passover Is Celebrated

21 And the king commanded all the people, "Keep the Passover to the Lᴏʀᴅ your God, as it is written in this book of the covenant." ²²For no such Passover had been kept since the days of the judges who judged Israel, or during all the days of the kings of Israel or of the kings of Judah; ²³but in the eighteenth year of King Josi′ah this Passover was kept to the Lᴏʀᴅ in Jerusalem.

24 Moreover Josi′ah put away the mediums and the wizards and the teraphim and the idols and all the abominations that were seen in the land of Judah and in Jerusalem, that he might establish the words of the law which were written in the book that Hilki′ah the priest found in the house of the Lᴏʀᴅ. ²⁵Before him there was no king like him, who turned to the Lᴏʀᴅ with all his heart and with all his soul and with all his might, according to all the law of Moses; nor did any like him arise after him.

26 Still the Lᴏʀᴅ did not turn from the fierceness of his great wrath, by which his anger was kindled against Judah, because of all the provocations with which Manas′seh had provoked him. ²⁷And the Lᴏʀᴅ said, "I will remove Judah also out of my sight, as I have removed Israel, and I will cast off this city which I have chosen, Jerusalem, and the house of which I said, My name shall be there."

Josiah Dies in Battle

28 Now the rest of the acts of Josi′ah, and all that he did, are they not written in the Book of the Chronicles of the Kings of Judah? ²⁹In his days Pharaoh Neco king of Egypt went up to the king of Assyria to the river Euphra′tes. King Josi′ah went to meet him; and Pharaoh Neco slew him at Megid′do, when he saw him. ³⁰And his servants carried him

---

23:21–23: 2 Chron 35:1–19. **23:30–34:** 2 Chron 36:1–4.

23:13 mount of corruption: A reference to the Mount of Olives, directly east of Jerusalem. For the pagan worship established there by Solomon, see 1 Kings 11:5–7.

23:14 pillars ... Asherim: Idolatrous cult objects. See note on 17:10. **the bones of men:** The use of bones to desecrate cultic sites is based on Mosaic teaching that contact with human death causes ritual defilement (Num 19:11–19).

23:15 Bethel: Roughly ten miles north of Jerusalem. Once within the bounds of the Northern Kingdom, the city of Bethel hosted one of the two golden calf idols that featured in Jeroboam's corrupt state religion (1 Kings 12:28–29). • Josiah's demolition and defilement of the Bethel altar fulfills a prophecy uttered against Jeroboam more than 300 years earlier in 1 Kings 13:1–2.

23:17 man of God: The prophet of Judah who was buried in Bethel (1 Kings 13:26–32).

23:19 the cities of Samaria: The towns of central Israel, formerly part of the Northern Kingdom and recently part of the Assyrian province of Samaria.

23:20 slew all the priests: Because they led the people away from Yahweh to the worship of other gods (Deut 13:12–18).

23:21–23 A summary account of Josiah's **Passover**. It is a national celebration of the feast in Jerusalem ordered by royal decree and observed in accordance with Deut 16:1–8. In the eyes of the Kings historian, the springtime festival had not been celebrated on such a grand scale since before the time of the judges (perhaps since Josh 5:10). A fuller account of Josiah's Passover appears in 2 Chron 35:1–19.

23:24 teraphim: Household idols (Gen 31:34) used to divine the future (Ezek 21:21; Zech 10:2).

23:25 heart ... soul ... might: Josiah loves and serves the Lord precisely as Deuteronomy prescribes (Deut 6:5; 10:12).

23:26–27 For the certainty of Judah's judgment, see note on 21:10–15.

23:28 Book of the Chronicles: See note on 1 Kings 14:19.

23:29 Pharaoh Neco: King of Egypt from 610 to 595 B.C. Most likely Neco marches north to join forces with Assyria in opposing the rising power of Babylon. Josiah unwisely interferes and gets himself killed in the process of trying to disrupt the alliance. A fuller account of his demise appears in 2 Chron 35:20–27. **Megiddo:** The Plain of Megiddo, southeast of Mt. Carmel, served as a battlefield in biblical times (Judg 5:19; cf. Zech 12:11).

23:30 the people of the land: See note on 11:14. **anointed him:** See note on 9:6.

ʲGk: Heb *he burned the high place.*

dead in a chariot from Megid'do, and brought him to Jerusalem, and buried him in his own tomb. And the people of the land took Jeho'ahaz the son of Josi'ah, and anointed him, and made him king in his father's stead.

31 Jeho'ahaz was twenty-three years old when he began to reign, and he reigned three months in Jerusalem. His mother's name was Hamu'tal the daughter of Jeremi'ah of Libnah. ³²And he did what was evil in the sight of the LORD, according to all that his fathers had done. ³³And Pharaoh Neco put him in bonds at Riblah in the land of Ha'math, that he might not reign in Jerusalem, and laid upon the land a tribute of a hundred talents of silver and a talent of gold. ³⁴And Pharaoh Ne'co made Eli'akim the son of Josi'ah king in the place of Josiah his father, and changed his name to Jehoi'akim. But he took Jeho'ahaz away; and he came to Egypt, and died there. ³⁵And Jehoi'akim gave the silver and the gold to Pharaoh, but he taxed the land to give the money according to the command of Pharaoh. He exacted the silver and the gold of the people of the land, from every one according to his assessment, to give it to Pharaoh Neco.

Jehoiakim Reigns over Judah

36 Jehoi'akim was twenty-five years old when he began to reign, and he reigned eleven years in Jerusalem. His mother's name was Zebi'dah the daughter of Pedai'ah of Ru'mah. ³⁷And he did what was evil in the sight of the LORD, according to all that his fathers had done.

Judah Overrun by Enemies

24 In his days Nebuchadnez'zar king of Babylon came up, and Jehoi'akim became his servant

three years; then he turned and rebelled against him. ²And the LORD sent against him bands of the Chalde'ans, and bands of the Syrians, and bands of the Moabites, and bands of the Am'monites, and sent them against Judah to destroy it, according to the word of the LORD which he spoke by his servants the prophets. ³Surely this came upon Judah at the command of the LORD, to remove them out of his sight, for the sins of Manas'seh, according to all that he had done, ⁴and also for the innocent blood that he had shed; for he filled Jerusalem with innocent blood, and the LORD would not pardon. ⁵Now the rest of the deeds of Jehoi'akim, and all that he did, are they not written in the Book of the Chronicles of the Kings of Judah? ⁶So Jehoi'akim slept with his fathers, and Jehoi'achin his son reigned in his stead. ⁷And the king of Egypt did not come again out of his land, for the king of Babylon had taken all that belonged to the king of Egypt from the Brook of Egypt to the river Euphrates.

Reign and Captivity of Jehoiachin

8 Jehoi'achin was eighteen years old when he became king, and he reigned three months in Jerusalem. His mother's name was Nehush'ta the daughter of Elna'than of Jerusalem. ⁹And he did what was evil in the sight of the LORD, according to all that his father had done.

Babylon Conquers Jerusalem

10 At that time the servants of Nebuchadnez'zar king of Babylon came up to Jerusalem, and the city was besieged. ¹¹And Nebuchadnez'zar king of Babylon came to the city, while his servants were besieging it; ¹²and Jehoi'achin the king of Judah gave himself up to the king of Babylon, himself, and

---

23:36—24:6: 2 Chron 36:5–8.   **24:8-17:** 2 Chron 36:9–10.

23:31 Jehoahaz: The 16th king of Judah (ca. 609 B.C.). He is Josiah's youngest son, also called Shallum (1 Chron 3:15). During his brief reign, Judah is reduced to a tribute-paying vassal of Egypt (23:33). **Jeremiah:** Not the famous prophet from Anathoth (Jer 1:1).

23:33 Riblah: A city on the Orontes River in Syria.

23:36 Jehoiakim: The 17th king of Judah (ca. 609 to 598 B.C.). His reign witnesses the first Babylonian invasion and subjugation of Judah (24:1), which are the first signs of God's judgment on the Southern Kingdom (24:3). It is unclear why Neco changed the name of this puppet king from Eliakim, meaning "God rises up", to Jehoiakim, meaning "Yahweh rises up" (23:34).

24:1—25:26 The fall of the Southern Kingdom of Judah. Judgment comes in several waves against Jerusalem and its surrounding territory. (1) In 605 B.C., the Babylonians march into Palestine and make Judah a vassal state after defeating Egypt at the Battle of Carchemish (24:1). (2) In 601 B.C., hordes from north and east of Judah make raids on the land to punish Jehoiakim for his rebellion against Babylonia (24:2). (3) In the early spring of 597 B.C., the Babylonians lay siege to Jerusalem, plunder its wealth, and drag the royal family along with skilled workers and soldiers to Babylon (24:10–17). (4) Finally, in the summer of 586 B.C., the Babylonians bring total destruction upon Jerusalem and its Temple, taking all but the poorest survivors into exile in Babylon (25: 8–12).

24:1 Nebuchadnezzar: Founder of the Neo-Babylonian Empire, which he ruled from 605 to 562 B.C. **his servant:** I.e., his political vassal. **rebelled:** Perhaps Jehoiakim took this bold step (ca. 602 B.C.) because Babylon had suffered a recent setback in its conflicts with Egypt. The king misread the situation as though the days of Babylonian dominance were over.

24:2 the LORD sent: A theological interpretation of history. Yahweh, the sovereign Lord of all nations, steers the course of world events toward the fulfillment of his purpose. Mighty Babylon is merely a rod in his hand, the instrument he uses to bring judgment on Judah for its crimes against the covenant (Deut 28:49-68; Hab 1:5-11). **Chaldeans:** Babylonians. **Syrians ... Moabites ... Ammonites:** Vassals of Babylonia compelled to support the military efforts of Nebuchadnezzar.

24:3 out of his sight: The same expression used to describe the exile of the northern tribes of Israel (17:18, 20, 23). **sins of Manasseh:** See note on 21:10-15.

24:5 Book of the Chronicles: See note on 1 Kings 14:19.

24:7 Egypt ... Euphrates: The full extent of the land promised to Abraham (Gen 15:18–20), once in the possession of Solomon (1 Kings 4:21), is now a part of the Babylonian empire.

24:8 Jehoiachin: The 18th king of Judah (ca. 598 to 597 B.C.). He witnesses the first Babylonian siege and capture of Jerusalem in the spring of 597 B.C. (24:10), at which time he surrenders himself and his royal administration to captivity (24:12). He is also known as "Jeconiah" (1 Chron 3:16) and "Coniah" (Jer 22:24).

his mother, and his servants, and his princes, and his palace officials. The king of Babylon took him prisoner in the eighth year of his reign, [13]and carried off all the treasures of the house of the LORD, and the treasures of the king's house, and cut in pieces all the vessels of gold in the temple of the LORD, which Solomon king of Israel had made, as the LORD had foretold. [14]He carried away all Jerusalem, and all the princes, and all the mighty men of valor, ten thousand captives, and all the craftsmen and the smiths; none remained, except the poorest people of the land. [15]And he carried away Jehoi'achin to Babylon; the king's mother, the king's wives, his officials, and the chief men of the land, he took into captivity from Jerusalem to Babylon. [16]And the king of Babylon brought captive to Babylon all the men of valor, seven thousand, and the craftsmen and the smiths, one thousand, all of them strong and fit for war. [17]And the king of Babylon made Mattani'ah, Jehoi'achin's uncle, king in his stead, and changed his name to Zedeki'ah.

Zedekiah Reigns over Judah

18 Zedeki'ah was twenty-one years old when he became king, and he reigned eleven years in Jerusalem. His mother's name was Hamu'tal the daughter of Jeremi'ah of Libnah. [19]And he did what was evil in the sight of the LORD, according to all that Jehoi'akim had done. [20]For because of the anger of the LORD it came to the point in Jerusalem and Judah that he cast them out from his presence.

25 And Zedeki'ah rebelled against the king of Babylon. [1]And in the ninth year of his reign, in the tenth month, on the tenth day of the month, Nebuchadnez'zar king of Babylon came with all his army against Jerusalem, and laid siege to it; and they built siegeworks against it round about. [2]So the city was besieged till the eleventh year of King Zedeki'ah. [3]On the ninth day of the fourth month the famine was so severe in the city that there was no food for the people of the land. [4]Then a breach was made in the city; the king with all the men of war fled[k] by night by the way of the gate between the two walls, by the king's garden, though the Chalde'ans were around the city. And they went in the direction of the Ar'abah. [5]But the army of the Chalde'ans pursued the king, and overtook him in the plains of Jericho; and all his army was scattered from him. [6]Then they captured the king, and brought him up to the king of Babylon at Rib'lah, who passed sentence upon him. [7]They slew the sons of Zedeki'ah before his eyes, and put out the eyes of Zedekiah, and bound him in fetters, and took him to Babylon.

The Babylonian Exile

8 In the fifth month, on the seventh day of the month—which was the nineteenth year of King Nebuchadnez'zar, king of Babylon—Nebu"zarad'-an, the captain of the bodyguard, a servant of the king of Babylon, came to Jerusalem. [9]And he burned the house of the LORD, and the king's house and all the houses of Jerusalem; every great house he burned down. [10]And all the army of the Chalde'ans, who were with the captain of the guard, broke down the walls around Jerusalem. [11]And the rest of the people who were left in the city and the deserters who had deserted to the king of Babylon, together with the rest of the multitude, Nebu"zarad'an the captain of the guard carried into exile. [12]But the captain of the guard left some of the poorest of the land to be vinedressers and plowmen.

13 And the pillars of bronze that were in the house of the LORD, and the stands and the bronze sea that were in the house of the LORD, the Chalde'ans broke in pieces, and carried the bronze to Babylon.

24:18—25:21: 2 Chron 36:11–21; Jer 52:1–27.

24:13 treasures: Precious metals looted from the Temple and royal palace (Jer 27:16). **as the LORD had foretold:** By the mouth of the prophet Isaiah in 20:16–18.

24:14–16 The Babylonians, like the Assyrians, execute a policy of "selective deportation", meaning that all persons of influence, wealth, and education are taken into exile and only a remnant of the peasantry is left behind in the land.

24:17 Zedekiah: The 19th and last king of Judah (ca. 597 to 586 B.C.). It is his foolish rebellion (24:20) that brings the final blast of Babylonian wrath that destroys the Southern Kingdom (25:8–12). Mattaniah/Zedekiah is the third son of Josiah (1 Chron 3:15) to wear the Davidic crown after Jehoahaz/Shallum (23:30) and then Eliakim/Jehoiakim (23:34). Ironically, the name Zedekiah means "Yahweh is my righteousness."

24:18—25:21 A nearly identical account appears in Jer 52:1–27.

25:1–17 The Babylonian conquest of Jerusalem. It begins with an 18-month siege (25:1–2) and ends in the summer of 586 B.C. with the city and its sanctuary in a blazing heap of destruction (25:8–9). This final blow topples the Davidic monarchy and marks the decisive end of the Southern Kingdom. The people of Judah will spend the next 48 years exiled in Babylon, cut off from their homeland and unable to worship at their sanctuary (25:21). Theologically, national catastrophe and exile are manifestations of the covenant curses that come with blatant defiance of God's Law (Lev 26:27–33; Deut 28:58–68). The aim of the curses is to humble and humiliate the covenant people so that they will acknowledge their sins and turn their hearts back to the Lord (Deut 30:1–10).

25:3 the famine: Starving survivors descend to the level of cannibalism (Lam 4:10).

25:4 the gate: In the southeast wall of the city. **the Arabah:** The wilderness of Judah east of Jerusalem.

25:6 Riblah: A city on the Orontes River in Syria.

25:7 put out the eyes: Physical torture as well as psychological torture. Zedekiah's last visual memory will be the violent execution of his sons. • The blinding of Zedekiah was foretold by Ezekiel, who said that the king would come to Babylon but never "see" it (Ezek 12:13).

25:8 the fifth month: August of 586 B.C. Subsequent generations mourned the Temple's destruction (25:9) by fasting in the fifth month (Zech 7:3).

25:11 carried into exile: See note on 24:14–16.

---

[k]Gk Compare Jer 39:4; 52:7: Heb lacks *the king* and *fled.*

¹⁴And they took away the pots, and the shovels, and the snuffers, and the dishes for incense and all the vessels of bronze used in the temple service, ¹⁵the firepans also, and the bowls. What was of gold the captain of the guard took away as gold, and what was of silver, as silver. ¹⁶As for the two pillars, the one sea, and the stands, which Solomon had made for the house of the LORD, the bronze of all these vessels was beyond weight. ¹⁷The height of the one pillar was eighteen cubits, and upon it was a capital of bronze; the height of the capital was three cubits; a network and pomegranates, all of bronze, were upon the capital round about. And the second pillar had the like, with the network.

18 And the captain of the guard took Serai′ah the chief priest, and Zephani′ah the second priest, and the three keepers of the threshold; ¹⁹and from the city he took an officer who had been in command of the men of war, and five men of the king's council who were found in the city; and the secretary of the commander of the army who mustered the people of the land; and sixty men of the people of the land who were found in the city. ²⁰And Nebu″zarad′an the captain of the guard took them, and brought them to the king of Babylon at Riblah. ²¹And the king of Babylon struck them, and put them to death at Riblah in the land of Ha′math. So Judah was taken into exile out of its land.

Gedaliah Made Governor of Judah

22 And over the people who remained in the land of Judah, whom Nebuchadnez′zar king of Babylon had left, he appointed Gedali′ah the son of Ahi′kam, son of Sha′phan, governor. ²³Now when all the captains of the forces in the open country[1] and their men heard that the king of Babylon had appointed Gedali′ah governor, they came with their men to Gedaliah at Mizpah, namely, Ish′mael the son of Nethani′ah, and Joha′nan the son of Kare′ah, and Serai′ah the son of Tan′humeth the Netoph′athite, and Ja-azani′ah the son of the Ma-ac′athite. ²⁴And Gedali′ah swore to them and their men, saying, "Do not be afraid because of the Chalde′an officials; dwell in the land, and serve the king of Babylon, and it shall be well with you." ²⁵But in the seventh month, Ish′mael the son of Nethani′ah, son of Elish′ama, of the royal family, came with ten men, and attacked and killed Gedali′ah and the Jews and the Chalde′ans who were with him at Mizpah. ²⁶Then all the people, both small and great, and the captains of the forces arose, and went to Egypt; for they were afraid of the Chalde′ans.

Jehoiachin Is Freed by Evil-merodach

27 And in the thirty-seventh year of the exile of Jehoi′achin king of Judah, in the twelfth month, on the twenty-seventh day of the month, E′vil-mer′odach king of Babylon, in the year that he began to reign, graciously freed Jehoi′achin king of Judah from prison; ²⁸and he spoke kindly to him, and gave him a seat above the seats of the kings who were with him in Babylon. ²⁹So Jehoi′achin put off his prison garments. And every day of his life he dined regularly at the king's table; ³⁰and for his allowance, a regular allowance was given him by the king, every day a portion, as long as he lived.

25:22–26: Jer 40:7—43:7.   **25:27–30:** Jer 52:31–34.

25:13–17 The Temple is plundered of its precious metals and sacred implements (see the inventory in 1 Kings 7:15–50). However, no mention is made of the Ark of the Covenant or of the golden altar of incense because the prophet Jeremiah hid them away in a cave before the onset of the Babylonian siege (2 Mac 2:4–5; cf. Jer 3:16).
25:18 Seraiah: The grandson of Hilkiah, high priest in the days of Josiah (22:3–4). **second priest:** A deputy high priest whose specific responsibilities are unknown. **keepers of the threshold:** See note on 22:4.
25:22 Gedaliah: A Jewish noble put in charge of Judah after the fall of the monarchy. With Jerusalem in ruins, he rules from Mizpah (25:23). His policy of peaceful cooperation with Babylon (25:24) angers some of his compatriots, leading to his assassination in the fall of 586 B.C. (25:25). A fuller account of his demise is given by Jeremiah (Jer 40–41).
25:23 Mizpah: About eight miles north of Jerusalem in the tribal territory of Benjamin.

25:26 went to Egypt: For fear of Babylonian reprisals in the wake of Gedaliah's murder. The fleeing refugees take Jeremiah and his secretary Baruch along with them (Jer 43:4–7).
25:27–30 A short postscript that brings the story of 2 Kings into the exilic period, offering a glimmer of hope for the future. The clemency shown to Jehoiachin, the king of Judah, hints that his fellow captives from Judah can anticipate a measure of mercy in the midst of exile. Also, it indicates that David's royal line remains intact despite the total collapse of the Southern Kingdom. Far from destroying the covenant people and their kings, the Lord will decree a release from exile in 538 B.C. (Ezra 1:1–4) and eventually raise up the heir to David's throne in Jesus the Messiah (Mt 1:1–16; Lk 1:32–33).
25:27 thirty-seventh year: About 560 B.C. **the exile of Jehoiachin:** Noted in 24:15. **Evil-merodach:** Son and successor of Nebuchadnezzar as king of Babylon (562 to 560 B.C.). The Babylonian form of his name means "Man of (the god) Marduk".
25:30 his allowance: A detail corroborated by the archaeological discovery of clay tablets from ancient Babylon that name Jehoiachin and his sons as recipients of food rations of oil supplied by the royal household.

---

[1] With Jer 40:7: Heb lacks *in the open country*.

Study Questions
2 Kings

Chapter 1

For understanding
1. **1:2.** Which king is Ahaziah? How much is known of him? How did he come into conflict with Elijah? What does the name Baal-zebub mean, and of what name is it a derogatory distortion? Where is Ekron?
2. **1:8.** Of whom are the garment of haircloth and the girdle of leather the distinctive dress? What does this clothing indicate? Centuries later, how will John the Baptist appear?
3. **1:10.** What comes down from heaven? For what was Elijah known? What does the incident show that God does? What two companions of Jesus appear to have this episode in mind in Lk 9:52–54?
4. **1:17.** Who is Jehoram? To what is his name sometimes shortened? What does his royal counterpart in the south share with him?

For application
1. **1:2.** Have you ever been seriously injured in an accident or known someone who has been? To whom did you (or they) look for healing and redress? How was the Lord part of this petition?
2. **1:8.** Judging from his tone, what do you think Ahaziah's attitude toward Elijah is? Of what other prophet does the description of Elijah remind you?
3. **1:9-15.** Note the change of approach of each of the captains in these verses. On whose authority do the first two rely when summoning the prophet? On whose authority does the third captain rely? How might his attitude help you approach persons in authority?

Chapter 2

For understanding
1. **2:1—8:15.** Who is the subject of these stories? How is he most remembered? What do scholars surmise about these stories? In what ways is Elisha a prophet after the likeness of Moses? How does Elisha also prefigure the Messiah?
2. **2:3.** Who are the sons of the prophets? How do prophetic guilds use the kinship language of "father" and "sons"? How does that language apply to both Elijah and Elisha? Where do communities of prophets live? Why is Elijah presumably making his final stops in these towns?
3. **2:9.** Why does Elisha request a double share of Elijah's spirit? What is the background for this request? How is Elisha confirmed as Elijah's successor?
4. **2:11.** What does Elijah's escort appear to be? What do raging flames and storm winds manifest? Who are the only two figures in the OT whose life on earth ended with a translation into heaven? What is fitting about John the Baptist's appearance as a prophet on the banks of the Jordan? How does St. Bede compare Elijah with Jesus? Elisha with the apostles?
5. **2:23.** What is significant about Bethel? What can the expression "small boys" designate? With what are these youths perhaps affiliated? Why are they mauled to death? What connotation does the Hebrew verb "go up" often have? What does it suggest that the boys are doing, and how does the Torah judge it? What does the insult "baldhead" insinuate?

For application
1. **2:9.** Read the note for this verse. Given your reception of the sacraments, what "portion" of the Holy Spirit have you received? How is that confirmed by changes in your relationship with God? What more do you think the Lord has in store for you? How much more do you want?
2. **2:15.** How does your parish or religious community respond to changes in its leadership? How do people greet new leader(s)? Are there any areas of resistance to new leadership, and how is submission manifested? What is your own attitude?
3. **2:21.** Read the note for this verse. How does St. Caesarius understand the spiritual meaning of the miracle? How has Christ, the new Elisha, restored you from evil ways to charity and righteousness?
4. **2:23-24.** If people dislike changes being made, how appropriate is it to initiate media protest campaigns or stage demonstrations of opposition? What are some ways they can make their dissatisfaction known legitimately?

Chapter 3

For understanding
1. **3:1.** How is the apparent discrepancy between the reference to Jehoshaphat's eighteenth year and the year mentioned in 1:17 best explained?
2. **3:5.** How might Moab's refusal to pay tribute to the Northern Kingdom of Israel be interpreted? Whom does the *Mesha Inscription* mention by name, and what does it celebrate about this event? What does the inscription fail to mention?
3. **3:17.** What does Elisha promise the king of Israel? What will happen to the dried-up riverbed?
4. **3:27.** What does Mesha do with his first-born son? For what is his action a desperate appeal? Whose wrath is meant by the phrase "wrath upon Israel"? What does the spectacle inspire Mesha's fighters to do?

For application
1. **3:3.** As a reminder, the "sin of Jeroboam" in 1 Kings 12 was to establish a state-devised religion for the Northern Kingdom to rival the true religion centered in Jerusalem. What does this verse in 2 Kings imply that Jehoram should have done? Why do people often cling to beliefs that a true religion brands as false?

111

2. **3:15.** What aids, such as music, do you use to help you concentrate? How often do you use them to focus your attention in prayer? If music helps you pray, what kind of music most appeals to you?
3. **3:27.** Read the note for this verse. Has a fit of anger or desperation ever prompted you to sacrifice a long-term resource, such as a savings account, to address a near-term need, such as hiring an attorney for a lawsuit? How did you come to the decision to make that sacrifice? To what extent was the sacrifice worth making?

Chapter 4

For understanding
1. **Chart: Elijah and Elisha.** How are Elijah and Elisha unlike the prophets Isaiah, Jeremiah, Ezekiel, and others? How many miracles does the narrative of Kings attribute to Elijah? to Elisha? What is this perhaps the author's way of demonstrating about Elisha?
2. **4:16.** What will God grant the Shunammite woman? For what is it a blessing? What danger would the lack of a biological heir cause the family? What promise do Elisha's words to her recall?
3. **4:29.** Why does Elisha tell Gehazi not to salute anyone on the road? Why does Jesus give the same instruction to 70 disciples?
4. **4:32–37.** What miracle does Elisha perform? Of what is restoration to life the result? What did Elijah and the Apostle Paul do to raise the dead? How does St. Gregory relate the spiritual meaning of this episode to salvation history?
5. **4:42.** Where is Baal-shalishah? What happened to the twenty loaves of barley? How will Jesus surpass the miracle of Elisha?

For application
1. **4:1–7.** Have you ever consulted anyone for financial advice? How critical was the need for help? How faithfully did you follow the advice given? How did your overall trust in God's Providence influence the way you sought and responded to help?
2. **4:13.** What do you think the Shunammite woman's answer to Elisha means? What resources exist among your own relations to care for you when you need support? What resources are you able to offer them?
3. **4:32–35.** What is the difference between resurrection and resuscitation? What do miracles of restoration to life like this say to us regarding the resurrection of the dead? (Refer to CCC 994 for help with this question.)
4. **4:42–44.** What is the purpose of miracles like this multiplication of food? The note for this verse refers to Jesus' multiplication of food. What might be the link between Jesus' miracle and that of the Eucharist?

Chapter 5

For understanding
1. **5:1.** Of what is the victory given to Syria a reminder? In this account, what kind of disease is Naaman's leprosy? What did it not prevent Naaman from doing?
2. **5:10.** What does Elisha's instruction to Naaman demand of him? What was Naaman expecting? What similar miracles does Jesus perform?
3. **5:14.** What does washing in the murky waters of the Jordan underscore? What is washing seven times perhaps imply that Naaman's body would experience? What does Leviticus stipulate that a person suspected of leprosy must do? According to Origen of Alexandria, how are men covered with leprosy cleansed? According to St. Ambrose, what are people like before Baptism, and what happens afterward? As a figure of future salvation, what does Naaman's immersion in the Jordan make us recognize?
4. **5:18.** What is the house of Rimmon? For what does Naaman hope by asking Elisha's pardon?

For application
1. **5:6–7.** Written correspondence such as letters and emails often miscommunicate for several reasons. What are some of them? Have you ever experienced correspondence that resulted in a miscommunication, and, if so, what problems resulted? How were any misunderstandings resolved?
2. **5:10–14.** What connection do these verses reveal between faith, pride, and humility? How does Naaman display all three? What was it about the advice of Naaman's servants that helped him change his mind? Have you ever received advice like that?
3. **5:20.** What is Gehazi's attitude toward Naaman? By implication, what is his attitude toward Elisha, given the latter's refusal to accept payment?
4. **5:22–24.** How many talents of silver did Gehazi ask of Naaman, and how many did Naaman urge him to take? Calculating from the note for v. 5, how heavy a load did the two servants have to carry for him? How was Naaman's generosity a problem for Gehazi? How is the success of a theft often a problem for the thief?

Chapter 6

For understanding
1. **6:5.** What was the axe head made of? What does the miracle of making it float to the surface show about Elisha? According to St. Justin Martyr, why did Elisha throw wood into the Jordan to raise the axe head? According to St. Ambrose, what does Elisha's invocation of the Lord have to do with our Baptism and the Cross of Christ?
2. **6:10.** What does Elisha do for the king of Israel by his prophetic knowledge? What does this make the Syrian king suspect?
3. **6:17–20.** What do these verses illustrate about the Lord? To whom is spiritual vision given, and from whom is it taken and restored again?
4. **6:25.** What does siege bring about, and what does it mean? What is the city eventually forced to witness?

For application
1. **6:15–16.** What is the difference between seeing and perceiving? What does Elisha's servant see, and what does his master help him perceive? How do you think the Lord might be leading you to perceive what he is doing in your life, despite what you see?
2. **6:22.** Read the note for this verse. What are some of the personal benefits of treating your enemies well? What does St. Paul say about getting revenge in Rom 12:19–21?
3. **6:31.** Why do you think the king of Samaria blames Elisha for the starvation and cannibalism taking place there? Where do we tend to place blame when an outbreak of disease or a sharp economic downturn—or even a long series of losses for a sports team—takes place?
4. **6:33.** How do you pray when things do not go your way or circumstances seem to conspire against you? What is the spiritual danger in getting impatient with God? Why will taking matters into your own hands not make things any better?

Chapter 7

For understanding
1. **7:1.** What does Elisha announce? What will happen the very next day? What could the city gate serve as during peacetime?
2. **7:2.** What happens to the captain who openly doubts the word of the Lord?
3. **7:6.** What did the Lord make the Syrian army hear? Into what did the sound of an approaching cavalry and chariotry send the army? Who are the Hittites?

For application
1. **7:2.** How do the captain's words betray his unbelief? Given dire circumstances like those in the previous chapter, how unreasonable is it to question promises of a sudden turnaround in fortune? Even so, how willing are you to trust the Lord to provide for you, even when circumstances look impossible?
2. **7:6–7.** What kind of event, phenomenon, or circumstance might make you panic? How do you react when you feel panic? How do you feel about yourself when the situation passes and the panic subsides?
3. **7:9.** What is the lepers' main motive for reporting the sudden good news to the king? If you stumbled on a fortune, what would motivate you to report it to the authorities rather than keep it for yourself?
4. **7:17–20.** How deserved do you think the captain's fate was? How might unbelief come to deserve death? Why does Jesus warn that those who do not believe the preaching of the Gospel will be condemned?

Chapter 8

For understanding
1. **8:3.** Why did the woman from Shunem have to appeal to the king for her house? What was the result of her appeal?
2. **8:10.** What is the meaning of Elisha's contradictory remark to Hazael? If sickness will not take the king's life, how will he die?
3. **8:16.** Who is the Jehoram mentioned here? For what is he criticized? What does his political marriage with Ahab's daughter occasion? When does Jehoram's independent rule over Judah come?
4. **8:25.** Who is Ahaziah? Why is his short reign judged an evil reign?

For application
1. **8:1.** Imagine a catastrophic failure of the electrical system in this country. What needs would you face? What kinds of arrangements would you have to make for your survival? How difficult an option would relocation become?
2. **8:12–13.** How has modern warfare become more or less humane than the evils Elisha narrates here? What military objectives lie behind the evils Elisha mentions? Why does Hazael think that doing them is for him a "great thing"?
3. **8:26–27.** Of how much of your family's history are you aware? What influence has your family's history had on your own outlook on life and your day-to-day behavior; for example, how like your parents are you? If your family has been harmed by a cycle of abuse and addiction, what can you do to break free of the cycle?

Chapter 9

For understanding
1. **9:1–10:36.** Why is Jehu the least criticized of all the northern kings? Nevertheless, why is he faulted? How long will Jehu's dynasty extend after him? How does the Black Obelisk of Shalmaneser III depict Jehu of Israel?
2. **9:6.** What does anointing symbolize? For whom was the rite performed? What does emptying the flask upon Jehu fulfill?
3. **9:13.** What is the meaning of placing garments on the steps under Jehu? In a similar way, what do the crowds do with Jesus on Palm Sunday, and why is this significant?
4. **9:22.** To what sorceries and harlotries is Jehu referring? What did Jezebel's corruption of Israel cause her name to stand for?
5. **9:31.** What does Jezebel mean by calling Jehu by the name of Zimri? What does she imply by this?

For application
1. **9:4–16.** The word *conspire* comes from the Latin for *to breathe with* or *together*. To what does it usually refer? How may it have a positive connotation? For example, how may it refer to the interaction between human beings and the Holy Spirit?

2. **9:17–20.** When touched by a "conspiracy of God", how quickly must a person act? Why can delay in responding to grace lead to its loss? Why, for example, did Jesus forbid a prospective disciple to bury his father first (in Lk 9:59–60)?
3. **9:30.** Why do you think Jezebel "painted her eyes and adorned her head" to confront Jehu, whom she knows is the murderer of his master (v. 31)? What does she know is about to happen to her? What message does she want to send by adorning herself?

Chapter 10

For understanding
1. **Word Study: Heads (10:6).** What various meanings does the Hebrew noun *ro'sh* have in the Bible? How is the flexibility of this term exploited in Jehu's letter in this verse? What does the inherent ambiguity in the word *ro'sh* enable Jehu to accomplish?
2. **10:11.** What does Jehu's violent action exceed? What had the Lord commanded him to do, and what does he proceed to do beyond that? Why does the prophet Hosea condemn him?
3. **10:15.** Who are the Rechabites? What did they idealize, and what did they deny themselves? For Jehu, what do they represent?
4. **10:19.** How are the prophets of Baal supported? What does the author of Kings acknowledge about Jehu's tactics? What do Christian moral standards say about using evil means to accomplish a good end?

For application
1. **10:9–10.** What is the implied answer to Jehu's question in v. 9? When people attribute evil (such as this massacre) to the Lord, how do you answer them?
2. **10:12–17.** Read the note for v. 11, and then look up Hos 1:4. What ultimate fate awaited the "House of Israel"? What is the difference between zeal and fanaticism?
3. **10:19.** Read the note for this verse. What examples can you think of where people use evil means to attain a good end? Does the end *ever* justify the means used to attain it?

Chapter 11

For understanding
1. **11:1–21.** With what do these verses deal? How was Athaliah's rule illegitimate from the start? What did Athaliah try to do, and whose example did she follow?
2. **11:2.** Who was Jehosheba? How did Joash survive? When does Joash come to the throne, and how long does he reign?
3. **11:4.** Who is Jehoiada, and what does he choreograph? What relation is he to the boy-king, and as what will he serve? Who are the Carites? What do they provide? When does the changing of the guard occur?
4. **11:12.** Of what is the royal crown a sign? What is the "covenant" referred to here?
5. **11:14.** What pillar is referred to here? Who do "the people of the land" appear to be? What about them has been seen on several occasions?

For application
1. **11:1.** Here, the queen mother usurps the throne of her son. How do you understand the role of Mary, heavenly Queen Mother and Mediatrix of all graces? How would you answer the objection that devotion to Mary usurps the authority of her divine Son?
2. **11:4.** Jehoiada the priest becomes the young king's protector and teacher (12:2). Who has been the most effective person (either a lay person or pastor) in your Christian life in terms of providing you with spiritual protection and instruction? How does that person's influence still manifest itself?
3. **11:17.** Have you ever joined or belonged to a renewal movement in the Church? If so, how effective has it been in renewing the parish to which you belong? What has been your role in it? If not, what prevents you from joining one? Why do such movements seem to arise in the Church from time to time?

Chapter 12

For understanding
1. **12:4–16.** What was needed on the Solomonic Temple? For what are the Temple revenues set aside? To whom is the task of repair first entrusted, but then who is later given responsibility for it?
2. **12:9.** What is the chest used as? Who served as sentries, and for what purpose?
3. **12:18.** What are votive gifts? Why are they given to the Syrians? Of what were gifts of silver and gold often the "price" in the days of the kings?

For application
1. **12:4–6.** How do you feel about priests who preach about the need for money? According to the *Catechism* (no. 2043), what does the fifth "precept of the Church" require? What is your own pattern of giving to the Church? How consistent is this pattern of giving? Have you ever considered giving a set percentage of your income or increasing the amount you give as your income increases?
2. **12:13.** What are some of the vessels used in the celebration of Catholic liturgy? How are they supposed to be made? Why would ordinary kitchen implements such as plates and bowls be unsuitable for use in the divine liturgy?
3. **12:16.** According to St. Paul, those who preach the gospel have a right to earn their living by preaching—in other words, to receive pay of some sort (1 Cor 9:14). What is the justice of this claim? What may be some of its dangers for the preacher?

Chapter 13

For understanding
1. **13:1.** Which king of Israel is Jehoahaz? For what does the narrator fault him? How did his cavalry and chariot corps come to be reduced?
2. **13:5.** What was the goal of the savior that the Lord provided Israel? Whom does the narrator have in mind?
3. **13:17.** What do prophetic actions such as this one announce? What does helping the king shoot the bow out the east window serve to prophesy? Where is Aphek?
4. **13:21.** How is Catholic teaching on the efficacy of holy relics illustrated by this episode? What do this and other passages affirm about the bodies and belongings of the saints?

For application
1. **13:3.** What does "the anger of the LORD" mean? What is the analogy used to describe it in this verse (hint: the word "kindled")? How might God's anger be considered an expression of his love?
2. **13:5–6.** When someone's behavior gets him into trouble and you rescue him from its consequences, what changes in the person's behavior would you expect to see? What would you think of the person who went back to the same behavior as before?
3. **13:19.** Imagine a boxing coach who wanted you to pretend that a punching bag was your opponent. How hard or how often would he want you to hit it? What would he say if you stopped after a few punches? Why would he ask you punch the bag in the first place?
4. **13:21.** Read the note for this verse. Why do Catholics venerate the relics of saints? What benefit would veneration of a relic be to you in your practice of the faith? What relationship should a popular devotion such as devotion to relics have to the liturgy (CCC 1675)? According to CCC 1676, why should popular devotions be purified when needed?

Chapter 14

For understanding
1. **14:1.** Which king of Judah is Amaziah? For what is he both praised and criticized? What do chronological factors suggest about his reign?
2. **14:7.** Who are the Edomites? What is Amaziah attempting to do with them? Where is the Valley of Salt?
3. **14:8.** What does Amaziah mean by calling on Jehoahaz of Israel to look him in the face? What is he about to learn?
4. **14:23.** Which Jeroboam is this? To his credit, what did he do? What made him a political "savior" of sorts? Nevertheless, why is his reign declared evil?

For application
1. **14:5.** What is your view of capital punishment? If it is to be allowed, what should be its purpose? If it is to be discontinued (see CCC 2267), what punishment should take its place and what should be its purpose?
2. **14:6.** Our culture readily punishes murderers for their crime, but little is said about what happens to their children. What would their children need from society, and what would they be more likely to get? How would you relate to the child of a convicted sex offender? How might you reach out to that child or exercise caution in relating to the child? Why would you do either?
3. **14:8–11.** *Hubris* is pride, a flaw of character that can lead to a person's downfall. Of what historical personages can you think whose hubris had that result? What, if any, hubris do you detect in yourself, and what might you do to rid yourself of it?

Chapter 15

For understanding
1. **15:1.** Which king of Judah is Azariah? What is he also known as? Although an admirable king overall, for what does the narrator criticize him? What does the parallel account in Chronicles indicate that Azariah/Uzziah did? What does Chronicles explain about the king's leprosy that is unexplained in Kings?
2. **15:8–31.** What happens in these verses? What events make for a time of power struggles and escalating violence? What do four of the last five kings of Israel do, and why? Why does the prophet Hosea condemn these final kings of the north?
3. **15:27.** Who is Pekah of Israel? Unlike his predecessors, who made Israel a vassal state of Assyria, what does Pekah do? What will his defiant stance against the Mesopotamian superpower eventually cause to happen?
4. **15:29.** Which Tiglath-Pileser is this, and what is his alternate name? What did he launch between 734 and 732 B.C., and what did he manage to do? With these lands made part of the Assyrian empire, what happens to the Northern Kingdom of Israel? What policy do the Assyrians execute at this time?

For application
1. **15:5.** Think of a person you know who is permanently disabled. How does that person handle the routines of daily life? What is his attitude toward life in general? How does the disability color that person's relationship to God?
2. **15:20.** Churches in many countries enjoy a tax-exempt status. What are the benefits they gain from that status? How great a hardship would result if the government were to remove it?
3. **15:25.** As the note to 15:8–31 points out, Israel undergoes a rather lengthy period of political instability as kings in succession assassinate their predecessors to gain power. If something like that instability were to affect this country, what impact do you think it would have on our cultural and economic life? How might it affect the religious life of the country? What has protected us from that instability so far?

Chapter 16

For understanding
1. **16:1.** Who is Ahaz? For what is he severely criticized? For what is he likewise faulted in his foreign policy and liturgical innovations?
2. **16:7.** What kind of language is Ahaz using by calling himself servant and son to Tiglath-pileser III of Assyria? What does Judah thus become? What did the prophet Isaiah advise?
3. **16:10.** What altar is referred to here? What does Ahaz commission, and what does he do there? What is the Damascus-style altar called?
4. **Chart: Near Eastern Kings and the Israelite Monarchy.** How does the history of Israel often intersect with the broader history of the ancient Near East? From a historical standpoint, with what kinds of testimony does the witness of Scripture closely cohere?

For application
1. **16:3.** Look up Is 1:12. What seems to be the attitude of Ahaz to the Israelite monotheistic religion, given his behavior in this verse? Why do some people—or, for that matter, some cultures—combine elements of Christianity with those of other religions (e.g., as in voodoo)?
2. **16:7-9.** What does the expression "Making a deal with the devil" mean? In what way is Ahaz doing that? How do many of us make similar "deals" in life that will eventually lead to our destruction?
3. **16:10-13.** What are some of the ways that Christians copy or imitate the spiritual practices of other religions, such as Buddhism? What are the potential benefits of such imitation? What are some of the dangers?
4. **16:14-18.** What are some principles that should govern why and how a church should be remodeled? What are some examples of good and bad remodeling of a church that you have seen? What standards lie behind your evaluations of these efforts?

Chapter 17

For understanding
1. **17:1-41.** With what do these verses deal? In what ways does the Kings account combine *historical* information with *theological* interpretation? *Eschatologically*, what happens to the northern tribes of Israel? What do several prophets envision about them?
2. **17:3.** Who is Shalmaneser? For what is he responsible, and how does Sargon II fit in? For what was Sargon II mainly responsible?
3. **17:24.** Who are the peoples listed here? What was the purpose of deporting and importing captives? What is the difference between what happened to Samaria and what happened to Galilee and the Transjordan earlier?
4. **17:29-34.** What is the main feature of Samaritan religion from the start? How do some understand the name Succoth-benoth? Who are Nergal, Ashima, Nibhaz, Tartak, and the others named here?

For application
1. **17:1-41.** Read the note for these verses. From the historical, theological, and even eschatological viewpoints, would you conclude that Christianity in the northern hemisphere is in a period of growth or decline? What hope do you see for its future? From the same perspectives, how do you view the growth of Christianity in the southern hemisphere?
2. **17:9.** The first half of this verse refers to things the people of Israel did "secretly" against the Lord. To what does the expression "Catholic guilt" refer? How might a person try to hide some violation of God's law? From whom is he really trying to hide it? What happens when a whole culture tries to hide its defection?
3. **17:14.** Psalm 95:8 warns us not to "harden your hearts" as Israel did. How has our culture hardened its heart against the Lord? How might practicing members of the Church do the same? Of which prophets are you aware who are warning us against such folly?
4. **17:34-40.** As Christians, what is our covenant with the Lord? How did we contract it? How do we tend to forget it?

Chapter 18

For understanding
1. **18:1—25:30.** What do these final chapters of Kings trace? Although Judah outlives Israel by more than a century, what happens? On the regional stage of Near Eastern politics, how does the balance of power shift?
2. **18:1.** Which king of Judah is Hezekiah? For what does the narrator applaud him? What do the high points of his kingship include?
3. **18:4.** What kind of reforms does Hezekiah undertake? What may have prompted his actions? What happened to the bronze serpent manufactured by Moses? What is the name Nehushtan a play on?
4. **18:13.** Who is Sennacherib? Why did his forces invade Judah in 701 B.C.? What do the surviving *Annals of Sennacherib* describe? Amid the duress of these circumstances, what did the prophet Isaiah counsel Hezekiah to do?
5. **18:32.** What does Sennacherib's delegation claim about the lands of Assyrian exile? What lesson does this hold for the spiritual life of believers, according to St. Ephraem?

For application
1. **18:4.** What is the most valuable object you own that is culturally or personally significant (e.g., a flag, a souvenir)? What would you do with it if you realized that it had become an object of superstition for you? How would you handle it if the object was a religious one?
2. **18:19-35.** Have any forms of psychological intimidation or other forms of bullying ever been leveled at you or people you know? If so, what effect did this intimidation have on you? How did you respond to it?

3. **18:22.** What is Sennacherib's messenger implying about the people's reliance on God in this verse? How does Satan try to undercut your faith in God?
4. **18:30–32.** What kind of proposition is called an "offer one can't refuse"? What do you think is attractive about the offer given by Sennacherib's messenger, and what is repulsive about it? When danger threatens, how much faith do you tend to put in the leaders who try to reassure you that all is safe?
5. **18:36.** Why would the king order his people not to answer the messenger? If you are intimidated by an adversary, what is the benefit to you of keeping silent?

Chapter 19

For understanding
1. **19:2.** Who are Eliakim and Shebna? Who is "the prophet Isaiah"? What aspects of Isaiah's distinctive language and style appear in this chapter? What does sending delegates to Isaiah indicate about Hezekiah?
2. **19:7.** What did Isaiah's prophecy say about Sennacherib? Why does Jerusalem have nothing to fear? What will happen to Sennacherib?
3. **19:9.** Who is Tirhakah? When did his reign as king begin, and what does that mean in the present situation in Palestine?
4. **19:29.** What sign does Isaiah offer the people of Judah? What does the miracle of the harvest illustrate?

For application
1. **19:1–2.** If you were in dire trouble or distress, to whom would you turn for counsel or direction? How do you seek spiritual direction? How regularly do you seek it?
2. **19:15–19.** Hezekiah's prayer consists of several parts. What are they? What seems to be his attitude to God as he prays? How can his prayer help you as you pray for deliverance from trouble?
3. **19:21–28.** What does Isaiah's prophecy have to say about God's control of historical forces such as Assyria's armies? Despite Sennacherib's role as God's instrument, with what vice does God charge him in v. 28? How is the sin of presumption associated with that vice?
4. **19:30.** How do you interpret Isaiah's meaning in this verse? In general, how does the Church "take root downward, and bear fruit upward"? How might you do the same in your own spiritual life?

Chapter 20

For understanding
1. **20:1–21.** How is the narrative sequence of 2 Kings 18–20 historically dischronologized? What are some of the observations supporting this?
2. **20:3.** What indication is given that Hezekiah expresses repentance? How powerful is a prayer of repentance, according to St. Cyril of Jerusalem?
3. **20:11.** On what does the miracle of sunlight and shadow take place? What does Hezekiah witness?
4. **20:12.** Who was Merodach-baladan, and when did he reign? What happened when he reestablished his kingship briefly in 704 B.C.? Why do many believe his envoys came to Jerusalem with more than a "get well" message for Hezekiah? For his part, what does Hezekiah do for the Babylonian dignitaries?

For application
1. **20:3.** In Is 38:10–20, read the prayer of Hezekiah during his sickness and compare his attitude there with his reasons for asking for healing here, in the current verse. What differences do you see? If you were terminally ill and prayed for healing, what reasons would you give for asking for it?
2. **20:8.** Why do people ask the Lord for signs that a divine promise will come true? What are some of the spiritual dangers in asking for signs?
3. **20:19.** What do you think of Hezekiah's reply to Isaiah in this verse? As long as we enjoy peace and security in our lifetimes, what concern should we have for the future?

Chapter 21

For understanding
1. **21:1.** Who was Manasseh? How is he judged as king? Under Manasseh's leadership, how does Judah sink into a time of unprecedented apostasy? What does the prism of the Assyrian king Esarhaddon mention about him? How long did he rule alongside his father, Hezekiah?
2. **21:3–7.** In what ways does Manasseh reverse the cultic reforms of Hezekiah? How does the Deuteronomic covenant label these actions?
3. **21:10–15.** What does the enormity of Manasseh's crimes guarantee? What effect will the heroic reforms of Josiah in chap. 23 have?
4. **21:16.** What does Jewish tradition hold about the prophet Isaiah's death?

For application
1. **21:2.** What do you think causes some children of virtuous parents to rebel openly and publicly against their parents' standards? What grief and even guilt might the parents feel? How can they retain their standards and yet keep open the lines of communication with their rebellious children?
2. **21:6.** What are some reasons that devotees of soothsayers, mediums, and wizards give for consulting them? According to CCC 2115–17, what forms of divination or occult activity are Christians to reject, and for what reasons? What virtue do these occult activities oppose?

3. **21:7-8.** According to these verses, what condition did the Lord place on his choice of Jerusalem? Why does God not give blanket promises but only conditional ones?
4. **21:14.** Read the note for this verse. According to CCC 710, how does the exile of this remnant play into the ultimate plan of God for his people? Of what is the remnant a prefiguration?

Chapter 22

For understanding
1. **22:1.** Which king of Judah is Josiah? As what is he hailed, and why? What do the admiring words of the Book of Sirach say about him? How much criticism does the Kings historian offer about him?
2. **22:4.** Who was Hilkiah? For what was the money donated? Who are the keepers of the threshold?
3. **22:8.** What is the "book of the law" referred to here? What had evidently happened to the scroll? What do scholars frequently claim, with insufficient warrant? What are three reasons why this hypothesis is problematic?
4. **22:14.** Who is Huldah? How is Josiah wise like other righteous kings before him? What is the Second Quarter thought to be?

For application
1. **22:7.** How trusting are you of those to whom you give your money for safekeeping? Whom do you trust with your money without the need for an accounting? By the same token, how trusting is the government of your honesty when you submit your tax returns? In banking or stock market situations, how airtight are the regulations designed to ensure honesty between parties in financial transactions?
2. **22:11-13.** How would you describe Josiah's emotions on being told of the contents of the Law? If you were in his position, how seriously would you take the danger that he saw in its discovery? If you have ever been in an analogous position, what was it, and how did you react?
3. **22:15-20.** The prophetess tells Josiah that doom will fall on Jerusalem, but because of his penitent attitude, Josiah will not live to see it. As a responsible king, what comfort might Josiah have taken at this word? How do you think his attitude might compare or contrast with that of Hezekiah in 20:19?

Chapter 23

For understanding
1. **23:3.** Which pillar is the one mentioned here? What does Josiah lead the nation in doing? What would both king and people have sworn? What did pledges of renewed commitment to Yahweh often entail?
2. **23:4-25.** What do Josiah's efforts at reform aim at accomplishing? Since Josiah's crusade is a rigorous enforcement of Deuteronomy, what does Deuteronomy forbid? What constitutes a king's service to God according to St. Augustine?
3. **Word Study: High Places (23:5).** How is the Hebrew word *bamah* often rendered? What does the word sometimes denote? In the majority of cases, to what does the term refer, and what happens there? What are otherwise admirable kings of Judah criticized for not doing? Who had the courage to shut the high places down? Why does Deuteronomy require their demolition? Where was the worship of Yahweh by sacrifice and incense to take place exclusively?
4. **23:36.** Which king of Judah is Jehoiakim? What does his reign witness? What name change did Neco make for the king of Judah?

For application
1. **23:1-27.** Since Josiah knew that disaster was threatened for Jerusalem no matter what he did, what do you think motivated him to such resolve? If you were responsible for a community on the verge of disintegration regardless of your efforts to keep it together, would you try to save it anyway or abandon it? Why?
2. **23:4.** If you were attempting to recover from an addiction like alcoholism or drug abuse, what would you do with all the paraphernalia associated with it? How thorough would you need to be? What kind of help would you want to have?
3. **23:8-9.** Why might some of the Levitical priests have refused to come to Jerusalem to perform their liturgical duties as required, preferring to remain where they were? Why does the Church often seem to be so slow to correct liturgical abuses? And when she finally does, why do some resist?
4. **23:21-23.** Of all your family traditions, which do you celebrate with the most elaborate preparations? What makes the celebration so special?

Chapter 24

For understanding
1. **24:1—25:26.** With what do these verses deal? In what four waves does judgment come upon Judah?
2. **24:1.** Who was Nebuchadnezzar? What does "his servant" mean? Why did Jehoiakim take the bold step of rebelling against Nebuchadnezzar? How did the king misread the situation?
3. **24:2.** What theological interpretation of history is the author of Kings making? What role does mighty Babylon play? Who are the Chaldeans mentioned here? Who are the others?
4. **24:17.** Which king is Zedekiah? What does his foolish rebellion bring about? What is ironic about his name?

For application
1. **24:2-3.** The author of 2 Kings attributes these attacks against Jerusalem to the command of the Lord. As you read CCC 311, does God command evil? If not, what is God's response sometimes to moral evil? How can good come out of it?
2. **24:13.** What kinds of material treasures does the Catholic Church possess? How might the Church respond if all the treasures of the Vatican were looted? What might be the minimum that the Church requires to keep alive her liturgical forms of worship?

3. **24:14-16.** Read the note for these verses. From Nebuchadnezzar's point of view, what was the advantage for himself of this "selective deportation" policy? What might have been the advantage for the deported citizens? Why leave a remnant of peasantry behind?
4. **24:20b.** Given the resources left him by Nebuchadnezzar, how could Zedekiah's rebellion hope to succeed? Why might a teenager rebel against his parents, even though he knows there is no hope of winning against them?

Chapter 25

For understanding
1. **25:1-17.** With what do these verses deal? What is the result for the Davidic monarchy and the Southern Kingdom? Where will the people of Judah spend the next 48 years? Theologically, of what are national catastrophe and exile manifestations? What is the aim of the curses?
2. **25:7.** How is the blinding of Zedekiah both physical and psychological torture? How did Ezekiel foretell it?
3. **25:13-17.** What happens to the Temple? Why is no mention made of the Ark of the Covenant and the golden altar of incense?
4. **25:27-30.** What does the short postscript to 2 Kings offer? At what does the clemency shown to Jehoiachin, the king of Judah, hint? What does it also indicate about David's royal line? Far from destroying the covenant people and their kings, what will the Lord decree and eventually raise up?

For application
1. **25:3.** Imagine that the electrical grid in this country were completely destroyed. What emergencies would result? For example, how would cities obtain food and water? How would a society like ours cope with such conditions?
2. **25:7.** Compare the fate of Zedekiah with that of his predecessor Jehoiachin (24:15; 25:27-30). Why the difference? Why is the punishment of an offender who resists often more severe than that of one who submits to it?
3. **25:9-17.** When a sacred place is desecrated, what kind of mourning is appropriate among the faithful? Although not guilty of the sacrilege, why is it appropriate for the faithful to do some kind of penance (cf. CIC, can. 1211)?

BOOKS OF THE BIBLE

THE OLD TESTAMENT (OT)

Gen	Genesis
Ex	Exodus
Lev	Leviticus
Num	Numbers
Deut	Deuteronomy
Josh	Joshua
Judg	Judges
Ruth	Ruth
1 Sam	1 Samuel
2 Sam	2 Samuel
1 Kings	1 Kings
2 Kings	2 Kings
1 Chron	1 Chronicles
2 Chron	2 Chronicles
Ezra	Ezra
Neh	Nehemiah
Tob	Tobit
Jud	Judith
Esther	Esther
Job	Job
Ps	Psalms
Prov	Proverbs
Eccles	Ecclesiastes
Song	Song of Solomon
Wis	Wisdom
Sir	Sirach (Ecclesiasticus)
Is	Isaiah
Jer	Jeremiah
Lam	Lamentations
Bar	Baruch
Ezek	Ezekiel
Dan	Daniel
Hos	Hosea
Joel	Joel
Amos	Amos
Obad	Obadiah
Jon	Jonah
Mic	Micah
Nahum	Nahum
Hab	Habakkuk
Zeph	Zephaniah
Hag	Haggai
Zech	Zechariah
Mal	Malachi
1 Mac	1 Maccabees
2 Mac	2 Maccabees

THE NEW TESTAMENT (NT)

Mt	Matthew
Mk	Mark
Lk	Luke
Jn	John
Acts	Acts of the Apostles
Rom	Romans
1 Cor	1 Corinthians
2 Cor	2 Corinthians
Gal	Galatians
Eph	Ephesians
Phil	Philippians
Col	Colossians
1 Thess	1 Thessalonians
2 Thess	2 Thessalonians
1 Tim	1 Timothy
2 Tim	2 Timothy
Tit	Titus
Philem	Philemon
Heb	Hebrews
Jas	James
1 Pet	1 Peter
2 Pet	2 Peter
1 Jn	1 John
2 Jn	2 John
3 Jn	3 John
Jude	Jude
Rev	Revelation (Apocalypse)